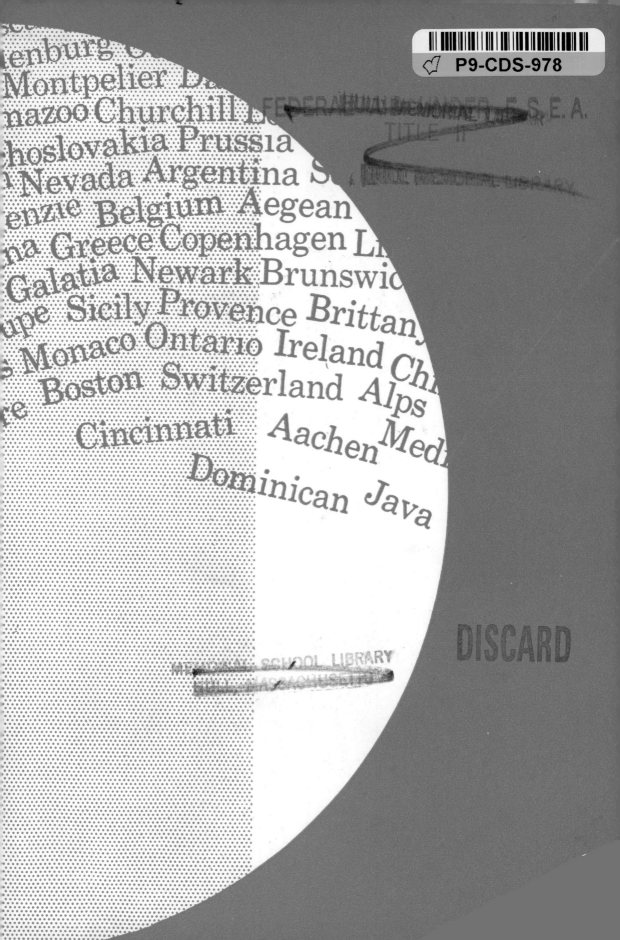

...enburg O...
Montpelier Da...
...nazoo Churchill L...
...hoslovakia Prussia
...Nevada Argentina S...
...enzie Belgium Aegean
...na Greece Copenhagen Li...
...Galatia Newark Brunswic...
...upe Sicily Provence Brittan...
...s Monaco Ontario Ireland Ch...
...re Boston Switzerland Alps
Cincinnati   Aachen   Medi...
Dominican Java

Words on the
Map

Non-Fiction books by the same author

in collaboration

Words on the Map

Isaac Asimov

Decorations by William Barss

Houghton Mifflin Company, Boston

The Riverside Press, Cambridge

To Manhattan

Introduction

NEVER BEFORE have Americans been so conscious of the map of the world. American responsibilities are world-wide and no corner of the globe can be neglected by us, if we ourselves are to survive.

It was only twenty years ago that "practical people" scoffed at any notion that we ought to worry about "milk for the Hottentots." Now, a stirring in the Congo or in Laos (who ever heard of Laos ten years ago?) draws an instant response from the White House and from every Main Street in the nation.

Africa has burst into independence and brought us new names — the Upper Volta, Mali, Ghana, and others. Where we used to hear of the Dutch East Indies, now we speak of Indonesia; Pakistan has emerged out of India; and the British Empire, proud legacy of the nineteenth century, has vanished to become something called the Commonwealth of Nations.

We may feel buried under the avalanche of strange and changing words, but, properly viewed, those names are truly romantic. They are bits of history frozen on the map; they echo the distant footfalls of explorers making their way through a wilderness. They breathe the passions and piety of men across the slow changes of the centuries.

They can even be surprising — or amusing. Hidden in New Jersey is Julius Caesar, though neither he nor most Jerseyites would ever suspect it. Troy, New York, is named after ancient Troy, but Troyes, France, is not. Worms, Germany, has nothing to do with worms, and Nice, France, may be nice but that's not what it means.

America was named, probably, by mistake, and there are two different "United States" on the North American continent (and two more in South America, plus two places where the United States used to be).

When you say "the Sahara Desert," you are saying "desert desert" and when you say "Lake Nyasa" (in Africa), you are saying "lake lake." The Sierra Nevada is not in Nevada and the section of American coast that was first named Virginia is now part of North Carolina. India was named for the Indus River, which no longer flows through India.

New Brunswick, New Jersey, was named for one British king, and New Brunswick, Canada, for another. Louisiana was named for one French king, St. Louis for another, Louisville for still a third. New Orleans has a Roman emperor hidden in it, while Philadelphia carries the mark of an Egyptian ruler.

Places on this earth are named for gods and saints, for kings and presidents, and politicians and warriors, and, often, for complete nonentities.

The map is a fascinating storybook and I've tried to trap some of that fascination and put it into this book.

ISAAC ASIMOV

Newton, Massachusetts

Words on the
Map

Aachen

IN THE DAYS before modern medicine, it was widely held that bathing in certain hot springs was very healthful, particularly if the water was full of dissolved minerals that made it smell and taste bad.

The Romans searched out such spots and found one in southwest Britain. They called it Aquae Calidae, which means, plainly enough, "hot springs." The Romans eventually left, but the hot springs did not and, in fact, they formed a health resort that was particularly popular in the 1700's. Since the place is important for its hot baths, it is only reasonable that its present name be the straightforward *Bath*.

Along the upper Rhine, the Romans found springs they named Aurelia Aquensis after the emperor of the time. This became part of Germany eventually, and the Germans made the same change the English did; that is, to their word for "bath," doubling it for good measure and making it *Baden-Baden* (bah'den-bah'den). The region along the east bank of the Rhine that includes the city was once the *Grand Duchy of Baden*. After 1870, this became part of unified Germany.

The Romans found a number of such spots in Gaul. One, in the northeast, they called Aquae Grani ("grainy water," because of its high mineral content) and this too, became part of Germany, just at its western border. This time, the "Aquae" persisted, for its present name is *Aachen* (ah'ken). It had its great moment of glory when, in the 800's, it served as capital of Charlemagne's empire.

The Romans located springs in areas which are now in France. Aquae Sextiae was twenty miles north of Marseille and is now known simply as *Aix* (eks), the first syllable of the Roman name being preserved. About 150 miles farther north was Aquae Gratianae, which is now *Aix-les-Bains* (eks-lay-ban'), meaning "Aix of the baths."

And, of course, there are towns named *Hot Springs* in the United States. The largest one, founded in 1807, is in Arkansas, and, since 1921, has had its area of hot springs reserved as part of *Hot Springs National Park*.

Acre

A CITY often grows up about a fortified place built on a hill for the sake of better defense. In Greek, a word referring to the peak of a hill is "akron," from "ake," meaning "a point." Thus, the central hill in Athens, which was probably the original site of the city, is the *Acropolis,* meaning "peak of the city."

On the north coast of what is now Israel is a city, built on a low promontory, which is named simply *Acre* (ah'ker). Through countless centuries, it has had forms of that name from the ancient Egyptian "Ak" to the modern Arabian "Akka" and undoubtedly the name has meant "peak" in every language. The small ocean inlet to its south is the *Bay of Acre.*

For a couple of centuries, from about 250 B.C. on, when the area was under the control of the Ptolemies of Egypt, the name was changed to *Ptolemais* (tol-uh-may'is) in honor of Ptolemy Philadelphus, the second of the line. Eventually, though, the Ptolemies vanished into history and the city went back to its older name.

Acre played an important role during the crusades. Richard the Lion-Hearted besieged and occupied it as his first important feat in the Holy Land. In the end, it was the last point held by the Crusaders, who lost it only in 1291, two full centuries after the Crusades had begun. The last defense was made by an organization called the Knights of St. John and the memory of this is still preserved in the French name for the city, which is *St. Jean d'Acre* (san-zhahn-da'kr).

There is a queer echo to this bit of Greek in American geography, although it has nothing to do with Acre. In 1825, a town was established along a projected route from Lake Erie to the Ohio River. The establishment was at the highest point along that route and the founders in a fit of classicism named the city *Akron.*

It might seem more natural to name an American town upon a height *Summit,* but only a few such towns exist in the United States. The largest is one in New Jersey, first settled in 1795.

Aegean Sea

THE IMAGINATIVE Greeks invented the most interesting myths of all time and they loved to make up stories to account for the names of places. These stories mask the true origins of the names, origins which the Greeks themselves had forgotten or never knew, but the myths have come to be so well known to the Western world that it would be a shame to look beyond them.

For instance, the *Aegean Sea*, between Greece and Turkey, was named, the Greeks maintained, after Aegeus, king of Athens. He threw himself into that sea when he spied the black sails of the ship of his son, Theseus, returning from a dangerous mission. Theseus was supposed to have changed the sails to white ones if the mission were successful, but, what with one thing and another, he had forgotten.

The *Atlas Mountains* in northwestern Africa are named for the giant Atlas, who, the Greeks imagined, stood in that area in ancient times, supporting the sky. His numerous daughters were known as the "Atlantides." They were water nymphs of the ocean just to the west of the mountains. That ocean came to be known, therefore, as the *Atlantic Ocean*.

The *Dardanelles*, a strait between Europe and Asia, southwest of Istanbul, is supposedly named for Dardanus, a mythical ancient king of that region. In early days, it was called the *Hellespont*, meaning "sea of Helle," because a girl, Helle, fell off the back of a flying ram and was drowned there.

The strait upon which Istanbul is located is the *Bosporus* ("cow-crossing") because one of Zeus's sweethearts, Io, in the form of a cow, swam across. Earlier, she had swum the strip of sea that separates northwestern Greece from southern Italy and that is known as the *Ionian Sea*. North of Crete is the *Icarian Sea*, named for Icarus, who, using wings of feathers held together by wax, flew too near the sun, which melted the wax, causing Icarus to fall into that sea and drown.

3

Africa

To THE ancient Greeks, the Aegean Sea (see AEGEAN SEA) seemed to divide the world into two parts, Europe and Asia. At first that seemed sufficient division. The land south of the Mediterranean — Egypt, for instance — was at first considered as part of Asia since it did connect with the region east of the Aegean by way of unbroken land.

By 150 A.D. Greek geography had advanced to the point where it was known that the land mass that included Egypt and areas west and south was large indeed and that the connection with Asia was by way of a very narrow isthmus. The geographer Claudius Ptolemy, therefore, recognized the southern land as a third continent. The Greeks sometimes applied the name *Libya* to this continent, a word of unknown origin.

Now the largest and most important city on this third continent, in Greek times, was Carthage. The Carthaginians called the area about their city by a word which the Romans wrote as *Africa*. At first Africa included only the Carthaginian neighborhood and the Arabs use the name in this limited fashion to this day. (They call the area Ifrikiya.) There is also a theory that *Africa* may come from "Aphros," the Greek word for "foam," because Africa to the Greeks was the land across the foam.

The Romans had an epic struggle with the Carthaginians in the third century B.C. and barely won out. The winner of any close fight often tries to make it out to have been a David-and-Goliath struggle, with himself as David, of course. The Romans, therefore, claimed that Carthage had brought all Africa against them and spread out Africa to include a wide region. The name expanded from a narrow region of the coast and came to cover the entire land mass behind it so that today *Africa* is the name of the second largest continent on the globe.

Libya remains, however, as the name of that section of northern Africa west of Egypt and east of Tunisia (the modern name of the original Africa). Between World War I and World War II, it was an Italian possession but in 1951 it became an independent nation.

Alaska

THE NORTHWESTERN corner of North America was discovered in 1741 by Vitus Bering, a Danish explorer in the employ of Russia. The value of the region and the seas about it lay in its furs, and fur traders swept over it, establishing Russian dominion over an area which, in the first half of the nineteenth century, was called *Russian America*.

In 1867, the American Secretary of State, William Henry Seward, arranged to have the United States buy the region from Russia. (This act was called "Seward's Folly" at the time, but I imagine we are all grateful for it now.) The region was then renamed *Alaska*, from a native Eskimo word meaning "great land." In 1959, Alaska entered the Union as the 49th State.

Traces of the Russian occupation can still be seen on the map. The *Pribilof Islands* (prib'i-lof), off Alaska, were first explored in 1786 by the Russian navigator Gerasim Pribylov. (The change of *y* to *i* comes through the fact that Russian is not written in the Latin alphabet, so that a Russian letter can often be expressed in more than one way in English.)

The Pribilof Islands proved to be the breeding ground of swarms of seals and other fur-bearing creatures. Their alternate name is therefore *Fur Seal Islands*, and included in the group are *Walrus Island* and *Otter Island*. Wild killings nearly ruined the islands as a source of fur. Special treaties were signed and, in 1910, the United States took over ownership of the islands, where hunting is now strictly controlled.

The first governor of Russian America was Alexander Andreevich Baranov. One of the larger of the over a thousand islands off the southeastern coast of Alaska is called *Baranof Island* in his honor. (The *v* and *f* interchange.) The entire group of islands is the *Alexander Archipelago*, named not after Baranov himself, but after Alexander I, who became Russian Czar two years after Baranov had become the governor.

Albania

A MOUNTAINOUS land is often a snow-covered land. Even in southern latitudes, the peaks are white with snow. The whiteness is spectacular and the region is often named for it.

The Latin word for "white" is "albus" and so *Albania* has come to be a name (often used only poetically) for mountainous areas. There was a region in the eastern Caucasus which, in ancient times, was called Albania. In the same way, northern Scotland (*The Highlands*) is fancifully called Albania, for it is the snowy peaks that distinguish it from southern Scotland (*The Lowlands*).

In one area of the world, however, the name appears on the map. The east coast of the Adriatic Sea was inhabited by a people whom the Greeks called Illyrioi so that the coastland came to be known as *Illyria*. After the passing of Rome's great days, the area was invaded first by Slavs, then by Turks. Nevertheless the Illyrians were never entirely beaten down but maintained their identity in the southern regions at least, although a good many of them turned Moslem.

The mountainous area of southern Illyria was known to the west as *Albania* (another one), but this time, when the region finally gained its independence of the Turks in 1913, the name appeared on the map. The Albanians themselves call their land by a native term, "Shqipni."

The Illyrian regions north of Albania became Slavic but not Turkish. In fact, one region north of Albania never entirely submitted to the Turks. The Slavs rallied about an area they called Crna Gora, meaning (an unusual reversal of form) "black mountain." In Italian, that becomes *Montenegro* (mon-te-nay'gro), the name by which the region is known to the west.

Montenegro was formally recognized as an independent nation in 1878, after Turkey lost a war to Russia. After World War I, it merged with other Slavic territories and is now a province of Yugoslavia.

Alexandria

THE ANCIENTS who named cities after themselves were inspired to do so partly by the case of Alexander the Great who, in his career of conquest from 336 to 323 B.C., founded numerous cities wherever his armies went, and who named almost every one after himself. The most famous of these was the *Alexandria* he founded in 332 B.C. on the westernmost mouth of the Nile in Egypt. It was the capital of the Ptolemaic kingdom of Egypt and was the center of intellectual advancement for 700 years, under them and under the Romans.

The Arabs captured it from the East Roman Empire in 640 A.D., but it still exists as an important town. However, since the Arabs had distorted Alexander's name to "Iskander," the official name of the town is now *al-Iskandariyah* (al-is-kan-da-ree'uh).

Because of the fame of Alexander the Great, *Alexander* has become a common name ever since. The various Alexandrias in the United States were therefore usually named for Alexanders other than the great conqueror. *Alexandria*, Virginia, for instance, the best known of the American towns of the name, was named for John Alexander, a settler who had originally owned the site in 1680.

The Roman emperors followed Alexander's example, but the names they gave their towns were often distorted unrecognizably with time. An example is that of the Emperor Hadrian, who established Hadrianopolis ("Hadrian's city") in northeastern Greece in A.D. 125. It is better known as *Adrianople*. The Turks captured it in 1361 and it has remained Turkish ever since. The Turkish distortion of the name is *Edirne* (uh-dir'nuh), in which *Hadrian* is no longer recognizable.

Nor does the *Adriatic Sea* bear his name, despite appearances. It comes from the town of *Adria*, established by the Etruscans in the days before Rome. With the passage of the centuries, however, the coast has silted up and Adria is no longer on the Adriatic to which it gave its name. It is fourteen miles inland.

7

Alps

THE MOST noticeable fact concerning mountainous areas is that they are white with snow (see ALBANIA). The Latin word for "white" is "albus" and some think the Celtic word for "white" was "alb." It is uncertain whether the Celtic-speaking Gauls or the Latin-speaking Romans first named the mountains that lay to the north of Italy and the east of Gaul, but, in any case, they are the *Alps* (the "whites"). The tallest peak in the Alps is *Mont Blanc*, concerning which there can be no doubt. In French, this means "white mountain."

A similar situation arose in the western hemisphere. The *Appalachian Mountains* (named originally for an Indian mountain village called Apalchen) are an old range not remarkable for height. In fact, the range in Virginia is known as the *Blue Ridge Mountains*, the bluish color in the distant haze being more impressive than any snowiness.

At the northern end, in New Hampshire, the range is unusually high. That combined with the northerly location increases the snow cover and gives the local range the name *White Mountains*. Included there are a group of peaks called the *Presidential Range* because they are named after Presidents of the United States. The highest is, fittingly enough, named *Mount Washington*. Then there are *Mount Adams*, *Mount Jefferson*, *Mount Madison*, and *Mount Monroe*, so that the first five Presidents are honored. Great statesmen who were not Presidents are also included. There are *Mount Franklin*, named for Benjamin Franklin, and *Mount Clay*, named for Henry Clay.

Not all mountains, by the way, have names with the prefix "Mount." In the *Rocky Mountains* (a name that was originally a translation of the French "Montaignes Rocheuses") there are a number of mountains named with the suffix "Peak." Of these, *Pike's Peak* in central Colorado is the best known. It gets its name from the fact that it was discovered in 1806 by the American explorer Zebulon Montgomery Pike.

Amazon River

THE GREEKS had legends of warrior women called Amazons, and ever since explorers of unknown regions have been on the watch for them. Only very rarely and then only under barbarous conditions have any battling ladies ever been found, but the notion of women fighting wars with men seems to be a fascinating one, and it was not forgotten.

For instance, in 1541, a Spanish explorer, Francisco de Orellana, explored the length of a long South American river that started in the Andes and traveled some 4000 miles eastward, across what is now Brazil, to the Atlantic Ocean. De Orellana started in Peru and worked his way downstream, making stands against hostile natives now and then. At one point in his journey it seemed to De Orellana that women joined in the fighting. That was enough; he named the river the *Amazon River* ("Rio de las Amazonas") at once. Others called it Orellana River after the explorer, but the more classical and romantic name won out.

The Amazon River is the largest in the world, delivering far more water into the ocean and draining a larger area of land than does any other river. The region it drains is sometimes called *Amazonia* and is one of the great tropical areas of the world.

The ancient Greeks had legends in which the equatorial regions were an unpassable blaze of fire. This was an exaggeration. The equator could be passed; it could be lived in. If land elevation was high enough, it could even be cool and pleasant.

On the western coast of South America, just beyond the origin of the Amazon, is a small country entirely centered about equatorial highlands, in fact. It named itself *Ecuador*, the Spanish word for "equator," when it became independent.

A second tropical region (in central Africa) advertises the same fact when it is termed, rather unofficially, *Equatoria*. This name is also applied, more specifically to the southern portion of Sudan.

9

America

WHEN, in the employ of Spain, the Italian navigator Christopher Columbus sailed westward across the Atlantic and reached land in 1492, he was convinced he had reached those parts of Asia which, in those days, were vaguely referred to as "the Indies." Even though this was found to be a mistake, the islands upon which he landed are still called the *West Indies* to this day. Its native inhabitants were called "Indians" by Columbus, and this term spread to all the natives of the new lands Columbus had discovered. It wasn't until 1498, on his third voyage, that Columbus got past the islands and landed on the mainland of the new territories.

Other explorers had been sailing westward meanwhile and some reached the mainland before Columbus did. One of these was another Italian explorer named Amerigo Vespucci, or, in the Latinized version, Americus Vespucius.

Vespucius described his explorations in two letters in which he claimed to have reached the mainland in 1497, a year before Columbus. In these letters he describes the territories he explored not as a part of the "Indies," but as a "new world." That began the habit of referring to the land of the western hemisphere as the *New World* and to that of the eastern as the *Old World*.

A German mapmaker, Martin Waldseemüller, was much impressed by Vespucius's letters. He was preparing a map of the world in which he showed the new lands as separate continents and not as parts of Asia. He felt that since Vespucius was the first to reach the mainland and the first to recognize them as separate continents, those continents ought to be named in his honor. In 1507, the name *America* first appeared on a map, therefore.

However, most modern historians strongly doubt Vespucius's truthfulness. It is quite possible Vespucius exaggerated his own achievements and that the proud name *America* is all a mistake.

10

Andalusia

DURING THE centuries from the fifth to the thirteenth, a succession of barbarian tribes stormed across Europe. Of the earlier groups, the most famous were the Goths, who, in the time of the late Roman Empire, banded in two groups, the Ostrogoths ("eastern Goths") and the Visigoths ("western Goths"). The Visigoths ravaged Italy and sacked Rome itself in 410. They then moved on into Spain while the Ostrogoths took over Italy and ruled it from 489 to 554. The Visigoths remained in Spain until 711, when that land fell to invading Moslems from the south. Thus, after about 300 years of power, the Goths faded from history.

They are not entirely gone from the map, however. The Goths originally started their migrations from a base in Scandinavia, and an island off the southeastern coast of Sweden is named *Gotland* ("land of the Goths"). The southern part of Sweden itself is similarly named *Götaland*, and Sweden's second largest city, on the southwest coast, is *Götaborg*.

Preceding the Visigoths into Spain were another Germanic tribe, the Vandals. Their behavior gave rise to our word "vandal" for anyone who engages in senseless destruction. They left a name with pleasanter connotations on the map, however. They passed from Spain into Africa, but the region through which they passed is still known as *Andalusia*, with only the initial *V* missing.

The Ostrogoths in Italy were conquered first by soldiers of the East Roman Empire and after that by a new barbarian horde that entered Italy in 568. They were the Longobards, so called, according to one theory, because of their long beards. This name was quickly twisted to "Lombards." The Lombards established a kingdom which lasted for two hundred years until, in 774, they were defeated and absorbed by Charlemagne. However, there is a province in north-central Italy that is still called *Lombardy*. The name of its chief city, *Milan*, is a shortened version of the Roman "Mediolanum," meaning "the middle of the land" because it is in the center of the north Italian plain.

11

Antarctic Ocean

SINCE THE South Polar regions lie on the opposite side of the globe from the North Polar regions, they are referred to as "Antarctic," meaning "opposed to the Arctic." The continent that occupies most of the Antarctic region is therefore naturally called *Antarctica*.

During the eighteenth century, explorers began to edge southward into the Antarctic area. In 1772, a French navigator, Yves Joseph de Kerguélen-Trémarec, searching for a mythical southern continent, came across a small island about 3000 miles southeast of the southern tip of Africa. It is named *Kerguelen Island* (kur'guh-len) in his honor, but the island is far enough south to be sub-Antarctic and its alternate name of *Desolation Island* shows that. It was nevertheless annexed to France in 1893, in those days when European powers were racing to annex all available land, however unimportant.

In 1819, the British navigator William Smith discovered islands about 500 miles south of the southern tip of South America and named them the *South Shetland Islands* because they were as near the South Pole as the Shetland Islands, north of Scotland, were to the North Pole. One of the South Shetland Islands was named *King George Island* after George III, then King of England. In 1821, islands not quite as far south were discovered and named the *South Orkney Islands*, after Scottish islands not quite as far north as the Shetlands. The sea between these groups of islands was fittingly named *Scotia Sea*.

Meanwhile, in 1820, a Russian navigator, Fabian Gottlieb von Bellingshausen, discovered islands still farther south and Russian monarchs got their chance. He named a large island *Alexander I Land*, after the reigning Czar, and a smaller one *Peter I Island*, after Peter the Great, who had reigned a century earlier. The ocean immediately about Antarctica is usually called the *Antarctic Ocean* and that portion of it between Alexander I Land and Peter I Island is called *Bellingshausen Sea*.

Antilles

BEFORE THE time of Columbus, the Atlantic Ocean was believed to be full of all sorts of islands endowed with mythical wonders. The oldest of all was a large island concerning which Plato wrote and which he called *Atlantis* because he described it as being located in the Atlantic Ocean.

Naturally, there are other and less mythical names derived from the Atlantic Ocean. For instance, the capital of Georgia, a city founded in 1837 and located 250 miles from the ocean, was nevertheless named *Atlanta* in 1845 because it then became the terminus of the Western and Atlantic Railroad. Earlier, *Atlantic City* had been established in New Jersey, but that is at least on the coast of the ocean for which it is named.

However, *Atlantis* is the really romantic name and although Plato made up the story out of whole cloth in order to teach a moral lesson, some people have believed in the existence of Atlantis from that day to this.

In the 1400's, when the Portuguese spoke of an Atlantic island of wealth and luxury, they named it Antilia which, many suspect, is merely a distortion of *Atlantis*. Naturally, Antilia was never found any more than Atlantis was. However, when Columbus located the West Indies (see AMERICA) these were identified with Antilia and since the West Indies consisted of a number of islands, the plural form had to be used. The West Indies are therefore often referred to as the *Antilles* (an-till'eez).

The Antilles are divided into two groups. The *Greater Antilles* include the four largest islands: Cuba, Hispaniola, Puerto Rico and Jamaica. The *Lesser Antilles* include the curve of smaller islands, sweeping down from Puerto Rico to the South American coast. Because these enclose the Caribbean Sea, they are sometimes called the *Caribbees*.

In this very indirect fashion, Plato's Atlantis may be found on the map after all.

13

Antioch

MOST OF the numerous cities founded by Alexander the Great during his career of conquest were named Alexandria (see ALEXANDRIA) but there is one important exception that arose as follows. Alexander, having invaded Persia in 334 B.C., promptly won a battle over the Persian provincial forces. This was good, but not decisive. The next year, however, he advanced to the point where Syria meets modern Turkey on the Mediterranean coast and there completely defeated the main Persian army. From that point on, victory seemed certain and the site of the battle was commemorated by founding the city of *Alexandretta* there.

Long afterward, the city fell to the Turks, along with all of Asia Minor, and the Turks called it Iskenderon. (Their name for Alexander was Iskander.) After World War I, the Syrian provinces of Turkey, including Alexandretta, fell to the French. In 1939, however, the French agreed to return the far northwestern portion of their Syrian possessions to Turkey, and Alexandretta became Turkish again.

After the death of Alexander, his general Seleucus took over control of most of the Asiatic dominions of the conqueror. In 300 B.C., he founded a city about forty miles south of Alexandretta and named it after his son, Antiochus (who was to succeed him twenty years later). We know the city as *Antioch* (an'tee-ok). Antioch is not quite on the sea and its seaport was named by Seleucus after himself, *Seleucia*. (Seleucus also built a capital city of the same name far to the east.)

During the time of the Roman Empire, Antioch was one of the greatest cities of the East. (Because of its prominence in the Bible, its name was given to a town in California in 1851.) However, it, too, fell to the Turks eventually, though for a time it was freed by the Crusaders. Politically, it shared the history of Alexandretta. The Turkish names of the two cities are Antakya and Süeydiye. The memory of the Macedonian general, Seleucus, is about wiped out in the new spelling, but his son, Antiochus, can still be clearly seen.

14

Argentina

In 1515, the Spanish explorer Juan Diaz de Solis discovered a wide ocean inlet on the western coast of South America well south of the expanding Portuguese dominions in Brazil. He thought at first it might be a sea route through the continent which would allow him to pass on to India (the goal of all good explorers in those days). However, the waters turned fresh when he sailed into it so he knew it must be a river and not a sea route. He called it *Mar Dulce*, meaning "Fresh-water Sea."

The Italian navigator Sebastian Cabot reached the same inlet in 1526 and noticed the natives along the shores wearing silver ornaments. He at once named the inlet *Rio de la Plata* (ree'o-duh-lah-plah'tuh), meaning "river of silver," and of course that dramatic name stuck. By 1776, virtually all the southern part of the continent was lumped together as the *Viceroyalty of the Rio de la Plata*. (A "viceroyalty" is a territory ruled by a "viceroy"; that is, someone who "takes the place of a king.")

In 1823, the viceroyalty gained its independence and then began a civil war that ended in the formation of several nations. The largest of these, which included the southern bank of the Rio de la Plata, called itself by the same silvery name — but in Latin. The Latin word for "silver" is "argentum" and the nation became *Argentina*.

The first settlement on the Rio de la Plata was made in 1536 by a Spaniard named Pedro de Mendoza. He named it *Santa Maria de los Buenos Aires* ("Holy Mary of Fair Winds"). The town is in the south temperate zone and its cool, pleasant climate contrasted very favorably with the tropic blasts of regions farther up the coast. It was a fair wind indeed that brought them there. It is now known simply as *Buenos Aires* (bway'nos-air'iz). It is the capital of Argentina and has a larger population than Chicago. In all the western hemisphere, only New York is clearly a larger city. Northwest of Buenos Aires is *Rosario*, Argentina's second largest city, founded in 1730 by Francisco Godoy. The name is the Spanish word for "rosary."

Ascension

THE MID-PACIFIC is noted for its tiny isolated islands, but the Atlantic Ocean has a few, too.

In the South Atlantic, just about halfway between the bulge of Brazil and the west coast of southern Africa is a small island which was discovered on Ascension Day, 1501, by the Portuguese navigator Joao da Nova. Ascension Day is celebrated forty days after Easter and is the anniversary of the day on which, according to tradition, Jesus Christ ascended to heaven. In honor of the day, the island was named *Ascension*. It is a bit larger than Manhattan Island.

About 750 miles to the southeast is another island, slightly larger than Ascension, which was discovered by Da Nova in the following year. This he named *Saint Helena*, after the mother of Constantine the Great. (He was the first Roman Emperor to turn Christian, partly through his Christian mother's influence, it is supposed.)

From 1656 on, the British occupied Saint Helena. In 1815, it gained sudden notoriety when Napoleon Bonaparte was taken into exile there and in that year Great Britain also annexed Ascension.

Farther south still, about halfway between Buenos Aires and Capetown, are a group of three small islands with a total area about twice that of Manhattan. These were discovered by the Portuguese navigator Tristan da Cunha and were named for him the *Tristan da Cunha Islands* (tris'tan-duh-coo'nuh). They were annexed by the British in 1810.

Ascension Island is noted for its giant sea-turtles but, on the other side of South America, about 650 miles west of Ecuador, are a group of islands noted for their giant land-turtles. These were discovered by the Spanish navigator Tomás de Berlanga in 1535 and he named them for the turtles he found, which, to his amazement, were large enough to carry men on their backs. The Spanish word for "land turtle" is "galápago" and so these bits of land became the *Galápagos Islands* (guh-lah'puh-gus).

Asia

THE ANCIENT Greeks could not help but notice the division of land into two parts separated by water (see AFRICA). There was their own land of Greece on the western side of the Aegean Sea and another land, which they quickly colonized, on the eastern side. They took to calling their own side *Europe* and the eastern side *Asia*.

The origin of the two names is uncertain. One theory is that the words are of Semitic origin and come from "Assu," meaning "east," and "Ereb," meaning "west." In other words, Asia and Europe are the east and the west. What could be better? Such a division still has meaning today.

At first Asia represented only the eastern coastline of the Aegean Sea. In 133 B.C., when the Romans took over control of that coastline and the area behind it, they set up the *Province of Asia*, which reached inland for about 200 miles.

Of course, the Greeks were fond of telling and retelling the story of how little Greece defeated huge Persia. It was a kind of war between Europe and Asia since Persia at the time controlled the Asian coast of the Aegean Sea. To emphasize the David-and-Goliath nature of the war, the Greeks took to applying the term *Asia* to the whole Persian Empire and then to the entire continent that lay behind the coast. The peninsula facing the Aegean Sea, which was the original Asia, now became *Asia Minor*, meaning "little Asia."

And so it is that *Asia*, from tiny beginnings, has become a name that covers Earth's largest continent, making up one third of all its land area.

As knowledge of northern regions grew in the times after the fall of Rome, it was found that Europe and Asia joined north of the Black and Caspian seas and that there was no real division between them. Europe is only a large peninsula sticking out of the western edge of Asia. Men continued to speak of Europe as a separate continent, of course, but the entire land mass is often called *Eurasia* now.

17

Assyria

IT WAS common for early peoples to name a city for their god; or perhaps to name their god for the city — it is hard to tell which is the true situation sometimes. About 2700 B.C., for instance, a group of men along the upper reaches of the Tigris River founded a city called *Asshur* after the name of the god they worshiped. For more than 1500 years it remained an obscure provincial town of Babylonia, but then, under a line of energetic kings, it became powerful and spread out its dominions.

By 800 B.C., Asshur had reached the Mediterranean and by 700 B.C. it had conquered all of Babylonia, with Syria, Israel, and Egypt to boot. The city ruled all the Middle East.

But the armies had overextended themselves and their cruelty made them hated and left them with restless subjects. In 626 B.C., they were attacked by the Medes from without while Babylonia rose in rebellion within. By 612 B.C., Asshur was totally wiped out.

To the Greeks, the empire (concerning which, vague rumors had reached their ears) was *Assyria* and that is the form in which we find it in the Bible.

About 700 B.C., the Assyrian Empire had moved its capital from Asshur to *Nineveh* (nin'uh-vuh) farther up the Tigris. This name is of uncertain origin, but the Greeks, who loved to name cities after mythical founders, even when they had to make up the founders, called it Ninus and insisted it was founded by Assyria's first king, whom they also called Ninus. (There was no such first king or any king by that name, of course.)

The Greeks, too, occasionally named cities after gods. The greatest of all Greek cities, *Athens* ("Athenai" being the Greek name) was named for the goddess Athena. Another and perhaps older form of the word, before it got twisted to match the goddess's name, is *Attica* and that is the name of the peninsula on which the city of Athens is located.

18

Asunción

WHEN THE southern part of South America became independent of
Spain, most of it ended as the republic of Argentina. Two small sections, however, formed separate nations. Both were named after
rivers flowing southward into the Rio de la Plata (see ARGENTINA).

To the north and in the interior is the land on either side of the
Paraguay River, which became *Paraguay* (par'uh-gwy). A city on
the Paraguay River was founded in 1537 by Pedro de Mendoza who,
the year before, had founded Buenos Aires. The new city was
founded on August 15, which is the Feast of the Assumption; that is,
the anniversary of the day on which, according to tradition, the
Virgin Mary was taken up to heaven. The city was consequently
named Nuestra Señora de la Asunción, meaning "Our Lady of the
Assumption." That is still its official name but it is referred to, invariably, simply as *Asunción* (ah-soon-syawn').

To the southeast and on the coast is the nation on the east bank of
the Uruguay River, which is therefore called *Uruguay* (yoo'roo-
gwy). It is about the size of Missouri and is the smallest nation in
South America. Its official name is Republica Oriental del Uruguay,
meaning "eastern republic of the Uruguay" because it was originally
the eastern part of the Viceroyalty of the Rio de la Plata. It was formerly also called Banda Orientale, meaning "east coast" because it
was on the east coast of the Uruguay River.

The capital of Uruguay is *Montevideo* (mon-tuh-vi-day'o), on its
southern coast. Its name is supposedly derived from a low hill near
by. The Portuguese navigator Ferdinand Magellan, during his voyage
around the world in 1519, explored the Rio de la Plata as a possible
sea route through South America and, on approaching the coast, a
sailor is supposed to have cried out, *"Monte vide eu"* (that is, "I see
a hill"). In this way, the city, settled two hundred years later, in
1726, was supposedly named.

Augusta

WHEN Octavius Caesar became the first Roman Emperor, he took the name Augustus, meaning "undertaken under favorable auguries." It was a "good-luck" name, in other words. However, it became associated with imperial power and it became therefore a popular name for rulers, especially among the Germans. The feminine version, Augusta, could be used for princesses.

There was one such in the British Royal House in the early eighteenth century. The British ruler, George II (himself a German), had a daughter-in-law who was a German princess named Augusta. She never became queen because her husband, the Prince of Wales, died before George II did. However, her son eventually became king as George III.

Well, then, in 1735, the English colonist James Oglethorpe laid out a town about 150 miles up the Savannah River from the coast of Georgia, his newly founded colony. It seemed appropriate to him to name it for the princess, and the town is now *Augusta*.

But these names are not confined only to royalty. In 1797, a town was founded in Maine and named after the daughter of Henry Dearborn, a New Hampshire man prominent in Maine politics at the time. His daughter was quite as much an Augusta as George III's mother had been and *Augusta* is now the capital of Maine.

Even more frivolous was the naming of a city sixty miles to the northeast of Augusta, Maine. In 1781, the region was petitioning for permission to form a town and they sent their minister, Seth Noble, to Boston (Maine was part of Massachusetts then) to file the necessary papers. He was humming a hymn while waiting and when asked for the name of the town, he thought he was being asked the name of the hymn, and he said "Bangor." Thus it is that Maine has a town named *Bangor*.

On the other hand, the easternmost city in Maine, and, therefore, the easternmost city in the United States, is simply and very appropriately named *Eastport*. No frivolity there.

Australia

WHEN THE ancient Greeks realized the earth was a globe, they also realized that all the land they knew of existed north of the equator. They felt it only symmetrical to suppose that there was also land south of the equator but felt that this southern land was unreachable because of the heat of the equatorial regions. This supposedly unreachable land became known as Terra Australis, which, in Latin, means "southern land."

During the age of exploration in the 1400's, it was discovered that the equator could be reached and passed, so men began to search for the southern land. Africa and South America extended south of the equator, but what was wanted was a continent that was entirely southern. As it turned out, a small one actually existed.

In 1606, a Spanish navigator, Luis Vaez de Torres, sailed around the equatorial island of New Guinea and just missed the continent to its south. The strait between the continent and New Guinea is still called *Torres Strait* (tawr'es).

Dutch navigators then landed in the western portion of the southern continent and called it *New Holland*. In 1642, the Dutch navigator Abel Janszoon Tasman circumnavigated the continent and discovered an island to its south which he called *Van Diemen's Land* (van-dee'menz) after Anton van Diemen, the Dutch governor of the East Indies who had commissioned the voyage. The island is now called *Tasmania* in Tasman's honor. Tasman went on to discover a group of islands to the southeast which he named Nieuw Zeeland or, in English, *New Zealand*. This was after a group of islands off the coast of his native land of the Netherlands which were referred to as *Zeeland*. The name was a good one for the low, flat Dutch islands, for it means "sea land," but not so good for the large mountainous ones Tasman had found.

In 1770, the English explorer James Cook (or "Captain Cook," as he is better known) landed on the southern continent, which was then gradually taken over by the English, who dropped "New Holland" naturally, and went back to the older Latin name of *Australia*.

Austria

THE LATIN word "australis" means "south" (see AUSTRALIA) but that does not account for *Austria*.

When Charlemagne established his empire in the eighth century, there were dangers from enemies on all sides. On the boundaries, then, he established special armed "marches" or "marks" (from an old German word meaning "boundary").

In the northeast, for instance, Dane Mark was established against the Danes and the land of the Danes themselves is now called *Denmark* as a result.

Again, the Ost Mark, meaning "eastern march," was established in the east against the barbarian Avars. This became the "eastern kingdom" or, in modern German, "Oesterreich." The English language twists this to *Austria*, which thus comes from the German word for "east" and not from the Latin word "south." (For a period after 1938, when Austria was part of Hitler's Germany, it was called Ostmark again.)

Just to the east of Austria is a plain which formed the center of the dominions of Attila the Hun, when he was attacking the broken remnants of the Roman Empire in 450. Though the Huns were defeated and have vanished, the plain is still called *Hungary* ("Ungarn" in German).

A new group of barbarians, the Magyars, occupied the plain beginning in 870, and it is their language which now dominates the area. In that language, the land is called Magyar-orszag, meaning "land of the Magyars."

From 1700 on, Hungary was under the domination of Austria. After numerous rebellions, however, Hungary won the right, in 1867, of self-rule. From then on, the nation was known as *Austria-Hungary*. After World War I, both nations (being on the losing side) were separated and reduced in size so that now there is both an Austria and a Hungary.

Azores

THROUGH THE 1400's, Portuguese explorers probed down the African coast in an endeavor to round the continent and reach India and the Far East. Almost at once, islands close at hand were discovered. In 1427, a Portuguese navigator, Diogo de Seville, came across a group of nine islands 750 miles west of Portugal. He was impressed by the hawks ("açor" in Portuguese) he found there and named them the Açores in consequence. We call them the *Azores* (uh-zawrz') and they still belong to Portugal.

Inching down along the barren coast of northwestern Africa, along the edge of the Sahara, was difficult and disheartening for the small ships of the time. Finally in 1445, Dinis Dias reached the westernmost project of Africa and found the desert was passed. The coast was populated, supplies could be obtained, trading could take place, and all this is reflected in the name he gave this westernmost cape. He called it *Cape Verde* (vurd), meaning "Green Cape." A group of islands 320 miles west are the *Cape Verde Islands*. They, too, belong to Portugal.

At one point, even in the desert regions, explorers had been able to barter material for gold dust. As a result, an area along the northwestern coast of Africa is named *Rio de Oro*, which means "river of gold" in Spanish. The region is now Spanish, but dreams of gold have long since evaporated. It has another name, the much more realistic one of *Spanish Sahara*.

A more appropriate sign of the type of trade possible in the area is to be found in the name of a region past the African bulge and on the southern shore of west Africa. This is the *Ivory Coast*, taken over by the French in 1842. It became an independent nation in 1960, retaining that name which, in French, is "Côte d'Ivoire."

Some of the trade was disreputable indeed, as is shown by the fact that a section of the coast east of the Ivory Coast was long known as the *Slave Coast*. Most of the Negroes brought to America originated from this section of Africa. That name, fortunately, has disappeared from the map.

Baghdad

AFTER THE death of Alexander the Great in 323 B.C., the huge empire which he had conquered was divided up by his generals. Most of the Asiatic portion fell to one named Seleucus, who thus founded the *Seleucid Empire*.

The largest city in the Seleucid dominions was Babylon on the Euphrates River (see MESOPOTAMIA). Seleucus, however, wanted a capital all his own, a Greek one. Therefore, in 312 B.C. he built a new city on the Tigris River about fifty miles north of Babylon and named it *Seleucia* (si-lyoo′shee-uh) after himself. He dismantled Babylon to build the new city and so Babylon disappeared while Seleucia became great.

Meanwhile, to the east of the Seleucid Empire, a Persian tribe which called itself Parthava, but is known to us in the Latinized version, *Parthia*, began to make head. By 150 B.C., the Parthians had conquered Mesopotamia. They found Seleucia too Greek for them and so they made their capital at *Ctesiphon* (which in Greek means something like "full of sound") just across the river.

The Parthians were in turn conquered by other Persian peoples under a line of kings who were descended from an ancestor named Sassan. In A.D. 226 the *Sassanid Empire* was established. Ctesiphon remained the capital and Seleucia fell into ruins.

In 642, the Sassanid Empire was defeated by the Arabs and wholly conquered. Persia turned Moslem and was ruled for a while by Arabian caliphs at Damascus. In 750, however, Abu-l-Abbas founded a new dynasty of caliphs that lasted five hundred years. The dominions of his line were termed the *Abbasid Caliphate* in his honor.

In 762, the second Abbasid caliph, al-Mansur established his capital in Mesopotamia, but Ctesiphon was too Persian for him. He picked on a small village, fifty miles up the Tigris, named *Baghdad* (from Persian words meaning "given by God") as the new capital. Now Baghdad grew great and Ctesiphon fell into ruins. Baghdad is, even today, the capital of Iraq.

Barcelona

In 264 B.C., Rome went to war with Carthage, the powerful commercial city across the sea in northern Africa. After more than twenty years of hard fighting, Rome was victor and assumed ownership of the islands of Sicily and Sardinia, which had previously been largely Carthaginian. The Carthaginians buckled down to build new power and empire in Spain (and from that as a base nearly — but not quite — destroyed Rome in a second war a generation later).

The Carthaginian leader in this project was their capable general, Hamilcar Barca (who was to be the father of Hannibal, perhaps the greatest general in history). According to tradition, he founded a town on Spain's eastern coast which was named Barcina in his honor. During Roman times, it came to be Barcinona and it is now known as *Barcelona.*

Barcelona is now the second largest city in Spain, just a hairbreadth behind the Spanish capital, *Madrid* (which was founded in 932 on the site of a newly conquered Moslem village named Magerit, of which *Madrid* is a distorted version).

In 801, Charlemagne took Barcelona from the Moslems, who had conquered Spain a century earlier, and for some centuries it was the center of an independent county. In 1137, however, it was absorbed by Aragon, a kingdom to the north.

The easternmost shore of Spain, of which Barcelona is the center, is known as *Catalonia.* This name, like *Andalusia* (see ANDALUSIA), represents a reminder of the Germanic invaders that swarmed into Spain after the breakup of the Roman Empire, for Catalonia is a distortion of "Gothalonia."

For a while in the fourteenth century, Catalonian mercenaries hired by the Byzantine Emperor Andronicus II to help against the Turks, made their mark in the east. They turned on their employer (as is usual with mercenaries) and for seventy years ruled Athens as an independent power called the *Catalan Grand Company.*

Belgium

JULIUS CAESAR, in describing Gaul, mentions the "Belgii" as living in the northeast and praises their courage. They did not survive as a separate people through subsequent history, but, thanks to Caesar, their name was not forgotten.

The home of the Belgii was part of the Netherlandish region that flourished through the Middle Ages. The portion nearest France and England was known as *Flanders,* from the "Flandri," another Gallic tribe living there in pre-Roman times.

During the period of the Reformation, the Netherlands rose in revolt against Spain, and the northern portion (Protestant) finally gained its independence. The southern portion (Catholic) remained under the control of Spain. Later, after 1701, they were under Austrian domination. After the fall of Napoleon, both parts of the Netherlands were united in order to form a strong barrier against a revival of imperial France. However, in 1831, the Catholic south, dissatisfied with the arrangement, broke away, and established its independence at last, taking the ancient name of *Belgium.* Within its borders, two languages are official, French and Flemish, and the name of the nation is "Belgique" in French and "Belgie" in Flemish.

Belgium's largest city is a river town, so tied to commerce that it was simply referred to at first as "aan het werf," meaning "on the wharf." This has become *Antwerp* ("Anvers" in French).

The capital of Belgium was founded during the barbarian invasions when natives fled into the marshes and established a village named Bruocsella, meaning "village of the marshes." This has become *Brussels* today ("Bruxelle" in French).

Southeast of Belgium there was in Roman times a little town named Lucilinburhuc, which, in the native language, meant "little town." By 963, when a German count took possession, that name had been twisted to *Luxemburg.* It avoided entanglements with the neighboring larger states and is still an independent Grand Duchy.

Bengal

THE SACRED river of the Hindus, the Ganges, flows southwestward across northern India and ends in a gigantic delta which constitutes one of the most densely populated portions of the world. In ancient times it formed the center of a powerful kingdom called Banga, but in 1200, the region was conquered by Moslem invaders.

The British first penetrated India in this region which became known as *Bengal,* a version of the old name of the area. The great inlet of the Indian Ocean into which the Ganges flows is therefore the *Bay of Bengal.*

The Moslem penetration of Bengal had important consequences in modern times. In 1948, when India gained its independence, the northwest section, being mainly Moslem, was set up as a separate nation. Since parts of Bengal were also largely Moslem, the eastern portion of that province was split off and added to the northwestern nation. That nation (Pakistan) thus came to consist of two parts separated by about a thousand miles of Indian territory.

The Bay of Bengal contains a group of narrow islands running almost due north and south inhabited by a dark-skinned pygmy race very low in the scale of civilization. To explorers from the more advanced lands of the surrounding mainland, they may have seemed a curious kind of large monkey, for it is possible that the name of the islands originally came from the Malayan word "hanuman," meaning "monkey."

To the Arabs, this name became "Angaman," and the Italian traveler Marco Polo referred to them as "Angamanian." In modern times, they are called the *Andaman Islands.* The three chief islands, in a straight line and nearly connected, are *North Andaman, Middle Andaman,* and *South Andaman,* lumped together as *Great Andaman.*

The chief town is *Port Cornwallis,* founded in 1792, and named for the general, Charles Cornwallis, whom George Washington defeated at Yorktown in 1781. However, five years later he was governor-general of India and far more successful there than he had been in America.

Birmingham

THE OLD English word "ham" means a "group of dwellings" and from it comes the word "hamlet" for a small village and that wonderful word "home." The suffix "-ham" is therefore often used in the names of English towns. An example is the large city of *Birmingham* in central England. One theory has it that, in Saxon times, the family ("ing" in old Saxon) of someone named Birm lived there so that the name of the city means "the home of the Birm family."

After the Industrial Revolution of the late 1700's, Birmingham began to change from a sleepy agricultural town into a bustling manufacturing center. It was the very model of the new industry.

When the Civil War was over, the Industrial Revolution hit the United States in earnest. Even the agricultural South was affected. One region which began to bustle with manufacturing activity was organized as a town in 1871 and deliberately took the name of Birmingham with the British example in mind.

Birmingham is now the largest city in *Alabama*, a state named after an Indian tribe that had once lived in the area. The capital of the state lies a hundred miles south of Birmingham. It is the city of *Montgomery*, founded in 1819, the year that Alabama entered the Union as the 22nd state. It was named after the Revolutionary general Richard Montgomery, who had been killed in a futile assault on Quebec in 1775.

Alabama has a short seacoast on the Gulf of Mexico and there the city of *Mobile* is to be found. "Mobile" is a French word and the city originated as a French settlement in 1711, so one might try to think of a reason for it to be called "movable." However, that's an illusion. The city was originally named Fort Louis de la Mobile. The first part of the name honors Louis XIV, then the aged king of France, but the "Mobile" part has nothing to do with "movable." It comes from a tribe of Indians of the vicinity that called themselves by a name that the French spelled "Mauvilla." That they converted further into the familiar (to them) word "Mobile."

Biscay

IN THE western Pyrenees live the remnants of an ancient people. Their language is not like any other language in Europe, or in the world. They seem to represent a racial group that lived in Europe before the Celts or any of the other Indo-European peoples had entered.

The people call their language Euskara, and the Romans used a version of that word when they called them Vascones. In Roman times, their territory was larger than it is today, but the invading barbarians of the fifth century drove them into the mountains. The French name for these people substitutes a *B* for the initial *V* and we inherit that when we call them Basques and speak of the three *Basque Provinces* in northern Spain. The Spaniards retain the *V* and call the chief of these provinces Vizcaya, a name that is, to us, *Biscay*. The section of the Atlantic Ocean north of Spain is therefore the *Bay of Biscay*.

In their attempt to escape from the invading barbarians, the Basques ("Vascones," remember) moved north of the Pyrenees and established a hold in what is now the southwestern section of France. This was a new "Vasconia." The region became completely French in time, but the name persists. The French substituted a *G* for the *V* this time and it became "Gascogne" or, in English, *Gascony*. For this reason, the Bay of Biscay is sometimes called the *Gulf of Gascony*. (The alliteration, you will notice, is retained.)

The chief of the modern Basque cities was established in 1300 by Diego Lopez de Haro at a place along a river where it could easily be forded. He named it Belvao, meaning "fine ford," and this has become *Bilbao* (bil-bah'o).

The *Pyrenees Mountains*, themselves, were supposed, by the Greeks, to be named for Pyrene, a young lady of the region whom Hercules, on one of his western voyages, carried on with. More likely, the word was originally derived from a Greek word meaning a "rounded knob," a phrase which seemed to describe some of the Pyrenees' foothills.

Black Sea

DURING THE early stages of their exploring, the Greeks found their way through the narrow straits between Europe and Asia to their northeast and entered the broad sea beyond. The new sea was not like their own Aegean with its many islands and short distances. Instead, it was an open stretch of water, stormy, foggy, and difficult for small ships to navigate, so they called it the "axeinos" or "bad to strangers."

However, the Greeks felt it was bad luck to speak ill of anything. If one were unkind to the sea, it might be unkind in return, so it was renamed the Euxine, meaning "good to strangers."

But later peoples who reached its shores were less superstitious than the Greeks, or more annoyed, for they went back to the use of an insulting name. The Russians, for instance, call it Chernoe More, meaning "black sea," the color referring to the ill fortune it brought sailors, no doubt, and we know it by that name, too. It is the *Black Sea*.

There are other seas of color, too. On the northern coast of European Russia is a large ocean inlet, choked with ice for more than half the year and therefore called Beloe More, meaning "white sea," by the Russians. We call it *White Sea*, too.

The reason why the narrow arm of the ocean between Egypt and Saudi Arabia is called the *Red Sea* is, in contrast, not known, but it was called that in both Latin and Greek. One theory is that certain reddish microorganisms sometimes increase in numbers and turn the water red, but that is not very convincing. The Arabic name is "Bahr-el-Hejaz," meaning "Sea of Hejaz," because the Arabian district of Hejaz forms its eastern shore.

The *Yellow Sea* is the large inlet of the Pacific Ocean between Korea and China. The turbulent waters of the *Yellow River* ("Hwang-Ho" is the Chinese name) pour into it. The river is yellow with the silt it continually strips from its banks, and the shallow sea is consequently yellow in those portions near the land. The colored name is appropriate.

Boston

THE VARIOUS American cities named for saints usually carry those names openly, with the word "saint" (or the Spanish "san" or "santa") making up part of the name. There are exceptions, though.

About 680, an English monk named Botolph founded a monastery near the east-central coast of England. Eventually, he was made a saint and about the monastery arose a town which, very naturally, was named St. Botolph's Town. The British, however, have a gift of slurring names they use often. The "saint" was dropped, plus a few other inconvenient letters, and the whole name was telescoped into *Boston*.

In 1630, a group of Puritan colonists sailed to the New World in search of a place where they might worship as they pleased and be the persecutors for a change. A number of them hailed from Boston, and when they arrived at their destination, they named the new town after the old so that there is now an American *Boston* some thirty times the size of the English one.

In this there was precedence, for in 1620 an earlier band of Puritans (the "Pilgrim Fathers") had come to the area. They landed first at a cape south of Boston called *Cape Cod* from the codfish that abounded in the waters about it. Here the winter was too severe so they moved up the coast and founded a settlement named *Plymouth* after the west channel port of *Plymouth* in England, from which their ship had sailed.

Earlier still, John Smith (the English soldier of fortune who had made the Virginia colony a success) had come exploring northward and in 1614 named the area about Boston *Massachusetts Bay*. This came from Indian words meaning "near the great hill" in reference to hills south of Boston where Indian tribes gathered for discussion.

As a result, the colony of which Boston was the center was called Massachusetts Bay, and the colony of Plymouth was merged with it in 1691. The name shrank to *Massachusetts* and under that name it was one of the thirteen original states, and the sixth to ratify the Constitution.

31

Brandenburg

FRANCE AND Spain developed strong central governments during the later Middle Ages, but Germany did not. That area consisted instead of virtually independent units, some of them made up of single cities or small patches of land, well into the nineteenth century.

One of the more important units was a region east of the river Elbe, which became German only in 936, when the Holy Roman Emperor, Henry I, attacked eastward and drove out the Slavs of the region. The chief Slavic town was Brennibor ("forest fortress" in the local tongue) and the incoming Germans called it Brennibor-burg, giving it a suffix meaning "town" in German. With time, that became *Brandenburg*, and this name was given also to the surrounding area.

Brandenburg gained a strong line of rulers when, in 1412, the house of Hohenzollern took it over. By the end of the century, they abandoned the town of Brandenburg as capital and established in its place a growing town to the east which was called *Berlin*. Berlin has come to be one of the great cities of the world, but its name remains of uncertain origin.

Other towns in the area date back to the Slavs one way or another. Southwest of Berlin is *Potsdam*, made famous in the eighteenth century by the greatest of the Hohenzollern line, Frederick II. Its name sounds as German as its associations, but that name is only a distortion of Postupimi (meaning perhaps "under the oaks"), the name of an early Slavic town on that site.

Sometimes completely German names occur, though. A fortified spot on a ford along the Oder River was established as protection against the Slavs in the thirteenth century, and in 1253, a group of merchants from Franconia (as southwestern Germany was then known) settled there. The town became the "Franconian ford" or *Frankfurt*. It is usually called *Frankfurt an der Oder* to distinguish it from a larger and older Frankfurt further west, one established by Franks on a ford on the river Main back in the 700's and therefore called *Frankfurt am Main*. (The English spelling is *Frankfort*.)

32

Brazil

AN OLD French word for glowing coals or embers is "braise" and that still survives with us in such words as "brazier," which is used for a pan intended to hold glowing embers.

There is a certain hard, red wood, valuable for the preparation of dyes, that was so brightly colored as to seem to be already burning. It was therefore named "braise-wood," which was eventually twisted into "brazilwood."

In the 1300's a story arose that out in the mysterious Atlantic there was an island rich in brazilwood and, of course, it was named Brazil. It was never found, however.

Now in 1493, after the discovery of Christopher Columbus, Pope Alexander VI tried to avoid quarrels over the new territories by drawing a vertical line (the "Line of Demarcation") about a hundred leagues west of the Azores, and allotted all new territories east of the line to Portugal and west of it to Spain. The next year, Portugal arranged to have the line moved 270 leagues farther west. Spain did not realize that South America bulged so far east that the new line crossed that continent. Perhaps Portugal did realize that, but there is no proof either way.

In any case, in 1500, the Portuguese navigator Pedro Alvarez Cabral, supposedly heading around Africa for the East Indies, somehow managed to get across the Atlantic and land on the South American bulge east of the Pope's line. He claimed it for Portugal, and settlers swarmed along the coast and inland, well beyond the Line of Demarcation, until the Portuguese dominion in South America covered a territory nearly half the continent.

The first traders found brazilwood in plenty and soon the land became known as *Brazil* ("Brasil" in Portuguese). Thus, at least one legend turned into reality, even though the land was not an island. It is just barely possible that the rumor concerning the mythical island of Brazil may have arisen through rumors about the South American coast originating out of voyages unrecorded and forgotten.

Brittany

THE CELTS who had inhabited Britain in Roman times slowly retreated before the invading Anglo-Saxons from the east, after the breakup of the Roman Empire. By A.D. 500, they were forced westward into Wales and into the smaller peninsula of *Cornwall*, south of Wales. This southern peninsula narrows like a horn, and "corn" is an old word for "horn." Cornwall therefore means "the Welsh on the horn."

Cornwall was finally subdued by the Saxon king, Athelstan, in 936. Wales, however, held out for several additional centuries and was conquered only after the Saxons themselves had been laid low by the Normans.

A number of the British Celts were forced out of their island altogether. Across the Channel in France, a peninsula lies to the south of Cornwall. In Roman times, it was called *Armorica*, from Celtic words meaning "upon the sea." To that peninsula, Celtic refugees from Britain made their way in such numbers that the very name of the land changed. In Latin, it came to be known as *Britannia Minor*, meaning "little Britain."

In French, the peninsula is now "Bretagne" while the island from which the refugees arrived is "Grand Bretagne." In English, the Armorican peninsula has become *Brittany*. An inhabitant of the island of Britain may be called a Briton and an inhabitant of Brittany is a Breton, which is the French version of the same word.

There is another similarity in the maps of Cornwall and Brittany. As one travels southwestward through Cornwall one eventually comes to the cape of land that marks the extreme tip of Great Britain in that direction. Very logically, it is termed *Land's End*.

Precisely the same thing happens in Brittany, except that there the French language is used. The westernmost point of Brittany, and, therefore, of France, is *Finistère*, which is "Land's End" in French.

And to cap it, the cape marking the westernmost point of Spain is called *Cape Finisterre*, which is still a third "Land's End."

34

Buffalo

IN THE nineteenth century, one of the most dramatic aspects of the West was the buffalo that roamed its plains in huge herds. The buffalo is a form of wild ox and its name can be traced back to "bous," the Greek word for "ox." A German word for a wild ox was "Wisent" and from this comes the alternate name of "bison." They were almost entirely slaughtered by the early white settlers, partly for food, partly for skins, partly for sport, and partly to wipe out the food supply of the Plains Indians. By the 1890's what few buffaloes remained were under protection and even now only a few protected herds exist, though there is no longer any immediate danger of extinction.

One might suppose that the West would have some sign of these large, shaggy creatures somewhere on its map, but nothing more than a county and village or two exists. But far in the east, in New York State, is the large city of *Buffalo*. It received its name from the small river on which it was founded and that in turn received its name as early as 1764 when, the story goes, some travelers felt they had seen signs of buffalo in the vicinity. That seems far east for buffalo, though, and perhaps the name was taken from some Indian tribal chief whose name meant "buffalo," or just sounded like it.

To the north, across Lake Ontario, in Canada, is an even larger city with a name that is unmistakably Indian. This is *Toronto*, from an Indian word meaning "a place of meeting" because on this site, in early days, representatives of the various Indian tribes of the region gathered for conferences.

Farther north still, at the boundary between the provinces of Ontario and Quebec, runs the *Ottawa River*, taking its name from a tribe of Indians who were called "adawe," an Indian word meaning "to trade." The city of *Ottawa*, on the river, was chosen in 1858 by Queen Victoria herself to be the capital of the united provinces of *Upper Canada* (that part on the upper St. Lawrence, i.e., Ontario) and *Lower Canada* (on the lower St. Lawrence, i.e., Quebec). When Canada became a dominion in 1867, including vast western territories in addition to the two provinces, Ottawa remained the capital.

Bulgaria

SOUTHERN EUROPE is divided into three peninsulas jutting south into the Mediterranean Sea. The easternmost of these includes Greece at its southern tip. North of Greece, there is a mountain range running east and west which the Greeks called Haemus, from their word for "blood," because of the ruddy color of the rocks composing it.

The Turks conquered the peninsula between 1350 and 1450 and, from their word for "mountain," the range became known as the *Balkan Mountains*. As a result, the whole peninsula is now called the *Balkan peninsula*, while the nations among which the area is divided are lumped together as the *Balkan States*.

Before the coming of the Turks, the Balkan peninsula had been invaded by Slavs from the north. About 700, these were followed by an Asiatic people called Bulgars, who had arrived from the east, possibly from the region of the *Volga River*, since "Bulgar" and "Volga" may come from the same source.

The Bulgarians set up a strong empire in the tenth century, one stretching over most of the Balkan peninsula. The Byzantine emperor, Basil II, after a long war, completely defeated the Bulgarians by 1018. Their great days were over and they melted into the Slavic population among which they lived. Nevertheless, the area retains the Asiatic name of *Bulgaria* ("Blgariya" in Bulgarian).

By the middle 1400's, the whole area had fallen to the Turks — Greeks, Slavs, Bulgarians and all. It wasn't until 1878, after Turkey had lost a war to Russia, that Bulgaria achieved independence once more.

The Bulgarian capital, *Sofia*, received its name from a medieval church dedicated to Saint Sophia. This was a popular name for eastern churches since the East Roman emperor, Justinian, had built the great cathedral of Saint Sophia in Constantinople in 562. "Sophia" is from the Greek word for "wisdom" so that the capital of one nation, at least, is named for that rather rare faculty among nations.

Burgundy

THE VARIOUS Germanic tribes who invaded the lands of the Roman Empire did not maintain their identity long. They faded into the population through intermarriage and by adopting the more civilized customs and culture of the people they had conquered. Their names persisted on the map, however.

Thus, one Germanic tribe was known as the Burgundians, and after they settled down in southwestern Gaul, shortly after 400, the region they inhabited became known as *Burgundy*, or, in French, "Bourgogne."

Burgundy was conquered by the Franks and through the Middle Ages remained under the domination of the French kings and of the German monarchs of the Holy Roman Empire. That section of the Holy Roman Empire immediately west of modern Switzerland was sometimes known as the *County of Burgundy*, but so Frenchified had it become that an alternate name was *Franche Comté* (frahnsh-konetay'), meaning "French county."

In 1362, King John II of France gave the Burgundian sections of his kingdom to a younger son, Philip, and made him Duke of Burgundy. Burgundy remained theoretically under the rule of the King of France, but, in actual fact, it became a virtually independent duchy, particularly since the descendants of Philip extended their rule over non-French lands in the Netherlands, and grew rich on the proceeds of Dutch commerce. In the 1470's, Charles the Bold, great-grandson of Philip, almost overthrew France, but was outmaneuvered by France's wily king, Louis XI.

After the death of Charles the Bold, the French portions of Burgundy became permanently French. Two hundred years later, the French king, Louis XIV, annexed Franche Comté as well.

Burgundy remained a province of France till the French Revolution and then the name of the old Germanic tribe vanished. One of the reforms of that revolution was to bring the nation under the centralized rule of Paris. The ancient provinces, including Burgundy, were divided up into small "départements" to weaken regional feelings and reduce the chances of civil war.

Cairo

THE HISTORY of Egypt fades far back into the centuries and it has cities that were old before the Pyramids were built. Among the oldest was one on the west bank of the Nile River near the point where the river first spreads out into the delta. Apparently the first pharaoh of a united Egypt, Menes, made it his capital about 3000 B.C. It may even have been named (or renamed) after him. The Greek version of this name was *Memphis* and from a Babylonian version of that name, the Greeks may have derived "Aigyptos," which to us becomes *Egypt*, as the name of the land.

Memphis held on to a measure of greatness for nearly three thousand years till the Ptolemies made their capital in Alexandria (see ALEXANDRIA) in 300 B.C. By the time the Arabs conquered Egypt in 641, Memphis was about done. The Arabs built new towns at the base of the delta, but ignored the actual site of Memphis. They built their cities on the east bank and used Memphis only as a source of building material. The Arabs built four cities in the area before they laid out a permanent Egyptian capital. The final one was built in 968 by the first of a new dynasty and is now the capital of Egypt and the largest city in Africa to boot. The Arabic name is "Al-Qahirah," meaning "the victorious," and the English version of that name is *Cairo* (kie′ro).

Yet Memphis is not entirely gone. In Tennessee, there is a spot where the Spanish explorer Hernando de Soto is supposed to have stood in 1541 and become the first white man to look upon the Mississippi River. In 1819, a city was laid out on that spot and, because the founders thought the spot as historic as that upon which Memphis had stood, they named the town *Memphis*.

Again, in southern Illinois, at the point where the Ohio meets the Mississippi, there is a strip of fertile land that seems as dependent on the broad waters of the Ohio as Egypt had been on the Nile. A gloriously fertile future was foreseen; the area is still sometimes called *Little Egypt* and where Ohio and Mississippi meet is another *Cairo* (pronounced kay′ro, however).

38

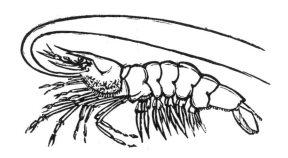

Cameroun

JUST WHERE the Atlantic coast of Africa makes a right-angle bend and begins to run north and south after having run east and west, there is a bay and, twenty miles offshore, an island about half the size of our own Long Island. The Portuguese explorer Fernando Poo, coming that way in 1571, discovered both. The island he called Formosa, meaning "beautiful," but later generations chose to honor the explorer and called it *Fernando Poo*. The Portuguese, Spanish, and English all occupied it in turn and abandoned it. Finally, in 1844, the Spanish tried again and this time they stayed and are still there.

As for the near-by bay, Fernando Poo found it to have prawns aplenty so he named the river running into it Rio dos Camerãos, meaning "river of prawns." The name did not stick, for the river now bears the native name of Wouri River. However, the Portuguese for "prawn" spread itself over that entire region of the west African coast which, in English, came to be known as *Cameroons*.

Great Britain, for some reason, neglected to appropriate that section of the coast though it lay adjacent to its colony of Nigeria. Consequently when Germany began a drive to find left-over portions of Africa to colonize, this region qualified. Germany took over the territory in 1884 and in German the land became "Kamerun."

After World War I, however, defeated Germany gave up most of Kamerun to France and the French spelling was "Cameroun." In 1960, when most of the French colonies received their independence, this region of prawns entered upon the world stage as the independent republic of *Cameroun*.

Not all of German Kamerun became French. Two strips in the northwest, adjacent to Nigeria, went to Great Britain and became the *British Cameroons*. Nigeria became independent in 1960 along with Cameroun, but the British Cameroons, lying between, remained a colony. Apparently, there is some indecision as to which nation this section ought to join.

Canary Islands

THE ANCIENT Greeks and Romans spoke of islands in the far west, which to them meant the Atlantic Ocean. These islands were viewed as a kind of earthly paradise and were called the Isles of the Blest, or the Fortunate Isles. Naturally, these were mythical but they served a useful purpose in encouraging navigators to head into the Atlantic in search of them. And if no Fortunate Isles existed, other islands, not quite paradises, but at least real, did exist.

Even in Roman times, tales of the real islands made themselves heard. For instance, the Roman writer Gaius Plinius Secundus (usually called simply Pliny) described islands which he claimed were called Canaria because of the large dogs found upon them. (The Latin word for "dog" is "canis.")

During the Middle Ages, these islands, about 800 miles southwest of Spain and Portugal, were lost sight of, but in the fourteenth century, when those two countries began their careers of exploration, the islands were rediscovered. For a while, both Portugal and Spain laid claim to them, but by 1400 they were definitely Spanish and have remained so ever since. The Spanish name, going back to the Roman, is "Islas Canarias" and, in English, that is *Canary Islands*.

A type of finch, native to the Canaries, was first domesticated in the 1500's and is now a popular household pet valued for its bright yellow color and its pleasant song. It is, of course, called "canary" and it is natural to think of the Canary Islands as having been named for the bird. As it happens, though, the bird was named for the islands and the islands were, as aforesaid, named for dogs.

The Portuguese, as a consolation prize, picked up a small group of islands north of the Canaries in 1418, when a Portuguese navigator, João Gonçalves Zarco, discovered them. They had been known to the Romans as the Purple Islands (purple in the distant haze of the horizon) but Zarco named the largest of the group *Madeira* (muh-dee'ruh), meaning "timber," because it was well wooded.

Cape of Good Hope

THE PORTUGUESE explorers who inched their way down the African coast searching for a route to India were delighted when they rounded Africa's western bulge and sailed eastward for fifteen hundred miles and more. Apparently, they were heading directly toward India. By 1472, when Fernando Poo discovered the island named for himself, the coastline had been followed back half the width of Africa.

But then it turned south again, and for a while all was despair and the Portuguese expeditions languished. In 1481, however, John II came to the Portuguese throne and he began pushing the project with new energy. Explorers advanced south again and, in 1487, the Portuguese navigator Bartolemeu Dias, venturing farther south than anyone before him, was caught in a tremendous storm and driven still farther south. When he beat his way out of it and back to the coast, he found it to be running toward the east again, and even toward the northeast. He called the point of land he had rounded during the storm Cabo Tormentoso, meaning "Cape of Storms."

Not so John II. When he heard the news, it seemed to him that this might be the southernmost point of the continent; that it would turn south no more but would finally allow the passage of ships to India. He renamed it Cabo da Boa Esperança, meaning *Cape of Good Hope*.

Good hope it proved to be, for, in 1497, the Portuguese navigator Vasco da Gama rounded that cape, kept on going, and reached India. He landed at a town on India's southwest coast which bore the native name of *Kozhikode* (ko'zhi-kode), which to Western ears sounded like *Calicut* (from which the type of cloth called "calico" was first obtained). Now that India is independent, the native name is coming back into official use.

Calicut is sometimes confused with *Calcutta*, a much larger city on India's northeast coast. It was founded by the English trader Job Charnock in 1690, and its name is the English version of Kalikata, the name of an Indian village which had existed on the site.

41

Caribbean Sea

JUST BEFORE the coming of Christopher Columbus, an Indian tribe, the Caribales, who lived on the north coast of South America, began to invade the smaller islands of the West Indies that curved upward from the South American coast. Columbus, when he reached the larger islands to the north, heard tales from the natives of the fierce Caribales to the south who fed on human flesh. The word "cannibal" arose at this time as a twisting of the word "Caribal."

When Europeans finally took over the West Indies in earnest, they exterminated the native Indians, including the Caribales, and repopulated the islands with Negro slaves brought over from Africa. Nevertheless, the name of the Indian tribe remains on the map, for the stretch of water enclosed by the West Indies, Central America, and South America is called the *Caribbean Sea*.

The line of small islands between Puerto Rico and South America still belong to various European powers. Most are British. The British first arrived in 1624 at an island that had been discovered by Columbus in 1493 and named *Saint Christopher* after his name-saint. To the British, somehow, the island came to be known by a rather irreverent pet-name version of the saint's name and it generally appears on the maps as *Saint Kitts*.

Other British islands of the group retain their original non-British name. One of the islands farther south was discovered by Columbus on a Sunday and he named it *Dominica* (dom'i-nee'kuh), which is the Spanish word for Sunday.

Still farther south is *Barbados Island* (bahr-bay'doze), meaning "bearded island," which was discovered by Portuguese navigators in the sixteenth century, who named it because of the beardlike growth of vines on the trees.

In 1958, the various British islands in the West Indies were grouped together as the *West Indies Federation* and their independence was being prepared for. The Federation fell apart, however. In 1962 the island Jamaica (see JAMAICA) became independent as did the islands Trinidad-Tobago (see LOS ANGELES) in the south.

Castile

THE ARABS invaded Spain in 711 and conquered the land, but Christian resistance was never entirely crushed. In the northern mountains a series of small Christian states arose. In the west was *León*, this being the Spanish word for "lion," a reference on the part of the inhabitants to their own bravery. (People invariably think well of themselves.)

East of León was *Castile*. This received its name from the fact that numerous castles ("castilos" in Spanish) were built as defenses against the Moslem enemy. As Castilian holdings expanded southward, the northern portion which had been Christian longest was called *Old Castile* while the southern portion became *New Castile*. By 1050, Castile had absorbed León.

At the western edge of the Pyrenees in Basque country (see BISCAY) there was established the kingdom of *Navarre* (na-vahr'), or "Navarra" in Spanish. This name is of uncertain origin, but may come from words meaning "land of the flat valley surrounded by hills," which is a lot to put into one word.

South of Navarre was *Aragon*, first formed on the Aragon River. This name may come from the Latin "Tarraconensis," a province established in eastern Spain by the Roman Emperor Augustus, meaning that part of Spain of which the city of Tarraco was most important. That city still exists on the northeast coast as *Tarragona* but is now far outstripped by the near-by city of Barcelona (see BARCELONA). In 1076, Aragon absorbed Navarre.

In 1469, Ferdinand II of Aragon married Isabella of Castile and this union between the two Spanish kingdoms was never broken thereafter; thus modern Spain was formed. At this time, the last remnant of Moslem territory in the south was *Granada* derived from "pomegranate," it is supposed, for these were numerous in the land. In 1492, the united Spanish kingdoms conquered Granada, and Moslem dominion finally came to an end.

Ceylon

SOUTH OF INDIA is a large teardrop-shaped island which was just within the ken of the ancient Greeks. Its northwestern section, the portion nearest to India, was the part best known to the Greeks. Its name in Sanskrit (the language of tribes which had invaded the Indian peninsula in 1500 B.C.) was Tamraparni, meaning "pool covered with red lotus." To the Greeks, this became *Taprobane* (tuh-prob'uh-nee) and that was the name used for the whole island through ancient and medieval times.

The Sanskrit-speaking people of Ceylon called themselves Sinhala, possibly meaning "lion." They called the island Sinhaladvipa, meaning "land of the Sinhalas." By the Arabs, this word was distorted to *Serendib* (ser-en-deeb') and that was the name used in the Arabian Nights.

In 1505, the first Europeans arrived at the island. These were Portuguese under Francisco de Almeida. To the Portuguese, the term "Sinhala" was twisted by the reversal of the *l* and *n* so that it became "Zeylan" and this has come down to us as *Ceylon* (si-lon'), which is the form we now find on the maps. In 1517, the Portuguese founded the town that is now the capital of Ceylon, and named it *Colombo*. Surprisingly enough, they chose to honor Christopher Columbus ("Colombo" in Italian), who had sailed for Spain, rather than Portugal. Thus, although Columbus had never reached the Indian waters, for which he had aimed, his name did.

Not all the island population, or all India, for that matter, is descended from the Sanskrit-speaking invaders. Northern Ceylon and southern India contain many people who speak "Dravidian" languages which existed in India before Sanskrit arrived. Nevertheless, the southern portion of India bears a Sanskrit name, for it is the *Deccan*, from a Sanskrit word meaning "south."

The Dutch succeeded the Portuguese in Ceylon and were in turn succeeded by the British. By 1815, all of Ceylon was under the control of Great Britain. In 1948, however, Ceylon gained its independence and became a dominion within the Commonwealth of Nations.

44

Charleston

THE NAME "Charles" comes from an old Germanic word that meant a lowborn fellow, though one who was not actually a slave. Our word "churl" comes from the same root. Nevertheless, since the time of Charles Martel and of his grandson, Charlemagne ("Charles the Great") in the eighth century, it has been a favorite name for royalty.

The first king of England to be named Charles was the second of the Stuart line, who succeeded to the throne as Charles I in 1625. He was an unfortunate king, for his subjects rebelled against him successfully and in 1649 actually executed him. Nevertheless, he reigned at a time when British settlers were beginning to colonize America and his name found its way prominently onto the map — if that can be considered consolation under the circumstances.

Charles I granted a stretch of land along the southern coast of what is now the United States, for purposes of colonization, to Robert Heath, the British Attorney General, and Heath promptly named the territory *Carolina* in the king's honor. (The Latin form of "Charles" is "Carolus.") No settlements were then made, but in the 1660's the project was renewed under new grants. By that time, Charles II, son of the executed king, had been restored to the throne and the name *Carolina* was kept and it served to honor both.

The stretch of coast involved in the grant was a long one and initial settlements were made at the northern end of the stretch and at the southern. So widely separated were these settlements that it seemed wise to administer them as two colonies: *North Carolina* and *South Carolina*. The first important settlement in South Carolina was founded in 1671 and, almost inevitably, it, too, was named for the king — *Charleston*.

Both North Carolina and South Carolina were among the original thirteen states of the Union, South Carolina being the eighth to ratify the Constitution and North Carolina the twelfth.

45

Chester

WHEN THE Romans first occupied the island of Britain, it was necessary to build many fortified places to hold the island. They called such places "castra," from which we get the English word "castle." About these fortifications, settlements grew up that often included "castra" in their names, or older settlements incorporated the Roman "castra" into their Celtic names. With time, this word became the suffix "-caster," "-cester," or "-chester."

In northwestern England, for instance, there is a town which, in Roman times, was "Devana Castra." In this case only the "castra" survived, for it is now called *Chester*. The English call their counties "shires," an old Anglo-Saxon word, so the county in which Chester is located is "Chester shire," or, as it is now abbreviated, *Cheshire*.

About sixty miles north of Chester was another "castra" on the River Lune. This has become *Lancaster*, which has given its name to the county of *Lancashire*. The largest city of Lancashire was named Mamucion in pre-Roman days. As a result of a fortification at the site, it became Mamucion Castrum, or *Manchester*.

In the same way, the ancient Glevum became *Gloucester*, Durobrivae became *Rochester* (only two letters saved). *Leicester*, *Worcester*, *Winchester*, *Dorchester*, and *Colchester* are other examples. And included among the counties are *Gloucestershire*, *Worcestershire*, and *Leicestershire*.

Some of these names were brought over to the American colonies. *Worcester*, Massachusetts, received its name in 1684 because some of the settlers had come from the English Worcester. There are also a *Gloucester* and a *Dorchester* (the latter now part of Boston) in Massachusetts, a *Manchester* in New Hampshire, a *Chester* in Pennsylvania, a *Winchester* in Virginia, and so on. *Rochester*, New York, is, however, named for the original owner of the land, who organized the laying out of the town in 1811—a man named Nathaniel Rochester.

Chile

WE USUALLY think of South America as being a tropical continent, but actually its southern tip reaches as close to the Antarctic Circle as Labrador does to the Arctic Circle. Except for Antarctica itself, South America is the southernmost of all the land masses, and the nation in whose territory the southernmost tip falls is *Chile*.

Chile is one of the most queerly shaped of all nations, for it is over 3000 miles long from north to south and less than 200 miles wide for almost all that distance. Its extreme north is deep in the tropics while its extreme south is in the frigid sub-Antarctic. Its name, it is thought, is from a native Indian word, "Tchili," meaning "snow," but, to be sure, this is not because of the coldness of its far south, but alludes rather to the snow-capped peaks of the Andes that line the full length of its long eastern border. (The connection between "Chile," meaning "snow," and the English word "chilly" is an interesting coincidence, but only a coincidence.) Its most important seaport, *Valparaiso* (val'puh-ry'soh) has a much pleasanter meaning, for it is the Spanish for "Paradise Valley."

The southernmost tip of South America is *Cape Horn* and one would almost think this was named because of the flaring, hornlike shape of that end of the continent. However, this is just another coincidence.

The name was given the cape in 1616 by the Dutch navigators Jakob Le Maire and Willem Cornelis Schouten, who were the first to round it. Schouten's home town was Hoorn in the Netherlands, and he named the cape in its honor except that, somehow, one *o* dropped out.

Another interesting piece of Chilean territory are the *Juan Fernandez Islands* (wahn-fur-nan'dez). These are in the Pacific Ocean about 380 miles west of the central Chilean shore. They are named for the Spanish navigator Juan Fernandez, who discovered them in 1563.

Their claim to fame rests in the fact that a Scottish sailor, Alexander Selkirk, was marooned on one of them (at his own request) from 1704 to 1709 and this inspired the English writer Daniel Defoe to write his classic novel *Robinson Crusoe*.

China

IN THE long history of China, there were many lines of rulers, some of them not native, and to each of them the Chinese have given a dynastic name. For instance, the dynasty of the Ch'in ruled from 221 to 207 B.C. This was an unusually short period of rule, but during it the land was first unified, and the principle of unification was never lost sight of in the two thousand years that followed. As the creation of the Ch'in, the united nation came to be called *China*.

The Greeks, hearing word of the distant Chinese via the trade routes across central Asia that brought in silk, used a twisted version of the name and called the land Sinai. This is still used when we speak of "Sinic civilization" or the "Sino-Japanese War."

West Europeans first gained real knowledge of China in the thirteenth century, when the Italian traveler Marco Polo made his famous visit to the Far East and then wrote up the tale of his travels on his return. At the time, the Mongols had conquered China, and a Mongolian dynasty ruled the land. One of the Mongol tribes living in the western part of the nation were the Khitans, and Marco Polo brought back the name of *Cathay*, which was a distorted version of the tribal name. In Russian, the name for China is still "Kitai."

After the revolution of 1912, the monarchy was overthrown and the *Chinese Empire* became the *Republic of China*. The provinces in the interior are truly Chinese in population and these are referred to as *China Proper*. The outlying areas, inhabited by Manchurians, Mongolians, Turks, and Tibetans (although Chinese immigrants keep moving in), are lumped together as *Outer China*. Since 1949, the Republic of China, as recognized by the government of the United States, is confined to the island of Formosa. It is sometimes called *Nationalist China*. The remainder of the huge land is under the control of the Chinese Communist Party, and calls itself the *People's Republic of China*. In order to avoid confusing it with the Formosa government, Americans commonly refer to it as *Mainland China*, *Communist China*, or *Red China*.

Churchill

THE FACT that almost all the globe was opened by the great explorations of the sixteenth to nineteenth centuries, and named, too, meant that nothing much was left with which to honor the leaders of the twentieth century. To be sure, in some nations, this is easily taken care of by renaming old sites. In the Soviet Union, for instance, there are cities named *Stalinabad, Stalingrad, Stalinir, Stalino, Stalinogorsk,* and *Stalinsk,* all named for Joseph Stalin, the Russian political leader during the industrialization of the 1930's and the war crisis of the 1940's. In 1961, however, the now-dead Stalin lost his popularity and names were changed. Stalino has become *Donetsk* and Stalingrad has become *Volgograd* after the rivers on which they are located.

In addition, the highest mountain peak in the Soviet Union was named *Mount Stalin,* but in 1961 was renamed *Mount Communism.* It is one of the ten highest mountains in the world and is in the *Pamir* Range (puh-mir'), this coming from a Persian word meaning "at the foot of the mountains." The native name is "Bam-i-Dunya," meaning "roof of the world."

For the remaining two of the big three of World War II, there was no such easy out. In the case of Winston Churchill, there was the compensating fact that his was a great family name in English history. Thus, toward the end of the seventeenth century, when the British controlled the fur-trading areas about Hudson Bay (even though France controlled the rest of Canada), they named one of the large rivers flowing into the bay *Churchill River.* A town at its mouth is *Churchill* and a point of land near by is *Cape Churchill.* This is in honor of John Churchill, Duke of Marlborough, an ancestor of Winston Churchill.

The best that could be done for Franklin Delano Roosevelt are some Antarctic islands known as the *Franklin Roosevelt Islands.*

Even the west can rename geographic sites, however. An innocuously named "Castle Mountain" in the Canadian Rockies was renamed *Mount Eisenhower,* in honor of the American general, in 1946.

49

Cincinnati

ONE OF the favorite legends of the Romans concerned a virtuous farmer of the early days of the Republic. About 500 B.C., the Romans were losing one of their wars and they called upon this farmer, Lucius Quinctius Cincinnatus, to assume emergency leadership of the army. He was found at his plow, which he left standing in the field in order that he might assume his new responsibility at once.

Within six months, he had defeated the enemy and saved Rome. Having done that, he refused all honors and returned to his plow. Cincinnatus was thus the model of the patriot who serves his country without trying to turn that service into personal power and without asking for any return.

At the end of the Revolutionary War, George Washington seemed a true American Cincinnatus. He, too, had been a farmer who had answered his country's call to lead its armies. And at the end of the war, he returned to private life. (It was not until six years later that he was elected President.)

Other officers of the Revolutionary army felt that they, too, were each and every one a Cincinnatus and, in 1783, at the close of the war, they organized "The Society of the Cincinnati" (using the Latin plural, of course). Washington remained the president of the society during his lifetime.

At the time, the territory north of the Ohio River and lying between Pennsylvania and the Mississippi formed the northwestern quarter of the nation and it was described, accurately enough for that time, as the *Northwest Territory*. The Cincinnati, as a constructive peacetime effort, interested themselves in the development of that territory.

In 1790, General Arthur St. Clair, member of the society, arrived as first governor of the eastern part of the territory. He made plans for the reorganization and enlargement of a small town upon the Ohio and renamed it for the society. It is now the great city of *Cincinnati*.

50

Cologne

ONLY THE westernmost part of Germany was ever under the direct rule of the Roman Empire, for the region west of the *Rhine River* formed part of Roman Gaul. In fact, the name of the river comes from the Gallic "Renos," which may perhaps come from a word meaning "rise"; that is, "sunrise," since the Rhine lay to the east of Gaul in the direction of the sunrise.

In A.D. 50, the Romans established a town on the Rhine River which the reigning emperor, Claudius, named after his current wife (his fourth), who had been born in the Celtic town that had occupied the spot previously. The wife's name was Agrippina, so the town became "Colonia Agrippina."

Agrippina had Claudius poisoned four years later in order that her son might become emperor. He did, but he happened to be Nero, and since Nero found his mother annoying he had her executed five years after that. In view of this poor example of home life, it is just as well that the "Agrippina" portion of the name dropped out. The "Colonia" part did not, however, and the city is known to Germans today as "Köln" and to us as *Cologne* (ko-lone').

That area of Germany which is west of the Rhine is popularly called the *Rhineland*. During the time of Napoleon, it was annexed to France, which for the first time since the breakup of the Roman Empire (and only for ten years or so) recovered all the territory of Gaul. After Napoleon's downfall, the Rhineland was awarded to Prussia in order that it might serve as a bulwark against France in future years. It did that, for through its industrialization in the nineteenth century, it made Prussia the strongest power in Europe and as dangerous to the rest of the continent as France had been earlier.

The Rhine is not entirely in Germany. Its mouth lies in the Netherlands and near that mouth a city grew up in the Middle Ages about a dam on a tributary stream called Rotte. The name of that city, naturally, is *Rotterdam*.

51

Congo

IN THE days before European penetration of Africa, there were stories of fabulous kingdoms deep in its interior. One such story concerned a kingdom spoken of by the ancients as "Congo." Naturally, European explorers never found civilizations as wonderful as the legends, but the romantic names of these mysterious lands lingered.

In 1482, the Portuguese navigator Diogo Cam, exploring Africa's west coast, came across the mouth of a huge river flowing into the Atlantic about 500 miles south of the equator. He set up a stone pillar and called the river Rio de Padrão ("river of the pillar"). This was quickly changed to Zaire, which is a distortion of a native word meaning simply "river." But the pull of the fabulous ancient kingdom eventually proved decisive. It became the *Congo River* and the whole area it drains, almost all of central Africa, became the *Congo*.

The river was first explored in its entirety, between 1874 and 1877, by the English-born explorer Henry Morton Stanley. Leopold II, King of the Belgians, grew interested in the area, organized an international corporation to exploit it, and by 1885 was recognized as having personal dominion over most of the basin, which then became known as *Congo Free State*. However, Leopold's methods for running the colony at a personal profit involved extremely cruel treatment of the natives and, in 1908, after a great scandal, the area was taken from Leopold's control and annexed to Belgium itself. It then became known as *Belgian Congo*. In 1960, the region gained its independence and became *Republic of the Congo*.

The map marks its past, however. A group of cataracts along the Upper Congo are called *Stanley Falls* and just downriver on the north bank is *Stanleyville*. Near the mouth of the Congo, on the south bank, is *Léopoldville*. Then, a city founded in the south of the nation in 1910, is named *Elizabethville*, after the wife of Albert I who, the year before, had succeeded his uncle, Leopold II.

Constantinople

EUROPE AND ASIA come together closely at the Bosporus (see AEGEAN SEA). In 658 B.C., a party of Greek settlers under a man named Byzas (according to legend, anyway) founded a town there and called it *Byzantium*. (Another theory is that the name means "close-pressed," because the town was so compactly built.)

Either way, it was a good spot for trading purposes and Byzantium did well for itself most of the time. In A.D. 196, it took the wrong side in a civil war and was besieged, captured, and largely destroyed by the Roman emperor Septimius Severus. However, in A.D. 330, another emperor, Constantine I, made up for that. Deciding that the eastern half of the Empire had grown more important, he shifted his capital from Rome to Byzantium. The latter town he rebuilt, beautified, and named after himself as "Constantinopolis" ("Constantine's city"), a name which is better known to us as *Constantinople*.

Under the barbarian invasions of the 400's, the western part of the Empire came to an end, but the eastern half, with Constantinople as the capital, held out for a thousand years. For a while, it can be best spoken of as the *Eastern Roman Empire*. However, after Arab conquests had reduced its area to Greece and Asia Minor, so that it included only Greek-speaking people for the most part, it came to be called the *Greek Empire* or, most often, the *Byzantine Empire* after Constantinople's old name. The people of the Empire called themselves "Roman emperors" to the very end.

When the Turks conquered most of Asia Minor about 1200, they established the Sultanate of *Rum* (room), for they felt they had conquered large parts of "Rome." Finally, in 1453, they took Constantinople itself and for nearly 500 years that city remained capital of the Turkish dominions. After World War I, however, the capital was moved inland and, in 1930, the Turkish version of Constantinople's name, *Istanbul* (is'tan-bool'), became official. This is a distortion of the Greek phrase "eis ten polin," meaning "to the city." It's as though we renamed New York "Downtown." One western version of Istanbul was *Stamboul*.

Copenhagen

FROM 800 to 1200, Northmen issuing out of Norway laid powerful hands on all the coasts of western Europe. They occupied northern districts of France and then conquered England. They took over Sicily and southern Italy, were powerful in Constantinople, and were among the leaders of the early Crusades. Yet Norway itself was only a small nation out of the main current of history and for the most part under the domination of Denmark, which ruled it from 1397 to 1814.

In the old Viking days, in 1048, a city was founded in southern Norway by Harold Siggurdson, and was named *Oslo* (a native word of uncertain origin). It was at the head of one of the narrow ocean inlets that are called *fjords* by the Norwegians, and this one was *Oslo Fjord*. Oslo was a wooden town and burned down every once in a while. It burned down in the 1620's and King Christian IV of Denmark (and Norway) had it rebuilt. It was then renamed *Christiania* in the king's honor.

In 1814, Denmark (which had sided with the defeated Napoleon too long) ceded Norway to Sweden (which had turned against Napoleon in time). In 1905, however, Norway peacefully and finally won its independence. By 1925, it seemed to the Norwegians that to have their capital named in honor of a Danish king was inappropriate. They switched back to the old name of *Oslo*.

The capital of Denmark itself originated as a small village shortly after 1000, which was called by the straightforward name of "Havn" meaning "harbor." With time, the word became elaborated to "merchant's harbor" or "Kjøbenhavn" in Danish and *Copenhagen* by the time English tongues were done twisting it.

About the same time as Oslo and Copenhagen were being founded, the capital of the third Scandinavian nation, Sweden, was also established. It was set up on an island just off the coast and the original town was surrounded by a fortification consisting of a wall built of logs (a "stockade"). So it was named *Stockholm*, meaning "island of the stockade."

Crimea

THE ANCIENT Greeks were always fearful of the nomads of the plains north of the Black Sea (what is now southern Russia). They were so many, so hardy, and so well mounted that they seemed irresistible. Moreover, since they had no cities or settled habitations, there seemed no way of striking back at them. The earliest inhabitants of the area of whom the Greeks knew were the "Cimmerians." These were mentioned in Homer. They were replaced later by the "Scythians" but the name of the earlier people has never entirely disappeared from the map. At least, north of the Black Sea is a peninsula which now bears the name of *Crimea*, a name which may be a dim memory of "Cimmeria." (On the other hand, the Tatars, when expelled from the rest of Russia, remained in control of the Crimea under Turkish protection, and Crimea may be a Tatar word with only coincidental similarity to "Cimmeria.")

The Russians did not take Crimea and the north shore of the Black Sea until the armies of Catherine II, under the Russian general Alexander Vasilievich Suvorov, defeated the Turks in 1774 and again in 1792. The Russian cities then founded in the far south are not the usual ancient towns of Europe but are no older than American cities. For instance, *Sevastopol*, meaning "the majestic city," was not founded till 1783, so that it is 160 years younger than New York.

The coastal waters northeast of the Crimean peninsula bear one of the most unpleasant names on the map. The Mediterranean Sea, you see, gets its oxygen from the current flowing through Gibraltar from the Atlantic. This is not a great supply and Mediterranean sea-life is therefore not as rich as that of the open ocean. The Black Sea is cut off still further, and the inlet past Crimea is almost entirely without oxygen. The lower layers of the Black Sea do not support life. Fish and vegetation in surface layers tend to die northeast of the Crimea and the odor of decay gives the coastal waters the name of *Putrid Sea*. However, it is a valuable source of salt and minerals. There is good in everything.

Czechoslovakia

Much of western Europe was Celtic during Roman times and before. About 400 B.C., for instance, a Celtic tribe which called themselves Boii emigrated from Gaul and settled in an area in central Europe. This new home of theirs was called Boiohaemia ("home of the Boiians") and this has become *Bohemia*. (In the Middle Ages, some people thought gypsies came from Bohemia. Consequently, people who lived in a vagabond fashion came to be called Bohemians.)

They also occupied land westward. This western portion was occupied by the Romans in the last days of the Roman Republic. The Romans called the tribe Bavarii, and from that we get *Bavaria*.

Neither portion remained Celtic. After the breakup of the Roman Empire, Bavaria came under the rule of the Franks, was gradually Germanized, and at times during the Middle Ages was the most powerful portion of the Holy Roman Empire. In early modern times, however, it was outstripped by both Austria and Prussia and, in 1870, it was incorporated into the newly formed German Empire.

As for Bohemia, a Slavic tribe known as the Czechs entered the land and established a kingdom which they called Czechy, during the 600's. They spread eastward into *Moravia*, that name coming from the Morava River that flows through it.

The Germans in their push to the east never succeeded in pushing the Slavs out of Bohemia-Moravia. From the late Middle Ages on, however, Bohemia-Moravia was ruled by Austria. After World War I, the Austrian lands disintegrated. Bohemia-Moravia combined with the Slavic land of Slovakia still farther east to form the independent kingdom of *Czechoslovakia* (chek-o-slo-vah'kee-uh).

This was broken up under Nazi pressure just before World War II. Slovakia was awarded to Hungary, while the remainder of the country became the *Protectorate of Bohemia-Moravia* under Nazi rule. After World War II, the protectorate vanished with the Nazis themselves, and Czechoslovakia was restored, losing only its easternmost tip (occupied by Ukrainian-speaking people) to the Soviet Union.

Dallas

ALTHOUGH THERE are many Americans who can name all the Presidents of the United States in order, there are probably very few indeed who can name more than a dozen Vice-Presidents in any order. The Vice-Presidency simply isn't a memorable position. For instance, at the time that James Knox Polk was President (1845–1849), the Vice-President was George Mifflin Dallas.

Who would remember him except that, in 1846, a new town was being laid out in Texas, which had just been admitted into the Union through the strong action of the Polk Administration. It was named for the Vice-President, and *Dallas* is now the second largest city in Texas.

Another Texan city memorializes a Spaniard even more securely forgotten. In the 1780's Bernardo de Galvez was the governor of the vast Louisiana Territory, which had just become Spanish and which, at the time, included Texas. An island on the coast of the Gulf of Mexico was named Galvez in his honor, and, when settled by Americans decades later, became *Galveston*.

The fact that Texas was once Spanish is all over the map. A small river in the southern part of Texas was discovered on St. Anthony's day in 1691. The river and a town founded upon it were therefore named *San Antonio*. On the southern coast is *Corpus Christi*, which, in Latin, is "body of Christ" and is the name of a feast day of the Catholic Church.

In the far west of the state, on the *Rio Grande* (which, in Spanish, means "great river"), is a place where that river can be forded. A settlement was founded there and called El Paso del Rio, which means, perfectly reasonably, "the ford of the river." It has been shortened simply to *El Paso*.

In the far south of the state is *Brownsville*, an English name again. It began as "Fort Brown" in 1846, and was named after an American officer killed in its defense in the early days of the Mexican War. It is at the mouth of the Rio Grande.

Dayton

ANYONE CAN name a new town after himself if he is doing the founding. With luck, he can then become the owner of an immortal name.

John Young, for instance, arrived in Ohio in 1797, bought land in the northeast of the state, and established a small town which he named *Youngstown.* John Young is unknown otherwise, but his name graces the seventh largest city in Ohio.

At the opposite end of the State is *Dayton.* It was named for General Jonathan Dayton when it was founded in 1795 and the choice seemed a good one at the time. The general had fought at Yorktown and had signed the Declaration of Independence for New Jersey. Ten years later, however, Dayton was implicated in Burr's conspiracy and was indicted for high treason. He was never brought to trial, but his political career was ruined. Nevertheless, Dayton kept its name and is the sixth largest city in the state.

In Indiana to the west, a city was founded on the Ohio River in 1817 in the southwestern portion of the state. The founder was General R. M. Evans, quite obscure otherwise, but securely placed in the name of *Evansville.*

The day of individual founding of cities, as of individual everything else, dimmed with the passing of the nineteenth century. In 1906, when a city was founded at the southern tip of Lake Michigan, it was the United States Steel Corporation that took charge of the swamps and dunes and beat it into a settled community. The chairman of the board of United States Steel at the time was Elbert H. Gary and the city was named *Gary* in consequence.

Cities can be named for merit, however. A city in northern Australia, founded in 1872, was originally named *Palmerston* for a British Prime Minister recently dead. It was renamed *Darwin* for Charles Robert Darwin, one of the great scientists of history. Nevertheless, the number of scientists on the map, compared to generals, politicians, and nonentities, is, alas, negligible.

Dead Sea

On the borders of modern Israel is a lake that is one of the most remarkable in the world. The ancient Hebrews called it by a name that in English means "the Salt Sea." This is not surprising since its waters are seven times as salty as the ocean. The Greeks called it by the equivalent of the *Dead Sea* for the very good reason that it is so salty that no living things are found in it. We know it by that name, but the Arabs go back to the Bible. The story of Lot and of the destruction of Sodom and Gomorrah involves the Dead Sea locale so the Arabs call it Bahr Lut, meaning "Sea of Lot."

The Dead Sea is also remarkable in that its surface is 1286 feet below sea level, making its shores the lowest land surface on the planet. This may give the name to the river that flows into it from the north, the *Jordan River*, which is perhaps the most famous small river in the world because of its connection with Biblical events. "Jordan" may derive from a Hebrew word meaning "to descend" because the river level drops so rapidly on its way to the low-lying Dead Sea.

The lowest land surface in the western hemisphere is 282 feet below sea level and it is to be found on the eastern boundary of California. Rather remarkably, it is only eighty miles from the highest mountains in the continental United States.

The California area may not be as low-lying as the Dead Sea, but it is just as unpleasant, if not more so. Its lowest places have remnants of salt water and, in fact, the lowest point of all is called *Badwater* for just that reason. Furthermore, it is unbearably hot, reaching temperatures of over 130° in the shade. In 1849, a party of "forty-niners" blundered into this valley and got out only after incredible hardships. They gave it the name it now bears — *Death Valley*.

Yet both the Dead Sea and Death Valley are valuable for the minerals they yield. The encrusted shores of the Dead Sea yield phosphate for fertilizers while the hot dry rocks of Death Valley yield borax.

Denver

THE MOUNTAIN STATES were the last to enter the Union and are still the least populated. Their initial prosperity was based largely on the mineral wealth dug out of the mountains. In the western part of what was then the Kansas Territory, for instance, traces of gold were found in 1858. At once settlements started springing up and a town of the area was named *Denver* after the territorial governor, James William Denver.

Some mining cities rose to dizzy heights of prosperity when the mines were rich, then sank to villages and even ghost towns when the mines petered out. *Virginia City* in Nevada is an example. Founded in 1859, it received its name from one of the early settlers who was nicknamed Virginia because he hailed from that state.

Butte (byoot), Montana (so named because it was located near a "butte," this being a flat-topped hill with steep sides), escaped the ghost-town fate, because, when its gold mines petered out, silver was discovered and, after that, copper.

Some western towns are now known for reasons other than mining. *Reno*, Nevada, was founded in 1859 and named a few years later for Jesse Lee Reno, a Union general killed in the Civil War. It became famous and prosperous in recent decades because divorces were granted there easily.

Again, near the southern tip of Nevada is *Las Vegas*, meaning, in Spanish, "the meadows," because it is located in a tract of open land. It was first settled in 1855 by Mormons and has grown tremendously during World War II and since because it is a glittering gambling resort.

Carson City, Nevada, is the smallest state capital in the nation and has a name that would be considered truly Western by those who read the dime novels of a couple of generations ago. It was settled in 1858 and was named for none other than that famous Western scout and trapper Christopher Carson, better known to one and all as Kit Carson.

Des Moines

THE DAKOTAS were a large group of Indians living in the Northwest, consisting of a number of smaller groups in alliance. The word "dakota" means "allies" in their language. In 1861, the area west of Minnesota was organized as *Dakota Territory*. In the 1880's, when the territory looked as though it would be divided into a northern half and southern half, both portions wanted to keep the name "Dakota." In consequence, a compromise was reached in which the two parts were named *North Dakota* and *South Dakota* and both entered the Union on the same day in 1889 as the 39th and 40th states.

In those days, the most remarkable man in Europe was Otto von Bismarck, the Prussian Prime Minister who had guided Prussia to victory over Austria-Hungary and France, then on to the unification of Germany, to alliance with Russia and the domination of Europe. In 1873, a town founded in the Dakota Territory was named in his honor by settlers, of whom many were of German descent. *Bismarck* is now the capital of North Dakota.

Farther south is a city that is French in name. In 1831, a fur trader named Pierre Chouteau, Jr., located a post on the west bank of the Missouri River. With fine lack of modesty he called it Fort Pierre Chouteau. The "Chouteau" being hard for Americans to pronounce, the name was shortened to *Fort Pierre*. Across the river, a town grew up in the 1870's and it adopted the still further simplified name of *Pierre*, pronouncing it, English-fashion, as "peer." It is now the capital of South Dakota.

Farther downriver in Iowa is another city with a name that at least looks French, *Des Moines*, although it is pronounced, English-fashion, as "duh moyn." In French, it means "of the monks" and, to be sure, monks had once lived in the vicinity. However, the name comes from the *Des Moines River*, which in turn comes from the Indian name "Moingana" for the river and for a native village upon it. Monks had nothing to do with the matter.

61

Detroit

THE GREAT LAKES are five in number, but included in the chain is a small lake, lying between Lakes Huron and Erie, not one-twentieth the size of Lake Erie. It was first seen by the French explorer Robert Cavalier de La Salle in 1679 and he named it Sainte Clair in honor of the saint on whose day he made the discovery. We call it *Lake Saint Clair*. La Salle went on to explore the Midwest and the Mississippi Valley. The town of *La Salle* in north-central Illinois, founded in 1827, is the largest of several named for him.

In 1701, another French explorer, Antoine de la Mothe Cadillac, passed that way. He established a fort and trading post on the strait that connects Lake St. Clair and Lake Erie and named it Fort Pontchartrain du Détroit, meaning "Fort Pontchartrain on the straits." The city that grew up on the site is now called simply *Detroit* and is the fifth largest city in the United States. The town of *Cadillac* in central Michigan, founded in 1875, is named in honor of this explorer.

Between Lake Huron and Lake St. Clair is the *St. Clair River* and between Lake St. Clair and Lake Erie is the *Detroit River*. (Both are really straits, of course.) Between Lake Erie and Lake Ontario is the *Niagara River*, that name coming from a French distortion of the name of an Indian village that stood upon its shores. The river drops over a precipice 167 feet high and this is the famous *Niagara Falls*. It stands on the boundary between the United States and Canada, and the Canadian portion is called the *Horseshoe Falls* from its shape.

The French Jesuit explorer Isaac Jogues visited the strait connecting Lake Michigan and Lake Superior in 1641. Like the Niagara, but much less so, it drops downward in a little "leap" of twenty feet in less than a mile. Jogues named it Saulte de Sainte Marie meaning "the leap of St. Mary." The strait is now known as *St. Mary's River*, but on either side of the river are towns called *Sault Sainte Marie*, pronounced, English-fashion, as "soo'saint-muh-ree."

District of Columbia

THE NAME of Americus Vespucius has been spread all over the western hemisphere (see AMERICA). It covers two continents, *North America* and *South America,* as well as the strip of land between them called *Central America* (which is usually considered part of North America). Very frequently, the United States of America is referred to simply as *America*.

What about Christopher Columbus, who deserves the real credit for opening the western hemisphere to European colonization? He is not entirely forgotten. His name appears in Latin America and even in the Far East (see CEYLON).

As for the United States, an alternate name for the nation, at least poetically speaking, is "Columbia" and there is evidence more concrete than poetry as well. In the first years of the Republic, the government wished to establish a new capital that would be part of no state and associated with no regional politics. In 1790, Maryland and Virginia granted a square of territory on the *Potomac River*, ten miles on each side. ("Potomac" is a twisting of the Indian name "Patowomek," which is, itself, of no known meaning.) The square was named the *District of Columbia.* The Virginian portion, south of the Potomac, was given back to Virginia in 1846, but the rest still holds the capital of the United States.

In 1792, moreover, an American sea captain, Robert Gray, in his ship the *Columbia,* discovered a large river flowing into the Pacific. He named it for his ship so that it became the *Columbia River.* In 1846, that section of the coast was divided peacefully between the United States and Great Britain. Most of the river was in the United States but it rose in Canada and, in 1858, Queen Victoria suggested that Canada's westernmost province be called *British Columbia,* and so it was.

The largest American town named *Columbia* was founded in 1786 and is the capital of South Carolina. The capital of Ohio was laid out in 1812 and named *Columbus.* So Columbus gets his due.

Dominican Republic

On his first voyage, Christopher Columbus, sailing in the employ of Spain, discovered an island he called Isla Española, meaning "Spanish island," a name that was quickly twisted to *Hispaniola*. He founded a settlement on the island in 1496 and named it *Santo Domingo* ("Saint Dominic") in honor of his father's patron saint. For a while, *Santo Domingo* was also used as the name of the entire island.

Spanish dominion over the island was weak. It became a haunt for pirates and, in 1697, the western section, and later the whole island, was taken over by France. The French called the island Saint Domingue but the original Indian name of "Haiti," meaning "Land of Mountains," became increasingly popular.

However, the native Indians had been wiped out and Negroes were brought in from Africa as slave labor. In 1801, the Negro slaves rose in a rebellion that was eventually successful, and by 1806, a Negro republic had been established with the name of *Haiti*. Spain re-established control over the eastern two-thirds of the island.

Thus, of the three names which were at one time or another used for the entire island, *Haiti* was restricted to the west and *Santo Domingo* to the east. Only *Hispaniola* remains for the entire island.

In 1844, Santo Domingo revolted from Spain and became independent under a Latinized version of the name — the *Dominican Republic*. The capital city, however, remained Santo Domingo for another century.

In 1930, a Dominican general named Rafael Leonidas Trujillo Molina took over the government after a successful revolt. Shortly afterward, a disastrous cyclone just about destroyed Santo Domingo, and Trujillo supervised its reconstruction. It was renamed *Ciudad Trujillo* (syoo-dad' troo-he'oh), meaning "city of Trujillo." Trujillo after long and despotic rule was assassinated in 1961. Before the end of the year, the city was Santo Domingo again. (The Haitians, in overthrowing the French, allowed the French name of their capital, *Port au Prince*, meaning "prince's harbor," to remain.)

Dover

A NARROW passage of water between two bodies of land, usually called a "strait," is sometimes called a "channel," the former word being from the Anglo-Saxon, the latter from the Latin. The best-known channel on the map is the one between England and France, which is called, simply enough, the *English Channel*, or, even more simply, *the Channel*. The French call it La Manche, meaning "the sleeve," because it widens from east to west in the fashion of a medieval sleeve.

At the narrowest point, England and France are only twenty-two miles apart and on the English coast, there, a town is located which, in Roman days, was called Dubris. This has now become *Dover*, while the narrowest bit of the Channel is the *Strait of Dover*. Dover has been an important seaport, glamorous for its stand in the forefront of danger in case of invasion, as in 1940.

It is not surprising, then, that the name of Dover was transplanted to the United States. A Dover, for instance, was founded in 1683 by William Penn, about seventy miles south of Philadelphia. It is now the capital of the state of Delaware. Other moderately sized towns of that name are in New Hampshire and New Jersey.

The English Dover, together with (originally) four other towns on the Channel coast, have been called *Cinque Ports* ever since Norman Conquest days, being organized for special defense against invasion. "Cinque" is French for "five" but is in this case pronounced "seenk," English-fashion.

Across the Channel in France is *Dunkirk* ("Dunkerque" in French), a city famous for the heroic retreat of the British in 1940. Its name is a form of "Dune-church," which originated in the seventh century when all there was to be found on the site was a church on the dunes. There is a city named Dunkirk in New York State, founded on the shores of Lake Erie in 1837. Its name is supposed to have originated because someone saw a resemblance in its harbor to that of the French Dunkirk.

Duluth

IT IS NOT surprising to find cities named Frankfurt in Germany (see BRANDENBURG). But why should there be a *Frankfort* in Kentucky?

Actually, the answer is plain enough and it involves no connection with the German cities. In 1780, a colonist named Stephen Frank was crossing a ford in the Kentucky River and was ambushed by Indians and killed. Six years later, when a town was established on the site, it was called Frank's Ford in his memory and that became Frankfort. When Kentucky entered the Union in 1792, Frankfort was established as its capital and has remained so ever since.

Even more obscurely named is another state capital. A town settled about 1840 in the Midwest had among its settlers some from a village in New York called Lansing. This name they transferred to the new town and since 1847, *Lansing* has been the capital of Michigan. And although there are other towns of that name here and there in the United States, the one in New York no longer exists.

But even important men, worthy of remembrance, can be forgotten, and then it is only right that they be preserved in a name upon a map. There was a French explorer who falls in this category, one among the many intrepid Frenchmen who moved far westward at a time when English colonists were still hugging the Atlantic coast. This Frenchman, in the late 1670's, reached Lake Superior, traveled to its westward tip, and penetrated deep into what is now Minnesota. His name was Daniel Greysolon, Sieur Duluth (or Dulhut or Du Luth — take your pick). A town was laid out at the western tip of Lake Superior in 1856 and it was rightly named *Duluth* in honor of the explorer.

But it is also possible for a city to be named in so straightforward a manner as scarcely to require explanation at all, either of forgotten men or forgotten cities. In 1826, a trading post was established at the site of some rapids on the Grand River. It gave rise to the city of *Grand Rapids*. Naturally.

Easter Island

THERE HAVE been territories discovered on special days which have received the names of those days. One case is that of Florida, which was discovered on Easter Sunday and named for it (see FLORIDA). A better example, at least for English-speaking people, is that of a small island 2200 miles west of Chile.

It was accidentally stumbled upon by a Dutch explorer, Jakob Roggeveen, on Easter Sunday in 1722 and it was named for the day, so that it is known to us as *Easter Island*. This little island, only about twice as large as Manhattan, was once part of a comparatively advanced culture, and giant statues (consisting mostly of a long face) still remain as evidence of the old days, and have roused much Sunday-supplement interest. Chile annexed the island in 1888 and in Spanish its name is "Pascua." That is simply a translation of Easter, which in Spanish is "Pascua Florida."

A similar case is that of an island, slightly larger than Easter Island, lying about a thousand miles south of Hawaii. It was also first sighted by Dutchmen back about 1650. In 1777, however, Captain Cook came upon it once again, on Christmas Day, and named it *Christmas Island*. It, too, remained neglected until 1888 but then it was Great Britain that annexed it. The United States disputed ownership with Great Britain in the mid-1930's and the two nations jointly possess the little bit of land now.

One "holiday land" antedates these two islands and even Florida. Vasco da Gama after he had rounded the southern tip of Africa (see CAPE OF GOOD HOPE) sighted a section of coast on Christmas Day of 1497. He named that coast Terra Natalis ("land of Christmas," since "Natalis" in Latin means birthday and is used particularly of Christmas). It became *Natal* and is the name, now, of one of the provinces of the Union of South Africa. It was also the name of the coastal town in that province, but that name was changed in 1835.

East Indies

EUROPE, in the Middle Ages, depended greatly upon the use of various spices. These help preserve meat and, failing that, cover up the bad taste of spoiled meat. The best source of spices was in certain regions of the Far East, which Europeans called the "Indies."

Before 1500, Europeans had to depend on middlemen, Arabs mainly, to bring spices from the Indies to Europe. In the 1500's, however, Portuguese ships began to penetrate the waters of the Indian Ocean (see CAPE OF GOOD HOPE) and reached the source.

Meanwhile, Christopher Columbus had sailed westward and was convinced he had reached the Indies in that fashion. He thought the earth was only about 16,000 miles in circumference and that Asia, in stretching eastward, reached to within 3000 miles of Europe. He was wrong in this but, for some decades, Europeans meant two different regions when they spoke of the "Indies," regions that were half a world apart.

Finally, this was realized and the two were distinguished. The Indies of the spices — the ones reached by the Portuguese — were named the *East Indies*, while those of Columbus were called the West Indies.

Beginning in 1596, the Netherlands gradually took over almost all the East Indies, which therefore became known through most of modern times as the *Dutch East Indies* or, better, the *Netherlands East Indies*. Dutch control was broken by the Japanese during World War II and never really re-established. Most of the Dutch areas were given their independence in 1949 under the name of *Indonesia*, a Greek phrase meaning "Indian islands." (This term had been introduced as early as 1884 by a German anthropologist, Adolf Bastian.)

At first, the separate islands of the new nation were allowed considerable self-government so that it was called the *United States of Indonesia*. However, movements toward separation of the various islands forced a strengthening of central authority and the name became simply *Indonesia*.

England

WHEN THE legions of the decomposing Roman Empire left the island of Britain in the fifth century, the invasion by Germanic tribes from the regions across the North Sea began. These tribes fell into three groups: the Angles, the Saxons, and the Jutes.

Of these, the Jutes were the most northerly, coming from the Danish peninsula, which still bears the name *Jutland* ("Jylland" in Danish), or "land of the Jutes." The Angles lived to the south in a region now called *Schleswig* ("Slesvig" in Danish), named from the "Schlei," an inlet of the Baltic Sea. Part of it is still called *Angeln*. The Saxons lived still farther south and their name is to be found over large sections of modern Germany (see SAXONY).

In Britain, seven Anglo-Saxon kingdoms were set up by 600, these being lumped together as the *Heptarchy*, meaning, in Greek, "seven governments." Of these, the three largest, covering the eastern half of the island from the Thames to the Firth of Forth, were settled by the Angles.

The northernmost Anglian kingdom was *Northumbria*, the land "north of the Humber River." South of that was *Mercia*, which may be a form of the word "march" (see AUSTRIA) since it was a borderland against the still active Celts to the west. East of Mercia was *East Anglia*, with a name that needs no explanation.

The kingdoms took turns at being dominant. Northumbria was strongest in the seventh century; Mercia absorbed East Anglia and became dominant in the eighth. In the ninth, however, Danish invasions conquered much of the Anglian kingdoms and the leadership passed to the Saxon kingdoms of the south. Nevertheless, the southern portion of Britain came to be known as "Anglia" in Latin. The equivalent term, "Angle-land," became the England of today.

Mercia disappeared from the map, but Northumbria remains as *Northumberland*, England's northernmost county.

Epirus

NORTH OF Greece in ancient times were two barbarian lands that felt the pull of Greek culture strongly enough to become semi-Greek in character. On the west coast lay *Epirus*. This is "Epeiros" in Greek, meaning "mainland," a name given the area by the Greeks of the islands off the coast. To its east lay *Macedon*, a name of which the origin is obscure.

Macedon rose from insignificance rather unexpectedly under Philip II, who began to rule in 359 B.C. By the time he was assassinated in 336 B.C., Macedon dominated all of Greece. The king's son, Alexander III (the Great), carried Macedonian arms into Asia and in a whirlwind campaign conquered the vast Persian Empire.

After Alexander's death, in 323 B.C., the *Macedonian Empire* quickly fell apart, but Macedon itself maintained a strong hold on Greece and remained an important power for another century and a half.

Meanwhile, Epirus itself had a moment of glory under its warlike king, Pyrrhus. In 280 B.C., Pyrrhus passed over into Italy to battle the rising Roman power on behalf of the Greek cities of the south. He won very costly victories (and such victories are still called Pyrrhic), but the tide of history was against him and the Greeks. A century later, Rome was strong enough to absorb Epirus, Macedon, and Greece.

Neither Epirus nor Macedon ever regained their independence but they did not disappear from the map. The northwesternmost province of modern Greece is still Epirus.

The matter of Macedon (or *Macedonia*, as it is usually called nowadays) is more complicated. In the nineteenth century, it was mostly Bulgarian-speaking, and in 1878, Russia, having defeated Turkey, awarded it all to Bulgaria. The western powers forced a reversal of that, however. After the Balkan war of 1912 and 1913, Macedonia was divided between Greece and Serbia. Serbia later became Yugoslavia and the result today is that Greece's northernmost province is called Macedonia — and so is Yugoslavia's southernmost province.

Estonia

THE ROMANS gave names to regions far beyond the territory they controlled, usually based on names of tribes they may have heard of at second hand. For instance, the Roman writer Pliny referred to the far north of Europe as "Baltia."

This persists in the name of the sea to the east of Denmark, the *Baltic Sea*. The Germans call it "Ostsee," meaning "East Sea," because it lies to the east of the section of the European shore (west of Denmark) where the main concentration of German population lay in the early Middle Ages. For similar reasons, the sea to the west of Denmark was called the "Nordsee," or *North Sea*, a name adopted by England (though the sea lies to England's east) and therefore by us.

The southeastern shores of the Baltic are inhabited by peoples that are neither Germanic nor Slavic. Immediately north of eastern Poland is a land called by the natives Lietuva. The people in the southern portion are called Lithuanians by us, those in the northern portions Latvians, both representing distortions of "Lietuva."

To the north of Lietuva are a group of people who call themselves Eestlased, from which we get "Ests" or "Estonians." A southern tribe of these was called the Livs.

Sweden ruled this area in the seventeenth century, but in 1721, Peter the Great of Russia defeated Sweden and took over the region. Under Russian rule it was divided into *Estland* in the north and *Livland* in the south. Because of the latter name, the southeastern Baltic coast was often referred to as *Livonia*.

In 1918, with Russia disorganized by revolution, three independent *Baltic States* were formed, these being — from north to south — *Estonia*, *Latvia*, and *Lithuania*.

Independence did not last long, however. All three were absorbed by the Soviet Union in 1940 and organized into "soviet socialist republics." Today, they form the *Estonian S.S.R.*, the *Latvian S.S.R.* and the *Lithuanian S.S.R.*

Ethiopia

THE GREEKS were always impressed with the dark complexions of the peoples of Africa, particularly of those from the regions below the Sahara. The people who lived south of Egypt, for instance, they referred to as "Ethiopians," from Greek words meaning "burnt faces," faces that had been burned black by the sun. From that day to this, there has always been a land named *Ethiopia* in east-central Africa.

Ethiopia is exceptional in many ways. Though named for its dark-skinned inhabitants and although "Ethiopian" is used as a synonym for Negro, the ruling tribes of that land are Semitic in origin and, in a broad sense, are "whites." Ethiopia had close connections with the Hebrew kingdom (also Semitic) in very early days and, for a time, beginning about 900, it had Jewish rulers. The present line of Ethiopian emperors considers itself to have descended from King Solomon and the Queen of Sheba and refer to themselves as the "Lion of Judah."

On the other hand, Ethiopia was converted to Christianity about 380 and when the Arabs conquered and converted the rest of Christian Africa, Ethiopia remained an unconquered Christian stronghold.

To the Arabs, Ethiopia was "El Habesha," meaning "the mixed," that is, a land where many races lived. In 1500 when the Portuguese began to arrive by sea, this was twisted to *Abyssinia*. Both names are popular in the west but Ethiopia is official. The capital city, *Addis Ababa*, is not ancient, but was built in 1887 and its name means "new flower."

During the nineteenth century, Ethiopia alone successfully resisted the incursions of European powers. It fought off the British in the 1860's and, in 1896, it actually destroyed an invading Italian army.

In 1936, the Italians, under Mussolini, undertook to avenge the earlier defeat. This time they had tanks and airplanes, which the Ethiopians did not, and the Italians took over the nation. They organized it, together with Italian colonies on the neighboring coasts, as *Italian East Africa*. In 1941, however, the British ousted Italy from eastern Africa and Ethiopia regained its independence.

Florence

A CITY in north-central Italy was known to the ancient Romans as "Florentia." This means "flowering," a common metaphor for "prosperous," which thus becomes a "good-luck name" to give a city. To the Italians, this name became "Firenze," but English sticks more closely to the Latin original and we call it *Florence*.

The name proved apt for at least one period of its history. Between 1300 and 1600, Florence was the center of artistic and literary endeavor for all western Europe. It represented the very flowering of the Renaissance.

After Italy was united in 1859, Florence served as capital of the nation until 1870, when Italy absorbed the papal dominions about Rome and made that city the capital.

On the western coast of Italy, about fifty miles from Florence, is Livorno. This has suffered "hobson-jobson" in English (a situation where a man, hearing a strange word in a foreign language, converts it into a word or words in his own language that sounds similar, whether it has meaning or not). Thus, to English sailors, Livorno became *Leghorn* and that is the name found on our maps.

North of Leghorn is *Pisa*, a smaller town famous for its "Leaning Tower." In Roman times, it was known as "Pisae" and one theory has it that it was founded by settlers from some Greek city of that name, but this is doubtful.

About sixty miles east of Florence is *San Marino*. This is an independent republic, the smallest in the world, for it is only a trifle larger than Manhattan Island. It was, according to tradition, founded by a Saint Marinus from across the Adriatic about 370. It maintained its mountain independence ever since barbarian times and even survived the unification of all the remainder of the peninsula. For six weeks during World War II, it was occupied by German troops, but that passed also and its independence remains unsullied.

73

Florida

IN MEDIEVAL times, the "Indies" were considered lands of marvels. When the New World was discovered, it was considered part of the Indies and it, too, was therefore full of marvels.

There were stories, for instance, of an island called Bimini on which was a miraculous spring that could remove illness and old age — a "Fountain of Youth," in other words.

The governor of Puerto Rico in 1513 was Juan Ponce de León, and the second largest city in the island is named *Ponce* (pawn'say) in his honor. He was commissioned to lead an exploring expedition to find Bimini. He didn't find the Fountain of Youth, of course, but he did reach a new coastland on Easter Sunday.

Now Easter is celebrated in Spain as a feast of flowers and so, in Spanish, it is called Pascua Florida or "Flowery Easter." In honor of the day, Ponce de León named the new land *Florida*. Nowadays, two small islands of the Bahamas, east of Florida, are called *Bimini* but, alas, neither contains the Fountain of Youth.

Oddly enough, the other "sunshine state" likewise possesses a mythical island in its history. The medieval French poem called the "Chanson de Roland" mentioned a nonexistent land called Califerne. About 1510, a Spanish writer, Garcia Ordonez de Montalvo, wrote a story in which Califerne became an island called California, far in the Indies. Because of this, the west coast of North America, at the northern end of the Spanish dominions, came to be called *California*.

The United States bought Florida from Spain in 1819 and annexed California in 1848 after a successful war with Mexico. Florida entered the Union in 1845 as the 27th state and California entered in 1850 as the 31st.

The portion of California that remained to Mexico is the barren peninsula, just south of our own state, that is now called *Lower California* (it is lower on the map). Between it and the rest of Mexico is a long narrow inlet of the Pacific Ocean, the *Gulf of California*.

Formosa

In 1590, the far-wandering Portuguese traders came across an island off the coast of China which impressed them with its beautiful scenery. They called it *Formosa*, meaning "beautiful."

The native name for the island was apparently "Ryukyu" and although it is only 150 miles off the China coast (*Formosa Strait* lies between) its inhabitants were not originally Chinese, but of Malayan origin. The Chinese referred to the island as "Taiwan" meaning "Terrace Bay," since the precipitous mountain slopes are carefully terraced. Though this replaced Ryukyu as the name, the chain of small islands running from Formosa to Japan still bear the name of *Ryukyu Islands* (ree-oo′kyoo).

In the seventeenth century, the Dutch established trading posts in Formosa and the Japanese attempted a conquest. Neither succeeded in taking the island. In 1644, however, when the Manchus conquered China, fleeing Chinese set up a kind of government-in-exile on the island that maintained itself for nearly twenty years before the natives drove them out. In 1683, the Manchu emperor finally seized control and Formosa remained part of China for two hundred years.

In 1895, China lost a war to Japan and was forced to cede Formosa and the Ryukyu Islands to the victor. Japan insisted on using *Taiwan* (tie-wahn′) as the official name, so that (and *Taiwan Strait*) began to replace Formosa on the map. The capital is *Taipei* (tie-pay′), meaning "Northern Terrace."

After World War II, however, the island was restored to China, and *Formosa* once more became popular. The Ryukyu Islands remained Japanese though the largest island in the group, Okinawa, is virtually under more or less permanent American control.

In 1949, a fleeing Chinese government set up headquarters in exile once again upon the island and Formosa now remains the only sizable section under the control of the only government which is recognized by the United States as the Republic of China.

Fort Worth

MANY AMERICAN cities began as military outposts or forts. However "fort" rarely remained in the title. Sometimes it was merely dropped, as when Fort Pierre gave rise to Pierre (see DES MOINES) or changed altogether as when Fort Dearborn became Chicago (see ILLINOIS). There are exceptions, however, and "fort" is sometimes retained.

Thus, in 1849, after the Mexican War, a fort was planned in northern Texas to protect the settlers of this newly American land from the Indians. It was to be named for Brigadier General William Jenkins Worth who had fought gallantly in the war and had just died. As it turned out, the fort wasn't built but the site was named *Fort Worth* anyway and a city grew up about it. It is now the fourth largest city in Texas and the largest "fort" city in the United States.

Earlier than that, other and more serious Indian troubles gave rise to another example. In 1794, General Anthony Wayne (called Mad Anthony because he attacked so impetuously) was carrying on a campaign against the Indians in Ohio. He defeated them at the Battle of Fallen Timbers near the western end of Lake Erie and pursued them farther west. (In 1820, a couple of towns were founded at the site of the battle, where Wayne had established "Fort Industry." That would have been a good name with or without the "Fort" but the towns combined and chose the name of *Toledo* [suggested by the Spanish city of that name] for no other reason than that it sounded good.)

In his forward march, Wayne established another fort in what is now Indiana. The fort was very naturally called Fort Wayne. It was abandoned in 1819 but by that time a town was growing up that took the name and *Fort Wayne* is now the third largest city in Indiana.

In western Arkansas is the city of *Fort Smith*, named for the fort established in 1817, which was in turn named for General Thomas A. Smith, who fought in the war of 1812. *Fort Dodge*, Iowa, is not named for any military hero. The original fort was named Fort Clarke after a military man but it had been renamed in honor of Henry Dodge, an American senator from Wisconsin who had only casual experience at Indian fighting.

France

OF THE various Germanic tribes who flooded over the western section of the Roman Empire in the fifth century, the most important were the "Franks." The name of this tribe is sometimes said to be derived from an old Germanic word meaning "free," indicating they considered themselves "free men," and sometimes from an old Germanic word meaning "spear," indicating they considered themselves "spear men." The Franks, for several centuries, formed kingdoms that governed the areas both west and east of the Rhine. Unfortunately, the rulers of that day divided their lands up among their sons, who invariably fought each other because each felt cheated. As a result, despite a temporary unification under Charlemagne, the western and eastern portions of Frankish territories became different in language and culture.

The western part was known in the early Middle Ages as *Neustria* (nyoos'tree-uh') or "new kingdom" because it represented the newer portion of the Frankish kingdom. The eastern part, *Austrasia* (aw-stray'zhuh) or "eastern kingdom," has a name that requires no explanation. Both parts clung to the name of the Franks, but the west did so more successfully, for it has become *France*, which the Germans themselves call Frankreich, or "kingdom of the Franks."

Austrasia was also called *Franconia* ("Franken" in German) but this name became obsolete in the later Middle Ages, though districts in Bavaria still bear the name.

The name *Germany* is that of a Germanic tribe whom the Gauls called Germani. The Romans, learning of these tribes from the Gauls, called the area to the east Germania, from which we take the name we use. The French call the area Allemagne, from an allied group of Germanic tribes called the Allemanni (meaning "all men").

The Germans call themselves Deutsch, from an old word meaning "people," and the land they live in Deutschland ("land of the Deutsch") or Deutsches Reich ("kingdom of the Deutsch").

Gabon

In 1839, French settlers moved into the equatorial regions of west Africa, along a river known by the name of *Gabon*. This name had been given it by the original Portuguese explorers of the coast who fancied some features of it resembled a cabin ("gabon" in Portuguese).

In 1849, the French founded a town in the area. Since the monarchy of Louis Philippe had been overthrown the year before and France was a republic again, the town was named *Libreville*, meaning "free town." Within two years, France lost its freedom to Napoleon III, but the city remained as a memorial to that brief moment between monarchs.

At first the French called the area *French Congo* because it lay north of the Congo River (see Congo) toward which French dominions had expanded. However, as they continued to expand farther and farther northward, some more general name was needed. The region became known as *French Equatorial Africa*, and its territory extended to *Lake Chad* (a name of native origin), which was a shallow and shrinking lake at the southern rim of the Sahara that had once been the center of a powerful Negro kingdom.

The capital of French Equatorial Africa was at the extreme south on the north bank of the Congo River and about 600 miles southeast of Libreville. It was founded in 1880 by the Italian-born French explorer Pierre Savorgnan de Brazza, and in his honor it was named *Brazzaville*.

In 1960, all of French Equatorial Africa gained its independence. Out of it four republics were formed. Southernmost were *Gabon Republic* on the coast and *Republic of Congo* to its east. (The latter is not the same as the much larger "Republic of the Congo" which lies across the river to its east and which was formerly Belgian territory; see Congo.) North of that is a nation with the rather unimaginative name of *Central African Republic* and north of that is the *Republic of Chad*. The Cameroons, associated with French Equatorial Africa after World War I, also gained its independence (see Cameroun).

78

Galatia

THE GAULS are usually associated with western Europe but they left their mark in Asia, too. In 279 B.C., a band of Gauls invaded Greece and spread devastation. The next year, a ruler over in Asia Minor named Nicomedes I hired some of these Gauls to help him fight a civil war against his brother.

The result was almost inevitable. The Gauls won the war for him, then became a far greater problem than his brother had ever been. It wasn't till 232 B.C. that they were brought under control and confined to a section in the interior of Asia Minor, a section known as *Galatia* thereafter.

Under the Romans, the province of Galatia included most of central and eastern Asia Minor, although, of course, the Gauls had melted into the general population long before. By 1100, Galatia was conquered by the Turks and the name vanished from the map.

The capital city of Galatia was *Ancyra*, possibly from a word meaning "valley." Under the Romans and Byzantines it was a sizeable and important city. In medieval and modern times, it was known to the West by the modified name of *Angora* (from the neighborhood of which come certain well-known varieties of cats and goats).

After World War I, defeated Turkey was in a state of collapse and seemed on the point of being divided by the victorious powers. In particular, Greece was getting ready to invade in order to regain the Aegean coast of Turkey, which had been Greek in ancient times, and still was to some extent.

Turkish patriots, planning their defense, used as their center Angora, which was far from the coast and the Greek danger. The Turks, rather unexpectedly, won the war and re-established a strong nation. In 1932, the capital of Turkey was moved from Constantinople to Angora, and in 1930, the name of the latter was changed officially to *Ankara*, a closer approach to the original. So although Galatia has disappeared, its city remains as a capital, and of a larger region, too.

Galilee

A LAKE in the upper reaches of the Jordan River is important because of its connection with events in the life of Jesus Christ. Its name arises out of the events that followed the destruction of the ancient kingdom of Israel by the Assyrians. The capital of Israel, founded in 887 B.C. by King Omri, was *Samaria*, named supposedly for the clan of Shemer, who owned the site on which it was built. The name was applied to all of Israel sometimes.

After the Assyrians had taken Samaria and deported the Israelites, they brought in foreigners who settled in and about the city and became known as "Samaritans." They accepted Judaism but only in a heretical form so that the orthodox Jews in the south disliked them cordially throughout the Greek and Roman period.

The area north of the Samaritans, in the neighborhood of the lake on the upper Jordan, was more successfully Judaized, but their population was still felt to be foreign. The area was therefore called "Galil haggoyim," meaning "the district of the foreign nations." The first word became *Galilee* and the lake became the *Sea of Galilee*. Most of the area is now included in the modern nation of Israel.

The Greeks were scarcely aware of the Jews at first. Herodotus in his history (written about 420 B.C.) did not even mention the Jews. To him, the shores of the eastern Mediterranean were important because of the coastal cities and their civilized inhabitants. The rude barbarians on the hills in the interior could be ignored.

The cities on the coast of the Jewish kingdoms had been inhabited by Philistines, and Herodotus called the region Palaistini therefore. This has come down to us as *Palestine*.

For Biblical reasons, the region was often called the *Promised Land* or the *Holy Land*. After World War II, when the land was divided between Israel and Jordan, those two names came to be used and the Bible-based names, and even Palestine itself, fell out of fashion.

Gallipoli

To THE north of the Aegean Sea, in ancient times, lay a land known to the Greeks as *Thrace*. The reason for the name is lost in history, but probably it originated as the name given to themselves by one of the native tribes of the region. Thrace made no great mark in history, but its name remained and still marks the area north of the Aegean Sea.

Jutting southwestward from the Thracian coast is a narrow piece of land called Chersonesus Thracica ("Thracian Peninsula") by the Greeks. On it, the Greeks founded *Callipolis*, which, in Greek, means "beautiful city."

The advancing Turks conquered that town in 1354, making it their first venture into Europe. They called the city Gelibolu and to us it became the intermediate *Gallipoli*, a name that came to be applied to the entire peninsula.

From Gallipoli, the Turks spread out farther and farther until, by 1600, *Turkey in Europe* was a vast area that included all the Balkans, Hungary, and much of southern Russia. Then Austria began to advance in the west and Russia in the north. Turkey in Europe shrank to the Balkans alone by 1800. The Balkan nations revolted in the nineteenth century and Turkey in Europe shrank further to a narrow strip across the middle Balkans.

The Balkan War of 1912 took away most of that. *Western Thrace* became a Bulgarian province and only *Eastern Thrace*, including the Gallipoli peninsula, remained as Turkey in Europe.

Turkey was on the side of Germany in World War I and, in 1915, the British Navy attacked at Gallipoli. There, at the site of their very first foray into Europe, the Turks made their last stand and succeeded. Even though the Turks were defeated in the end, eastern Thrace remained Turkish. Bulgaria had also been defeated in World War I, and it was forced to cede western Thrace to victorious Greece.

Gibraltar

THE MOST important portion of the ocean in the history of modern man is the *Mediterranean Sea*, for on its shores there developed the civilizations of Egypt, Israel, Phoenicia, Greece, and Rome. It is a nearly enclosed inlet of the Atlantic Ocean, bounded on the north by Europe, on the east by Asia, and on the south by Africa, so that its name, which in Latin means "between the land," is quite appropriate.

The Mediterranean Sea opens into the Atlantic Ocean through a narrow strait which is no more than eight miles wide at one point. On each side of the strait is a rocky promontory and the Greeks called these the Pillars of Hercules. The myth they invented to account for those rocks was that Hercules on one of his adventures in the far west found the sea closed off and tore the mountain range apart to make the connection with the ocean.

The straits were an easy highway for the invasion of Europe from Africa (or vice versa). In 711, the Arabs, who had conquered their way across the length of North Africa, were ready to cross into Europe. The Arab general, Musa ibn Nusayr, sent a force across under his officer, Tariq ibn Zayid. Tariq landed his army at the Spanish Pillar of Hercules, which was named thereafter Jebel al-Tariq, meaning in Arabic, "mountain of Tariq." By European tongues this was twisted into *Gibraltar*, and the strait is now known as the *Strait of Gibraltar*.

The African Pillar of Hercules was named *Jebel Musa* for the general who remained behind (though later he followed Tariq and joined in the campaigning).

Spain was conquered by the Arabs quickly and it then took the Spanish Christians seven hundred years of a foot-by-foot advance to undo the deed. Finally, in 1462, Gibraltar was recaptured. However, it was captured in 1704 by British forces and it has been retained ever since by them. Beginning in the 1400's the Strait of Gibraltar began to serve as a highway in the opposite direction and Christian armies moved periodically into Africa.

Great Britain

THE ISLAND off the north coast of France was called *Britannia* by the Romans, this being their form of some native word. The Roman word has come down to us as *Britain,* although Britannia is still used poetically.

After the breakup of the Roman Empire, the name *Britain* could still be used for the island, but not for any nation upon it, for no nation was to control all of it for over a thousand years thereafter. By 1000 the southern portion of the island had become England (see ENGLAND).

A peninsula on the western side of the island was inhabited by non-English people, descendants of the Celts (the original "Britons") who had been driven there by the invading Anglo-Saxons. To the English, they were "wealh," an old word of non-Germanic origin meaning "stranger" or "foreigner." This western area therefore became *Wales.* Its conquest was begun by Edward I of England in 1277 and it became part of England thereafter. The southern part of Britain is still referred to sometimes as *England and Wales.*

The northern portion of Britain remained largely Celtic and the inhabitants, originally called Picts, from a Latin word meaning "to paint," because they painted themselves, came to be called Scots, from an old word for the Irish, since western parts of the region were regularly invaded by the Irish in early times. The northern areas were called *Scotland* therefore.

Scotland was never conquered by England, despite a number of efforts, but in 1603, when Queen Elizabeth I died, King James VI of Scotland proved to be the legal heir (he was her first cousin twice removed). He succeeded as James I and thereafter the whole island had a single king. In 1707, it was decided to unify England and Scotland into the single nation of *Great Britain* and Queen Anne was the first monarch of the enlarged land. To include other near-by islands subject to the British crown (notably Ireland) one speaks of the *British Isles.*

Greece

THE PEOPLE we think of as "Greeks" thought of themselves as "Hellenes," insisting that they were descended from a mythical Hellen. The land in which they lived they called *Hellas*.

The Romans, however, met their first Hellenes in the form of a group in the western part of Hellas, just across the narrow strait at the heel of the Italian boot. These were called Graikoi or, in Latin, Graeci. The Romans proceeded to apply this limited tribal name to all Hellenes (a common practice) and this habit has been inherited by us so that we call them Greeks and their land *Greece*.

The ancient Greeks were never united but were separated into individual independent cities. Vague cultural ties were recognized between groups of these cities. The Greeks considered themselves descended from Hellen's three sons, Aeolus, Ion, and Dorus, to account for the existence of the three chief Greek dialects.

The Aeolians and Ionians entered Greece first but the Dorians arrived shortly after the Trojan War and conquered most of Greece. A region in central Greece, named *Doris*, may mark an early conquest. Many of the Aeolians and Ionians fled across the Aegean to the Asian coast, establishing cities there. The northern cities were lumped together as *Aeolia*, while cities to the south of these formed *Ionia*.

For several centuries, beginning about 800 B.C., the Greeks sent out colonists to settle regions of the Mediterranean coast. One place where colonies were very successful was in the southern portion of Italy (where Greek influence remained dominant throughout the Roman period). In fact, so flourishing were the Greek colonies in Italy and so much wealthier than the towns of Greece itself, that the region came to be called, in Latin, *Magna Graecia* or "Great Greece."

After four centuries of Turkish subjugation, Greece emerged into independence again in 1821. The disagreement over names still exists. We still write *Greece* while the modern Greeks write *Ellas*.

Greenland

THE MOST daring explorer of the Greek world was Pytheas of Massilia. About 300 B.C. he brought back stories of the far north, including mention of an island six days' sail north of Britain. The Romans called it Thule or ultima Thule, meaning "last Thule," because it was the last bit of land on the planet, supposedly. The name may be derived from a Gothic word meaning "farthest land." (In Greek times, the Goths lived in northern Europe.)

During the early Middle Ages, Norse raiders sacked the coasts of Europe but destruction and pillage were not their only accomplishment. In their flight from overpopulation at home, the bold navigators penetrated new lands. In 870, for instance, they reached the island that was very likely the Thule of Pytheas. They named it Island (ees'lahn), meaning "land of ice" and we call it *Iceland* in consequence.

Despite Iceland's northerly position, the Gulf Stream and hot springs make portions quite livable. It was under the rule of Denmark until recent times, but in 1944 it received its independence.

In 982, an Icelander, Eric the Red, sailed west in search of new land and reached the southwest coast of a much larger and still more northerly island which he called *Greenland*. This name was an attempt to attract settlers with false notions of fertility. (Eric the Red was centuries ahead of his time in advertising know-how.) The settlers came and for four hundred years, life struggled along. However, weather grew gradually colder and some time in the 1300's, the last settlers gave up and either died or left.

A scattering of Eskimos still live there, plus a few Danish officials, for Greenland is still a possession of Denmark. During World War II, Greenland became strategically important and the United States established airbases there. One was at a small Eskimo settlement in the northwest, which is now the most northerly permanent settlement in the world and, thanks to modern technology, is fitted up with all modern conveniences. The name of the place is *Thule* so the ancient notion of "ultima Thule" has become a reality.

Guadeloupe

ALTHOUGH MOST of the smaller islands of the West Indies are British, some are not. Two of the islands are still French and remind one of the days of the eighteenth century when the French were as actively engaged as the British in opening up the western hemisphere. The names of the islands, however, go even farther back than that.

One of them recalls the Spaniards, for it was discovered by Christopher Columbus in 1493 and he named it for the monastery of Santa Maria de Guadelupe back in Spain. It came to be known by the shortened name of "Guadelupe" and when the French occupied it in 1635, the name took on the French spelling, *Guadeloupe*.

The name of the second island, occupied by France at the same time as Guadeloupe, goes farther back still. It sounds French, for it is *Martinique*, but that is an illusion. Actually, it is merely a French distortion of a native Indian name, "Madiana" or "Mantanino."

Another group of islands, off the Venezuelan coast, belong to the Netherlands and make up what are called the *Netherlands Antilles* or the *Dutch West Indies*. These islands were first discovered by the Spanish explorer Alonso de Ojeda in 1499 and were Spanish for over a century. The Dutch took possession by force in 1634 and, for a while, Peter Stuyvesant, later famous as the last Dutch governor of what is now New York, ruled them. The islands retain their Spanish names, though the largest island, *Curaçao* (koor-uh-sow'), has a name that is a distortion of a native Indian name.

The names of the cities are clearly Dutch, however. The largest is *Willemstad*, meaning "William's town." It was founded in the 1640's and named for William II (the Dutch version of the name is "Willem"), who then ruled the Netherlands. Similarly, *Oranjistad* ("Orange town"), on one of the other islands, is named for the House of Orange of which William II, and the later rulers of the Netherlands, too, was a member.

Guiana

AFTER THE revolt of the Spanish colonies in the Americas and the enunciation of the Monroe Doctrine in 1823, no further permanent European colonization took place in the western hemisphere. However, the Monroe Doctrine also stated that the United States would have no objection to the continued existence of colonies already in being. In all South America, the only colonies that then remained (and still do today, for that matter) were in a small area in the north between Brazil and Venezuela.

The area is lumped under the name *Guiana*, which is of obscure origin and may have been derived from some native word meaning "wild coast." The original Guiana extended farther west and south than does the Guiana on the modern map, lapping over into eastern Venezuela and northern Brazil. (In fact, in 1895, Great Britain and Venezuela were in dispute over the Guianese boundary and the United States was almost drawn into a war with Great Britain.)

Guiana is now divided into three regions: *British Guiana*, *Netherlands Guiana*, and *French Guiana*. The exact boundaries weren't settled without fighting. In the middle seventeenth century, the British captured Netherlands Guiana (also called *Surinam* from a river that flows through it) but exchanged it for New York. That was a shrewd bargain for the British. In 1803, the British founded the present capital of the colony, naming it *Georgetown* after the reigning British monarch, George III.

Off the coast of French Guiana are three small islands called *Safety Islands*, perhaps because any one imprisoned there was safely held. The French did, in fact, use these as penal islands, the most famous of them going by the expressive name of *Devil's Island*. This last was made particularly famous by the fact that the French army officer Alfred Dreyfus was wrongfully imprisoned there for several years. France began to dismantle Devil's Island as a penal institution in 1938. The war interfered, but by 1951 Devil's Island was through.

Guinea

THE SOUTHERN coast of the large western bulge of Africa early received the name of *Guinea*. The origin of the name is uncertain but it may be a form of "Ghana," a strong native state that had earlier flourished in that region and concerning which the early explorers must have heard stories. As Africa was gradually split up among European nations, various portions of the coast added a European adjective to the name.

There was *French Guinea*, for instance, just south of the westernmost bulge of Africa. In 1958, French Guinea voted for independence and received it, adopting the name of, simply, *Guinea*. A year earlier, a section of the coast, 300 miles east of Guinea, had obtained its independence from Great Britain (though remaining in the Commonwealth of Nations as a dominion) and took the older name of *Ghana* (gah'nuh). Before that, it had been called the *Gold Coast* because some gold had been picked up by panning the local streams.

Spain and Portugal came earlier on the scene and are leaving later. Both still retain their portions of the coast. *Portuguese Guinea* is just to the northwest of Guinea, while *Spanish Guinea* (now called *Rio Muni* after the Muni River that passes through it) is a small patch of territory at a spot where the African coast starts bending southward again. The portion of the Atlantic Ocean that bathes the entire coast is, naturally, the *Gulf of Guinea*.

The name spread to the other side of the world when, in 1546, the Spanish navigator Ynigo Ortiz de Retez landed on a large island in the East Indies and noted the dark coloring of the natives. To him, they seemed much like the dark natives in West Africa and so he called the island *New Guinea*.

The western half of the island is still under Dutch control, for the Netherlands retained it even when the rest of the East Indies became independent in 1949.

Hanover

IN 861, shortly after the time of Charlemagne, a son of the Duke of Saxony, named Bruno, founded a city near what was then the eastern frontier of German territory and named it Brunswich ("the district of Bruno"). In English it is now called *Brunswick*, but in German it has slowly twisted to *Braunschweig* (brown'shvige).

In the seventeenth century, Brunswick absorbed the territory centered about a town fifty miles to the west called Hannover, from the word "hohenufer" meaning "high bank," referring to the fact that it was originally built on the high bank of a river. In English, the city is *Hanover*. Brunswick was only a duchy but Hanover was an electorate (which meant its ruler was one of those entitled to vote in the election of a Holy Roman Emperor) so the combined territory was known as the *Electorate of Hanover*.

In 1714, the House of Stuart, descended from King James I of England by way of his son Charles I, was extinct except for Catholic members who were disqualified, by act of Parliament, from the throne. The closest Protestant to the line of descent was George Louis, Elector of Hanover, whose grandmother had been the daughter of James I. He ascended the throne as King George I, first of the new "House of Hanover."

Hanover did not become part of Great Britain but it remained a separate possession of the British kings until 1837 when Victoria became British queen. A woman could not succeed to the throne of Hanover (which was a kingdom by then) so the two were separated. In 1866, Hanover was annexed to Prussia.

Hanover became a patriotic name in the colonies during the early eighteenth century and it showed one's loyalty to the new dynasty to give towns that name. None of the towns or counties so named grew large or populous but *Hanover*, Virginia, served as the birthplace of Patrick Henry and of Henry Clay, and surely this is a kind of fame.

89

Hawaii

CAPTAIN COOK, who combed the Pacific in a fine-tooth series of explorations, landed on a group of islands in the mid-Pacific in 1778. He named them the *Sandwich Islands*, in honor of John Montagu, the fourth Earl of Sandwich, who happened at that time to be First Lord of the Admiralty and is also said to have eaten meat between bread so as not to have to leave the gaming tables, thus inventing the "sandwich." It was at the Sandwich Islands, the next year, that Captain Cook was killed and eaten by the natives.

The native name for the island on which Cook was killed was something like "Owhyhee." The origin of the name is unknown. One story is that it was the name of the ancestral discoverer of the islands, but that sounds purely mythical. Another is that it was the name of the land from which the first native settlers arrived, which is perhaps more likely. In any case, the native name is now spelled *Hawaii* and it spread to the other islands of the group, which came to be the *Hawaiian Islands*. These were annexed by the United States in 1898 and became America's 50th state in 1959. The region is referred to only as Hawaii and the name *Sandwich Islands* is dead.

The main islands of the Hawaiian chain all have native names of uncertain origin, but one of the tiny islands at the northwestern end, over a thousand miles from Hawaii itself, is named *Midway Island*. This name is literally correct, for it is just about midway in the Pacific Ocean, 4500 miles due west of North America and 4500 miles due east of Asia.

However, the Earl of Sandwich was not left entirely bereft. In 1775, Captain Cook had discovered a group of islands in the far south which he called the *South Sandwich Islands* and those islands have retained the name. The largest of these islands, which have remained British ever since, is *South Georgia* in honor of George III.

Nor was Cook himself unremembered. In 1773, he had come across some small islands about 2500 miles south of Hawaii. They were later named *Cook Islands* in his honor and they now belong to New Zealand.

90

Hebrides

WHEN ONE speaks of the British Isles, one thinks mainly of Great Britain and Ireland, but actually there are a number of small islands also included. Between northern England and northern Ireland, for instance, is the *Isle of Man,* which was known as "Mona" to the Romans, but which may come from an old Celtic word meaning "little" because, after all, compared to the islands between which it lies, it is a little island indeed. The adjective derived from the island is the unusual one of "Manx," as when one speaks of a "Manx cat." This is supposed to be derived from what was originally the Scandinavian adjective, "Manisk."

Just off the center of England's Channel coast is an island the Romans called Vectis. This could be spelled "Weghtis" if we remember that in Anglo-Saxon the *w* is pronounced like a *v* and the *gh* like the German *ch* so that the pronunciation would then be much the same. It has now become the *Isle of Wight* (wite), which in modern English pronunciation gives it the illusion of being a "white island," which is not the meaning at all.

West of northern Scotland are the *Hebrides,* also called the *Western Islands.* To the Romans, they were known as "Hebudes" and the present name is supposed to be the result of a misprint. Perhaps the misprint was due to the thought that the Greek for certain nymphs of the western sea was "Hesperides" and that may have induced the insertion of an *r.*

To the Norwegians, they were "Southern Islands" or, in their language, "Sudreyjar." This became Latinized to "Sodorenses." The British still speak of the churchman in charge of the area including the Hebrides and the Isle of Man as the "Bishop of Sodor and Man."

The Hebrides are divided into two groups. Those just off the Scottish shore are the *Inner Hebrides.* Those farther off are the *Outer Hebrides.* All are bleak islands and nothing like the blissful and beautiful sea nymphs of the Greeks.

Holland

In 1240, a dam was built across a river in the low-lying coastal areas between France and Germany by Giesebrech van Amstel. The town at the site of the dam became known as "Amstelredamme" ("Amstel's dam") and, eventually, *Amsterdam*. The city flourished and so did the region about it, which was known as *Holland*, or "wooded land" in the local language.

Toward the end of the sixteenth century, the Netherlands rose in revolt against Spain, and the northern portion gained its independence in 1648. Because Holland had been the richest and most active member of the regions in revolt, it is very common (but incorrect) to apply the name *Holland* to the Netherlands.

The area of Holland had been occupied by the Germanic tribe of the Batavi in Roman times, so that *Batavia* remains a Latin name for the Netherlands. In 1795, when the armies of the French Republic conquered the Netherlands, they established the *Batavian Republic* for a few years, until Napoleon put his brother on the throne and made the *Kingdom of Holland* out of it. (This was the only time when the area was officially called Holland rather than the Netherlands.)

Dutch explorations spread these names to the other side of the world. For a while Australia was known as *New Holland* (see Australia) and though that disappeared, there is still a town on the northern coast of New Guinea called *Hollandia*.

In 1619, a Dutch explorer, Jan Pieterszoon Coen, founded a city in Java on the site of a native village named Jacatra. He named the new city *Batavia* in classical honor to his homeland. It served as the nucleus of the Dutch Empire in the East Indies and is still the capital of Indonesia. However, when the people of the islands gained their independence in 1949, they changed the name back to *Jakarta* in a move to destroy unnecessary reminders of Dutch colonialism.

Holy Roman Empire

THE IDEA of the Roman Empire lingered on in western Europe for centuries after the Empire had broken up. In 800, Charlemagne was crowned Roman Emperor by Pope Leo III and this began a custom that continued for a thousand years. Because the "Roman Emperors" of the Middle Ages were crowned by the Pope and because it began under religious auspices, the new version of the Empire was the *Holy Roman Empire*.

The Holy Roman Empire was largely German, consisting of many small and independent states. The Emperors were mere figureheads except in their own lands. In 1806, Napoleon finally forced an official end to it. The last Holy Roman Emperor was Francis II and, to preserve his title, he converted Austria (his own kingdom) into the *Austrian Empire* so that he remained Emperor.

Austria remained dominant among the German-speaking territories until it was defeated, in 1866, by Prussia. In 1870, Prussia absorbed the German lands outside Austria and formed the *German Empire*, with William I as "Kaiser" (a word derived from "Caesar").

The German Empire was defeated in World War I and a republic was established by a national assembly held in the central German town of Weimar. The new democratic Germany was therefore frequently called the *Weimar Republic*.

In 1933, Adolf Hitler took power and established a dictatorial "Third Reich" (the first being the Holy Roman Empire, the second being the German Empire). This Third Reich, or "realm," did more poorly than the first two. It lasted only twelve years before its total destruction in World War II, a war it had itself deliberately brought about.

What was left of Germany after the war was divided among the four chief victors in 1945. In 1949, the American, British, and French portions were joined to form the *West German Federal Republic*, usually called *West Germany*. The Soviet portion became the much smaller *East German Democratic Republic*, or *East Germany*.

Honduras

On Christopher Columbus's fourth and last voyage, in 1502, he finally touched the coast of North America, at a point of land which was eventually named *Cape Honduras*. This name came to be applied to the land area behind the cape, and *Honduras* is now one of the six independent republics of Central America. The word is Spanish for "the deep" but whether that refers to the depths of the ocean offshore or the depths of the valleys on the land is unknown.

The ocean inlet on the north shores of Honduras is the *Gulf of Honduras* and upon it is the port city of *Puerto Cortes*, founded in 1525 and named for the Spanish soldier Hernando Cortes, who had gained fame a few years earlier through his conquest of Mexico.

North of the Gulf of Honduras lay a section of coast only feebly held by Spain so that it became a favorite haunt of pirates. At one point along the coast a beacon ("belice" in French) was maintained as a guide at night. The town that grew up there was named *Belize* and it lent its name to the whole territory. However, the British made landings as early as 1638 and by 1798 were in full possession. They came to call the territory *British Honduras*. When the rest of Central America won its independence from Spain, British Honduras remained a colony.

If the meaning of *Honduras* is vague, that of the name of the nation to the west, *Guatemala*, is vaguer. The name is an old Indian word, but its meaning is mysterious. Some theories are that it means "Land of the Eagle"; others that it is "Volcano of Water." Whatever the meaning, it would account for the capital, too, which is *Guatemala City*.

South of Honduras is the republic of *Nicaragua*, which is named for an Indian chief who was prominent in the area at the time the Spaniards first arrived. This name applies also to *Lake Nicaragua*, in the nation's south, which is the largest body of fresh water between the United States and Peru.

Hudson Bay

THE ANCIENT Greek astronomers noticed that as one traveled northward, constellations near the North Star, such as the Great Bear and the Little Bear, rose higher in the sky. The Greek word for bear is "arktos." For that reason, they called regions of the far north "arktikos" and the word comes down to us as the *Arctic*.

In the seventeenth century, a whole series of intrepid men searched for the "Northwest Passage," the route by sea about the northern end of the Americas. One of these was the English explorer William Baffin, who, during expeditions from 1612 to 1616, sailed farther north than anyone else did till the latter part of the nineteenth century. He gave his name to *Baffin Land*, which became *Baffin Island*. It is the largest island in the frozen archipelago north of Canada. Between Baffin Island and Greenland lies *Baffin Bay*.

We are familiar with Henry Hudson for his discovery of the *Hudson River* in 1609. He was in the employ of the Netherlands, then. However, he made three expeditions into the Arctic in the employ of England, dying there at last. As a result, the water passage between Baffin Island and Canada is *Hudson Strait* and Canada's large northern ocean inlet is *Hudson Bay*.

The archipelago that includes Baffin Island is included in the Canadian *District of Franklin*. This is named after the British explorer John Franklin, who headed four expeditions into the Arctic in the early nineteenth century, dying on the fourth. He found the Northwest Passage at last but also found it to be unusable because of Arctic pack ice.

The climax of Arctic exploration was the trek in which the American explorer Robert Edwin Peary finally reached the North Pole itself in 1909. In his earlier attempts he explored the north coast of Greenland and that coast, the most northern land area in the world, is called *Peary Land* in his honor.

Illinois

A TRIBE of American Indians, living in the Midwest called themselves by the name "Iliniwek" which, in their own language, meant simply "people." The very first European explorers of the Midwest were two Frenchmen, Father Jacques Marquette and Louis Joliet, who penetrated the area in the 1670's. To their French way of speaking, "Iliniwek" became "Illinois," pronounced "il-in-wah'."

After the French and Indian War, the region became British and after the American Revolution it was part of the United States. In 1818, it entered the Union as the 21st state, with the name of *Illinois*, pronounced, in compromise, "il-in-oy'." The French *oi* was lost but at least the *s* remained silent.

The largest city in Illinois (and second largest in the United States) is *Chicago*, a name which is also derived from Indian words meaning, according to one theory, "wild onion place." The first settlement on the site of Chicago was a military establishment, *Fort Dearborn*, first set up in 1804, and named for Henry Dearborn, an American officer who fought in the Revolutionary War and who was Secretary of War under Jefferson at the time of the founding of the fort. The city of *Dearborn*, in Michigan, is also named after him, and the capital of Maine (see AUGUSTA) was named for his daughter.

About thirty-five miles southwest of Chicago is a sizable town that honors one of the pair of explorers I mentioned earlier, for its name is *Joliet*, pronounced English-fashion, of course, as "jo'lee-et." In northern Michigan, on the shores of Lake Superior, is the smaller town of *Marquette*, honoring the other.

Chicago is the largest city on the connected series of lakes that stretch across nearly a thousand miles of east-central North America. These are the largest inland bodies of water next to the Caspian Sea. Since the Caspian Sea is salty, these American lakes represent the largest bodies of fresh water in the world and are rightly called the *Great Lakes*.

India

MOST OF the early civilizations of man began in large river basins where agriculture could be conducted with an unfailing supply of water. One civilization grew up along a large river in southwestern Asia which to the people on its banks was simply "the river."

About 1500 B.C., people speaking Sanskrit invaded the region and, in that language, the word for river was "sindhu" or, in one of the western dialects, "hindu."

When the Greeks penetrated the region under Alexander the Great in 325 B.C., they called the river the *Indus*, the name still used by the West. This has given its name to the large southern peninsula of Asia that lies east south of the river, which is now called *India*, and to the *Indian Ocean* into which the river flows.

The older name of the river is not forgotten. The inhabitants of India are frequently called Hindus and the name of the land is sometimes given as *Hindustan* ("land of the Hindus").

A whole series of strong native nations ruled India during its history, while strong rule was set up on occasion from the outside by Moslems or Mongols. During a period of weakness in the eighteenth century, Great Britain was able to move in and slowly establish its rule over the entire land. Those portions which it ruled directly were called *British India*. The remaining portions, under princes of their own, but dependent on Great Britain anyway, were the *Indian States*. Together they made up the *Indian Empire*.

During the twentieth century, agitation for Indian independence began and strengthened. The difficulty was that regions of India were strongly Moslem and these did not want to be under Hindu rule. The matter was settled in 1947 when the region became independent as two nations. The larger portion remains the *Republic of India*. The Indus River, however, which gave India its name, no longer flows through India. It flows through the Moslem portion, now a separate nation named Pakistan.

Indochina

To THE Europe of the Middle Ages, the lands of the Far East were filled with wealth and luxuries that Europeans did not possess. They had silk, sugar, cotton, spices and, as if the reality were not enough, European imagination filled the lands with still greater wonders. The term "India," originally applied to the land about the Indus River (see INDIA) came to be applied to the East in general. In the form "Indies" it applied to eastern islands.

By the eighteenth century, however, Europeans had explored the Far East quite well and the term "India" came to be applied specifically to the large peninsula in south-central Asia. Regions to the east of that peninsula and south of China were referred to at first as *Farther India.*

This was not a satisfactory name since it implied the area to be part of India, which it wasn't. The Danish geographer Conrad Malte-Brun suggested in the early nineteenth century that the region be called *Indochina* instead. This name won out though it merely makes the area sound as if it were part of both India and China.

From 1858 onward, France spread its control over portions of the northeastern half of the peninsula. This area came to be called *French Indochina,* so that the term "Indochina" fell out of use as a name for the entire peninsula and was restricted only to the French portions.

During World War II, French control of the area was destroyed by Japan and although it was restored after the war, it was truly at an end. In 1949, three nations of the area gained their independence. The word "French" therefore disappeared and even "Indochina" was an unwelcome reminder of colonial days. Besides, a name was wanted to include not only the independent nations of the peninsula but also those of the islands offshore, such as Indonesia and the Philippine Islands. The logical and straightforward decision was made to apply the term *Southeast Asia* to the entire region.

Ireland

To THE WEST of the island of Britain is a smaller island that has remained Celtic throughout its history. An old Celtic word for the people of that island was "Eire" and it is from that that the name *Ireland*, "land of the Eire," is derived. From it also, with the insertion of a *b* somehow, came the Latinized name *Hibernia*, used only poetically now. (This does not arise from "hibernum," the Latin word for "winter.") The conquest of Ireland by England was begun in 1169 under Henry II and for 750 years the Irish remained conquered without ever once reconciling themselves to the fact.

In 1801, the British Parliament decided to unite the two islands as a single nation, and the official name of the new combination became the *United Kingdom of Great Britain and Ireland*, or, as it was usually termed, simply the *United Kingdom*. (It is difficult to get the various names straight. England is the southern portion of the island of Britain and Scotland is the northern portion. Great Britain is the whole island and the United Kingdom is that island plus Ireland.)

Finally, in 1921, the centuries of rebellion and unrest were climaxed by the granting of virtual independence to most of Ireland under the name *Irish Free State*. Six of the northern counties, which were largely Protestant in religion and which were reluctant to join the largely Catholic remainder of the island, remained an integral part of the United Kingdom. It was called *Northern Ireland* so that the kingdom is now the *United Kingdom of Great Britain and Northern Ireland*.

The Irish Free State broke most of what ties remained with England in 1937 and adopted the old Celtic name *Eire* (ay'ruh), of which "Erin," by the way, is another form. In 1948, it declared itself completely independent of Great Britain and became the *Republic of Ireland*.

The capital of Ireland is *Dublin*, a name derived from "dubh linne," Celtic words meaning "black pool." By coincidence, across the *Irish Sea*, on the English coast opposite, is a British port city named *Blackpool*.

Israel

IN THE BIBLE, the various nations that are mentioned usually have their names traced back to some ancestor of the same name (an "eponymous" ancestor). This was the usual habit in ancient times and the Greeks, for instance, followed the same system. The Hebrews traced their own ancestry back to Jacob, whose alternate name was Israel, and his twelve sons. The land which they inhabited they therefore named *Israel* and divided it into twelve districts named for the various sons. The inhabitants of these districts are the "twelve tribes."

Ancient Israel was strongest under King David, who died in 973 B.C. In the time of David's grandson Rehoboam, Israel split in two, forming a *Northern Kingdom* and a *Southern Kingdom*. The northern, being the larger, retained the name of Israel. The southern, consisting chiefly of the tribe of *Judah*, one of the sons of Israel, took that name (and from it "Jew" is derived).

Israel was wiped out by Assyrian conquest in 722 B.C., but Judah survived even though it was conquered by the Babylonians 150 years later. Judah endured the exile of its leaders and revived under the Persians. They revolted against the Greek successors of Alexander the Great, and for a while in early Roman times there was an independent Judah again, known by the Greek version of the name, *Judea*. That was finally destroyed by the Romans during the first century and its population was scattered — yet retained their identity.

In the nineteenth century, Jews began to drift back to Judea and after World War I, Great Britain, in taking over the area from Turkey, more or less promised to re-establish a Jewish national state. This was not done until 1948, after World War II, and then only as a result of a Jewish rebellion. It was decided to rename the new nation *Israel*.

Although not the capital, *Tel Aviv* is the real metropolis of the nation. Its name means "hill of the spring" and it was founded in 1909 on the Mediterranean shore.

Istria

THE SECOND longest river in Europe formed the northern boundary of the Roman Empire from the Alps to the Black Sea. The Romans called it Danubius, a name of uncertain origin, and it is interesting that none of the modern nations through which it flows calls it by a name as close to the Latin as does the English language. We call it the *Danube River*, but to the Austrians it is "Donau," to the Czechs "Dunja," to the Hungarians "Duna," to the Serbians "Dunav," and to the Rumanians "Dunarea."

The Greeks had a knowledge of the river, especially of the point where it flowed into the Black Sea, and they called it Ister, another name of uncertain origin. Some Greeks had the vague notion that a portion of the water of the river flowed off in a stream that ended in the upper reaches of the Adriatic Sea and, for that reason, the peninsula in those upper reaches is called *Istria*.

In early modern times, it was part of the Venetian Republic, but in 1797, when Venice finally crumbled after centuries of decay, Austria annexed Venice, Istria included. After World War I, when Austria in its turn crumbled, Italy and Yugoslavia squabbled over it, with Italy winning out. After World War II, however, defeated Italy had to give it up to Yugoslavia.

The chief town of the peninsula, one on its northwestern shore, was called by the Romans Tergeste. This has become *Trieste* now. After World War II, in order to compromise the conflicting claims of Italy and Yugoslavia to the area, Trieste and the area about it was made independent as the *Free Territory of Trieste*. This lasted only from 1947 to 1953 and then the city itself was turned over to Italy while the surrounding areas went to Yugoslavia.

About 640, a Slavic tribe called the Hrvati conquered the area east of Istria. Non-Slavs found the Hrv hard to pronounce and the tribe came to be called Cravats, or, in English, Croats. The land they inhabit is *Croatia*. It is now part of Yugoslavia.

101

Jamaica

CHRISTOPHER COLUMBUS quickly found that his first landfall in the west was a small island. He passed on therefore to another land with shores that seemed to stretch indefinitely to either side. This, he thought at first, was finally the continent of Asia. Unfortunately, he was wrong. It was another island — but the largest island in the area, at least.

The native name of the island was "Cubanacan." The Spaniards adopted the first two syllables (which happened to be a familiar Spanish word meaning a "tub") and the island is now called *Cuba*. It remained Spanish until 1898, when, with American help, it gained its independence.

The first Cuban governor, Diego Velásquez, founded a city in 1519. Because of its beautiful harbor he called it La Habana ("the haven") or, as we spell it, *Havana*.

(This is not the only "haven" in the Americas. In 1638, a group of Puritans landed on the Connecticut coast after leaving England the year before. They named the town they founded *New Haven*, after the English channel port of Newhaven from which they had embarked. By spelling it as two words, they also emphasized the spot as a "new haven" for their religious views.)

Columbus discovered another island south of Cuba, in 1494, and named it Santiago, which is Spanish for St. James, the patron saint of Spain. In 1655, however, the British, under Admiral William Penn (father of the Penn of Pennsylvania), captured it. They changed the name of the island closer to the native one of "Xaymaca" ("island of fountains") but, in a happy compromise (perhaps unintentional) wrote and pronounced it as *Jamaica*, which remains reminiscent of St. James.

At the time Jamaica was captured, England was a republic, but the monarchy was soon restored and, in honor of that, the chief English town on the south shore of the island was named *Port Royal*. When that was destroyed in 1692 by an earthquake, it was rebuilt as *Kingston*. In 1962, Jamaica gained its independence.

Japan

UNTIL THE coming of the Europeans, China dominated the entire Far East. Even where its domination wasn't political, its culture was admired and imitated. To itself, China was the "Middle Kingdom," for there were other lands to the east and to the west. To the east was an island nation which the Chinese called "land of the east."

The people of the island nation took their point of view from the Chinese and also thought of themselves as the land of the east. (At that, there is no important land farther east for some nine thousand miles or so.) In their own language, then, they called themselves Jih-pen-kuo, or "nation of the origin of the sun." To us the name has become well known in translation as "land of the rising sun."

(Oddly enough, this is not the only region so called. The Greeks applied the same phrase, in Greek of course, to the land to their east. They called the peninsula across the Aegean *Anatolia*, from their word for "sunrise." This peninsula has been Turkish for nearly a thousand years now, but the Turkish name is a clear adaptation of the Greek, for it is "Anadolu.")

Marco Polo, in his description of his eastern travels, spelled "Jih-pen-kuo" *Zipangu*, and that was the name by which the nation was known in the later Middle Ages. Once Europeans reached the Far East, however, a closer approach was made and the nation was known as *Japan*. Actually, the Japanese pronunciation of the name of their land is closer to *Nippon*.

Beginning in the 1890's, Japan embarked on a period of expansion that led them from Formosa to Sakhalin, to Korea, Manchuria, and much of China. Finally, in 1941, they attacked Pearl Harbor and began a quick offensive that brought them Southeast Asia, the East Indies, the Philippines and vast areas of the Pacific which they called, grandiosely, the *Greater East Asia Co-Prosperity Sphere*. But they were defeated in 1945 and stripped back to their 1890 beginning once again.

Java

THE ARAB chroniclers spoke of the East Indies in the 1300's as "Jawi." This may come from a Sanskrit word, "Javanna," which was applied to foreign lands generally, but that is uncertain. In any case, in modern times, the name has narrowed down to mean the most southern of the large Indonesian islands and it has become *Java*. This island is only the fifth largest of the group in area, but it is the most populous of all. In fact, it is the most densely populated agricultural region in the world. The part of the ocean to the north of the island is the *Java Sea*.

The fact that *Java* had a more general meaning at first is reflected in the fact that Marco Polo, in the thirteenth century, referred to the island lying to Java's northwest as "Java Minor," meaning "little Java." It was much larger in area, of course, but much smaller in population. However, in 1505, an Italian explorer, Ludovico di Varthema, gave it a version of its native name so that it has since been called *Sumatra*.

One of the racial groups in western Java is called Sunda. From this, the narrow strait between Java and Sumatra is called *Sunda Strait*. In fact the name has sometimes been given to the entire group of islands, which may then be called the *Sunda Islands*. The large islands are the *Greater Sunda Islands*, while the smaller ones east of Java are the *Lesser Sunda Islands*.

On Java's northeast is the large island of *Celebes*, a name that is a distortion of the native name "Sulawesi." When Indonesia became independent, Celebes was dropped and *Sulawesi* became the official name of the island. The largest city on Celebes is *Macassar* which, again, is a distortion of a native name, "Mangkasar." Macassar oil, to slick down hair, comes from that island. To protect furniture from the grease, strips of cloth called "antimacassars" were used a couple of generations ago.

All three islands, together with most of Borneo and many smaller islands, were occupied by the Dutch beginning in the early 1600's. The entire area, however, gained its independence in 1949, so that the islands are component parts of Indonesia.

Jerusalem

In the Book of Genesis, mention is made of Melchizedek, King of *Salem*, and the place is never mentioned again. However, when King David established a strong Hebrew kingdom a thousand years after the time of Melchizedek, he made the newly captured city of *Jerusalem* his capital. Tradition identified Salem with Jerusalem and in the 76th Psalm, for instance, *Salem* is definitely used as a synonym for Jerusalem. Since *Salem* comes from the Hebrew word for "peace," Jerusalem probably means something equivalent to "city of peace."

Since Jerusalem is the Holy City of the Bible, it has always seemed sacrilegious to name any other site after it and there is no other Jerusalem of any importance at all. However, this did not hold for *Salem*, which is a short and simple name, unlike many in the Bible.

The oldest Salem in the United States was founded in Massachusetts by Roger Conant in 1626 (four years before Boston). In 1692, this Salem made itself forever notorious through its trials and executions of men and women accused of witchcraft.

In 1833, a group of missionaries under Jason Lee was sent out by the Methodist Episcopal Church to convert the Indians in the Northwest. A town was founded upon their arrival which, in line with their calling, they named Salem. This Salem is now the capital of Oregon state.

The Salems of Massachusetts and Oregon are of roughly equal size. A third Salem, twice the size of either, is to be found under an obscured name. In 1753, a Moravian Church community from Pennsylvania founded a city named Salem in North Carolina. In 1849, some land was bought from the community and a second city, named *Winston*, was founded, honoring Joseph Winston, an American general of the Revolutionary war.

In 1913, the two symbols of war and peace were combined and the two towns were consolidated into *Winston-Salem*. The symbol of war came first.

105

Kalamazoo

THE NAMES of certain towns in the United States have somehow become associated with the unsophisticated backwoods so that use of their names can often raise a laugh. For some reason or other, *Peoria* is often used in big cities as an example of a small "hick" town. This is rather a ridiculous thing to do, since Peoria is a sizable town and, in fact, the second largest city in Illinois. It derives its name from the tribe of Peoria Indians who once lived in the vicinity.

Sometimes names are humorous because of the sound, and most of these seem to contain the letter *k*. Thus, there is the city of *Kalamazoo* in Michigan, founded in 1829 and taking its name from the *Kalamazoo River* on which it is located. The river was named from Indian words meaning "boiling pot," because of gas bubbles in the water at one turbulent point. *Keokuk*, Iowa, was founded in 1837 and was named for an Indian chief of the area.

Dubuque, Iowa, settled in 1834, is another city usually considered typically small-townish. The French sound of the name is legitimate, for it was named for a French settler, Julien Dubuque, who came to the region in 1788 in search of lead mines.

Large cities often have suburbs with names that are considered funny by the "sophisticated" big-towners. New Yorkers, for instance, are invariably amused at the name of *Hoboken*, New Jersey (though it is no funnier a name, actually, than New York). This was first founded by the Dutch in colonial days on the site of an Indian town named something like "Hopoakan-hacking." Hoboken is what the Dutch made out of that.

Again, a town to the north of New York was once part of the estate of a Dutchman who was called Jonkheer (or "squire") as a title of respect. (In Dutch it means, literally, "young sir.") The area came to be called Jonkheer's and since the Dutch *j* is pronounced *y*, the name was easily twisted to form *Yonkers*.

The *k* seems to do it.

106

Kaliningrad

Iᴛ ɪs quite usual for the official name of a city or region to change spellings when it shifts from the political control of one nation to another. For instance, the Franks, about 700, built a city on the upper Rhine which they called Strateburgum. This became *Strassburg* (shtrahs'boorg) in modern German and *Strasbourg* (stras-boor') in French. The spelling and pronunciation depends on which nation is in control. Right now the city is French.

On the other side of Germany, the same thing happens with respect to Poland. The Baltic town of *Gdansk* (gdahn'yisk) was taken over by the Germans in the thirteenth century and the name was twisted into *Danzig* (dahn'tsik), which was pleasanter to German ears. It was completely Germanized with time.

After World War I, those sections of eastern Germany which were largely Polish in speech were included in the new nation of Poland that was formed. These sections divided Germany in two, leaving its easternmost part (East Prussia) separated from the rest. The strip of Polish territory was called *Pomorze* (paw-maw'zhuh), meaning "on the sea," because it reached to the Baltic. To the English-speaking world it was the *Polish Corridor*.

Danzig was too Germanized to be made part of the Corridor, although it lay right upon it. Since Poland seemed to need a seaport, Danzig was made independent as the *Free City of Danzig*. It was over Danzig and the Corridor that World War II began, and when it was over, Poland took Danzig, giving it back its original Polish name of Gdansk.

The Soviets were more thoroughgoing, changing names altogether. After World War II, they annexed a strip of Germany's easternmost portion including the city of *Königsberg*, meaning "king's mountain." In 1946, they renamed it *Kaliningrad* (kuh-lee'nin-grad), meaning "Kalinin's town" after Mikhail Ivanovich Kalinin, who had been president of the Soviet Union for twenty-three years and who had just died.

Kansas

A TRIBE of Indians known as "Kansa" lived along the banks of a river flowing from the west into the Missouri. When explorers reached it, they called it the *Kansas River*. The region, under the name of *Kansas*, was admitted into the union in 1861 as the 34th state. At the eastern border of the state, where the Kansas meets the Missouri, is *Kansas City*. Right across the river in Missouri is another and much larger Kansas City.

About seventy miles upstream from the two Kansas Cities is *Topeka*, the capital of Kansas. It was founded in 1854 and was named from an Indian word meaning nothing more glamorous than "a good place to dig roots."

South of the Kansas River is a much larger one called the *Arkansas River*. The similarity to the Kansas River in name is a delusion, for it arises only through the twisting and retwisting of the name of an Indian tribe that was originally spelled "Quapaw." It is for this reason that Arkansas is pronounced "ahr'kan-saw" except by Kansas people, who insist on saying "ahr-kan'zas."

In 1836, the region through which the Arkansas River flows, under the name of *Arkansas*, was admitted into the Union as the 25th state. In the upper reaches of the Arkansas River, while it is still flowing in the state of Kansas, is *Wichita*, a city established in 1864 and named for an Indian tribe of that name which once occupied the territory.

In the lower reaches of the river, in the state of Arkansas, there is a city that abandons Indian names for ordinary English. Actually it is a translation that came about in this way. In 1722, a French explorer, Bernard de la Harpe, sailing up the Arkansas River observed two rocky formations on the riverbank. He called the smaller one La Petite Roche, meaning "the little rock." In 1820, a town was established on that spot and the name was turned to English. It is *Little Rock* and capital of Arkansas.

Key West

IN THE 1760's, Indians of the tribes living in Georgia and Alabama moved down into Florida, which at that time also belonged to England. They were called Seminoles, from an Indian word meaning "renegade." After the Revolutionary war, Florida was ceded to Spain and under the weak Spanish rule, the Seminoles were free to raid the southern United States. After a number of reprisal raids by American soldiers, the problem was settled by the purchase of Florida from Spain by the United States in 1819.

Reminders of the Indian days remain clearly marked on the map, however. The state capital, *Tallahassee*, in the extreme north of the state, was founded in 1824 on the site of an old Indian village and the name is from an Indian word meaning "old town." *Tampa*, on the west coast, is also named after an Indian word but here there must be some mistake or misunderstanding, for the Indian word seems to mean "near it."

Pensacola in the far west is named after an Indian tribe. So is *Miami* on the southeast, though here a comedy of errors seems to have brought in a tribe from Ohio for the purpose.

The first European city on what is now American soil was established on Florida's east coast by the Spanish admiral Pedro Menandez de Aviles, in 1565. He first sighted land on the day dedicated to St. Augustine and the town has been *Saint Augustine* ever since.

Off the southern tip of Florida is a line of low islands sweeping to the southwest. These are called the *Florida Keys*. The word "key" is from the Spanish "cayo," meaning "small island." The most westerly of the keys is *Key West* and it would seem certain that the name is derived from its location, but that is not so. "West" is a mispronunciation of the Spanish "huesco," meaning "bone," because human bones were found there. What *Key West* really means then is "Bone Island." The largest and longest of the keys is *Key Largo*, just off Florida, which means "Long Island."

Kherson

THE GREEKS, in ancient times, colonized all the shores of the Black Sea, including the Crimean peninsula on its northern coasts. The southern coast of Crimea seems at the time to have been populated by a group of people called Tauri, and so the Greeks named the land *Tauris*. The whole peninsula they called Chersonesus Taurica ("the Taurian peninsula").

Now a settlement on the southwestern shore of the Black Sea was named *Heraclea Pontica*. This was named in honor of Heracles (Hercules) and since the Black Sea was sometimes known as "Pontus" (meaning "sea"), the city's name was equivalent to "Hercules-on-the-Black-Sea." (It still exists today as a Turkish town named *Eregli*, in which name "Heracles" can still be recognized.) Colonists from Heraclea Pontica founded another city in Tauris which they named *Chersonesus Heracleota* ("Heracles-on-the-peninsula").

Long afterward, in 1778, the Russians were founding new cities on the Black Sea coast, which they had just conquered from the Turks. They founded one at the mouth of the Dnieper River, northwest of the Crimea. Under the wrong impression that this was the original site of Chersonesus Heracleota, they named the city *Kherson* (kher-sawn').

A Greek city had once existed on another part of the north shore of the Black Sea, about eighty miles to the west of the site of Kherson, and that city had been named Odessus. When that position (the correct one this time) was settled by the Russians in 1789, it was named *Odessa*.

When the Greeks first penetrated the Black Sea region, they heard of a mountain to its east which they called Mount Caucasus. As their explorations continued, they came to realize that not one mountain existed there but a whole range of lofty peaks. These are now the *Caucasus Mountains* (the highest in Europe) and the whole area between the Black Sea and the Caspian Sea is known as *Caucasia*.

Kiev

THE FIRST important civilization to arise in what is now Russia did so in the southwestern portion and centered about the city of *Kiev* (kee'ef). The meaning of the name of the town is obscure but, according to legend, it was founded in 864 by three brothers of whom one, Kiy, gave his name to the settlement. The importance of Kiev arose from its strategic location on one of Europe's large rivers, which the Romans had called Danapris. The modern Russian name "Dnepr," or, in English, *Dnieper River* (nee'per) is a distortion of that.

For four hundred years, Kiev flourished so that the period is called that of *Kievan Russia* and modern Russians give Kiev the nickname of "mother of cities."

For the first century of the period, the Russians remained pagan, but in 990, the Kievan ruler, Vladimir, having been impressed by the beautiful ritual in Constantinople, accepted Christianity according to the Eastern fashion, and saw to it that his subjects accepted it also.

The Kievans kept the use of pagan names, however, many ending with the suffix "-slav." For instance, the son of Vladimir and the greatest ruler of the Kievan period was Yaroslav the Wise. In 1026, during his reign, a town was founded some two hundred miles northeast of modern Moscow and named *Yaroslavl* (yahr-o-slahv'l) in his honor. This is an indication of how far north Kievan influence was felt. The town still bears that name.

Another son of Vladimir was Mstislav, who ruled that portion of Russia about the upper Dnieper. His son was Rostislav. Even today there is a small town in the region called *Mstislavl* (moo-sti-slahv'l) and a larger one called *Roslavl* (ru-slahv'l).

In 1240, however, Kiev fell to the invading Mongols and was utterly destroyed. Kievan culture came to an end. When Russia struggled out from under the Mongol yoke two centuries later, supremacy had passed to Moscow.

Korea

THERE IS a peninsula on the northeast of China that stretches from Manchuria toward Japan. It has long been a source of dispute between China and Japan, but is neither Chinese nor Japanese in language or background, though of course it has been strongly influenced by Chinese culture.

The name of the peninsula to the people themselves is "Cho-son," a name which usually appears on the map as *Chosen*, meaning "The Land of the Morning Calm." This name, like that for Japan (see JAPAN), reflects the fact that it was viewed as a land of the east from China and that the people of the land itself accepted the Chinese point of view.

In 918, Chosen came under a native dynasty of emperors called the Koryu, and these endured until the coming of the Mongols in the thirteenth century. To Marco Polo, who visited the Far East in the thirteenth century, the name of the dynasty seemed the name of the land, so that Europe heard of it under the name of *Korea*.

In the 1600's, Korea was forced to fight off a devastating Japanese invasion from the east and a Manchu invasion from the west. It therefore cut itself off from the outside world for 250 years, finding peace and the name of the *Hermit Kingdom*. In the late nineteenth century, however, the nations of Europe began to press in upon it and yet, strangely enough, it was not a European nation that took it over. In 1904, Japan went to war with Russia, partly over the question of which was to control Korea and (to the surprise of the world) won. In 1910, she annexed Korea and established the older name of Chosen on the map. After World War II, Korea was freed and divided into two parts, the south under American administration and the north under Soviet.

A war between the two sections was fought from 1950 to 1953, with American forces aiding the south and Chinese forces the north. It ended in a draw, and the peninsula is now divided between two nations: the *South Korean Republic* and the *North Korean People's Republic*, usually known, simply, as *South Korea* and *North Korea*.

Kuwait

THE TWENTIETH century saw the shift from coal to oil as the chief fuel for heating homes. Oil was also the source of fuels such as gasoline, which runs automobiles and airplanes, and of kerosene, which runs Diesel-powered trucks, trains, and ships. It is also the source of innumerable chemicals. Consequently, areas which produced the much-desired petroleum became suddenly important. In the 1930's, it appeared that the richest oil-bearing countries in the world were the dry and backward lands of the Middle East.

Suddenly, Arabic nations grew strategically important and filled headlines, where previously they had vegetated in unnoticed obscurity. Even tiny lands grew famous.

Thus, at the head of the Persian Gulf is the small sheikdom of *Kuwait* (koo-ite'), which is only about twice as big as Rhode Island. (Its capital city is *Al-Kuwait*.) The name is from an Arabic word meaning "little fort," presumably because of some little fort that was in the vicinity.

Since 1914, Kuwait had been under British control, and in 1938, it was found to be swimming on the top of the biggest oil reserves in the world. The sheik grew rich indeed. In 1961, the British granted Kuwait its independence and withdrew their forces. At once, the also oil-rich but larger land of Iraq to the north announced that it would annex Kuwait, and British forces were hurriedly brought back.

In the Persian Gulf itself, 350 miles south of Kuwait, are the *Bahrein Islands* (buh-rine'). The name, in Arabic, means "two seas," perhaps because (as in all islands) there is sea on either side. Great Britain has exercised some sort of control here since 1820 and it was in 1932 that oil was discovered there. Although its area is less than that of Greater New York, it is one of the major oil-producing areas of the coast. Bahrein and some areas about the rim of the Arabian peninsula that have some sort of truce or treaty arrangement with Great Britain are lumped as the *Trucial Coast*.

Lebanon

MANY OF the place names of the Bible have long since joined the dust heap of history, but not all have. In Biblical times, the Syrians to the north of Israel had their capital in a city which, in Hebrew, was called Dammesek. The city still exists today, is still the capital of Syria and is still known to us by the Greek version of the original name, *Damascus*.

On the coast southwest of Syria was a region named *Lebanon*, famed for its cedars in Biblical name. Its most fertile part is a valley between two mountain ranges so that the Greeks called it *Coele-Syria* (see'luh-sir'ee-uh), meaning "hollow Syria" with reference to the valley. The word "lebanon" is from a Semitic word meaning "moon" or "white" (the moon is white, after all), probably with reference to the snowy mountain peaks.

France occupied Syria after World War I and when the region became independent in 1944, the coastal section formed a separate nation so that Lebanon, or the *Lebanese Republic*, returned to the map.

The capital of Lebanon is *Beirut* (bay-root'), a name which stems from Roman days, when Augustus Caesar, the first emperor, founded the city and named it Berytus after one of the names of his daughter.

The Hebrews (to return to the Bible) spoke much of their neighbors, with whom they fought constantly. Most are now completely gone, but traces of one, the Ammonites, persist and so does the enmity. To the east of the Jordan is the city of *Amman*, a clear reminder.

In 1921, when the British took over the area, they organized the territory east of the Jordan River as *Transjordania*, meaning "across the Jordan," with Amman as the capital. In 1949, after Israel became independent, Transjordan annexed some of the Arabic portions west of the Jordan River and was no longer entirely "across" it. The name of the country was changed to *Jordan*. Because the ruler is supposedly descended from Mohammed and is therefore a member of the "Hashemite" family, it is called *Hashemite Kingdom of Jordan* in full.

Leningrad

SINCE THE 1917 revolution, the Soviet Union has been eagerly breaking with the past. One way in which it has been doing so is by renaming its towns and cities.

Thus, in 1703, the Russian czar, Peter the Great, founded a city on the Gulf of Finland on territory he had just conquered from Sweden. It was to be the new Westernized capital of Russia, replacing Moscow. He named it *Saint Petersburg* ("St. Peter's City" in German) after his patron saint.

In 1914, at the start of World War I, it seemed wrong to have a capital city named in the language of the enemy, so the city was renamed *Petrograd*, which is "Peter's City" in Russian. But then came the Revolution and to the new Soviet government it seemed wrong to have an important city (it was no longer the capital, for they had moved back to Moscow) named for a czar. The first Soviet leader, N. Lenin, died early in 1924 and at once the city was renamed *Leningrad* ("Lenin's city") in his honor.

Again, there was a town founded on the bend of the Volga River in southeastern Russia at the point where the *Tsaritsa River* ("Princess River") enters. The city was named *Tsaritsyn* for the river. During the Civil wars that followed the Revolution, Tsaritsyn was successfully defended by the revolutionary armies under Joseph Stalin. In 1925, when Stalin succeeded Lenin as leader, the town was renamed *Stalingrad* ("Stalin's city"). In dramatic fashion, it was at Stalingrad that the Soviet armies in World War II finally turned, defeated the Germans, and fought their long way back to the border, then on to Berlin. Nevertheless, in 1961, with Stalin downgraded, the city was renamed Volgograd.

In the same way, the Russian city of Tver, northwest of Moscow, had its name changed to *Kalinin* (kuh-lee'nin) in 1932, in honor of the Soviet president (see KALININGRAD). Again the city of Samara, on the easternmost bend of the Volga River, was renamed *Kuibyshev* (kwee'bi-shef) in 1935, after Valerian Vladimirovich Kuibyshev, an important Soviet official who had died that year.

115

Liberia

IN THE first half of the nineteenth century, Negro slavery was an established institution in the United States. There were always some Americans, however, who felt this was a shameful thing. There was continuous pressure for the ending of the institution and the freeing of the slaves, but this was not accomplished without the fighting of a bloody war between the northern and southern states.

Another kind of effort was also made, that of returning the Negroes to Africa. For this purpose an organization called the American Colonization Society was formed in 1816. They negotiated the purchase of a section of the west African coast and then began to obtain Negroes who had been freed by their masters and persuade them to return to a land they might make their own. In 1820, they made their first shipment of eighty-eight Negroes. Others followed and, by the time the Civil War had ended, 6000 free Negroes had been transported to Africa.

In 1824, the name *Liberia* was given to the section, from the Latin "liber," meaning "free." At the same time, the first settlement was founded and named *Monrovia*, after James Monroe, then President of the United States. It is now the capital of the nation.

The United States always maintained a lively interest in the one African nation it had managed to found and Liberia maintained its independence, thanks to our interest, throughout the height of the European penetration of Africa. In the early part of the twentieth century, Liberia and Ethiopia were the only independent portions of the continent.

It is strange that so wonderful a gift as liberty is not more often commemorated in geographic names, particularly among those nations that have won it only after hard fighting. There are provinces in El Salvador and in Peru that are named *La Libertad* (Spanish for "liberty"). In the United States, four states have counties named Liberty and there are a few small towns by that name. The largest of these is *Liberty*, New York, in the heart of the Catskill resort area.

Lima

In the centuries before the coming of the Europeans, the Indians on the west coast of South America had built up an amazing empire, strong and efficient despite the fact that its population was still in the Stone Age and had not yet invented writing. This was the "Inca Empire" with its capital at *Cuzco* (a native name of obscure origin).

For three hundred years, beginning about 1230, the Incas flourished and then the Spanish "conquistadores" ("conquerors") came. In 1533, Spaniards under Francisco Pizarro executed the last Inca for refusing to accept Christianity and went on to capture Cuzco. The Inca Empire came to an end and vanished from the map.

In 1535, Pizarro founded a new city which he named Ciudad de los Reyes, meaning "City of the Kings." Yet although a people may be physically defeated, their ideas live on with curious tenacity. The city was founded on the site of an Inca temple dedicated to the god Rimac. Oracles were issued from this temple to pilgrims from everywhere in the Inca Empire and the name was not forgotten. The Spaniards might call it City of the Kings, but the Peruvians called it Rimac and the latter name held on, although, in time, it was twisted to *Lima* (lee'muh).

During the centuries of Spanish occupation, the region about Lima and Cuzco became known as *Peru*, apparently from a small river known to the natives as "Piru."

To the east of the Inca Empire lies the long mountain range of the *Andes*, higher than any other range outside Asia. An idea of its height can be had from the fact that a pass across it between Chile and Argentina is nearly three miles high. That is the valley between two mountains. Its name, by the way, is *Paso del Inca*, meaning "Inca Passage" — about the last reference to the old empire on the map. *Andes* itself may come from an old Incan word meaning "east." The range is along the western edge of the continent, but it was to the east as far as the Incas were concerned.

117

London

THE ROMANS first invaded Britain in 55 B.C. under Julius Caesar, but it took a hundred years for a permanent Roman occupation to be set up. In A.D. 43, a Roman general, Aulus Plautius, established a fortification on the site of a small British settlement on what is now the *Thames* (temz) *River*, called Tamesis by the Romans and possibly from a Celtic word meaning "dark."

The British settlement was "Londinion," a name of obscure origin that has resisted all attempts to find a meaning for it. The Romans used a Latin ending and called it "Londinium." When the Romans left, the incoming Anglo-Saxons used no ending at all and it became *London*.

Although London grew with Great Britain's power and has been for long periods the largest city in the world, the old Roman "Londinium" still keeps its boundaries. It is known at the present time as the *City of London*, or simply *The City*, and makes up one square mile of territory with a population of a little over 10,000. *Greater London*, however, covers an area nearly three fourths that of Rhode Island.

London has spread its name through some of the lands that have come under British sway, though not perhaps to the extent one might have suspected. There are a few tiny towns named London in the United States, but the largest in the western hemisphere is in the Canadian province of Ontario. That London was at first selected as the site of the provincial capital but the selection was put aside in favor of Toronto. London, Ontario, is also on a Thames River.

In Connecticut a town founded in 1646 received the name *New London* in 1658. It, too, is on a Thames River, but this one is often pronounced "thaymz." Larger than either the Canadian or the American city is a town of Northern Ireland originally called *Derry*, from a Gaelic word meaning "place of oaks." In 1613, after suppressing an Irish revolt, it was given to the city of London, which organized a Protestant settlement and renamed the town *Londonderry*.

Lorraine

CHARLEMAGNE WAS survived by only one son, Louis the Pious, who inherited the large Frankish empire intact. Louis had three surviving sons, however, and he divided the empire among them. His second son, Louis the German, got the eastern portion (modern Germany) and his third son, Charles the Bald, got the western portion (modern France). His eldest son, Lothar, got northern Italy plus a strip of land running between the dominions of his brothers. This strip was called *Lotharingia*, from the Latin "Lotharii regnum," meaning "realm of Lothar."

Lotharingia was an artificial creation and in perpetual dispute between France and Germany. It shrank in area as it lost on both sides until the name covered only a rather small region south of modern Belgium. Under the name *Lothringen* (lo'tring-en) it became part of the Holy Roman Empire, which was chiefly German in character. France continued to nibble at it and by 1766 it was under French domination entirely (but then the inhabitants were French-speaking). The French name was the clipped version, *Lorraine*.

South of Lorraine, along the west bank of the upper Rhine, is a region which, after the breakup of the Roman Empire, was under the domination of certain Germanic tribes known as the "Allemanni" and "Suevi." (The latter give their name to *Swabia* or, in German, "Schwaben," an outmoded name once applied to that part of Germany east of the upper Rhine.)

The region west of the Rhine came to be known as *Alsace*, a name that seems to combine "Allemanni" and "Suevi" in itself. Alsace, though German-speaking, was annexed to France in 1690.

These areas, part of the original Lotharingia, seemed to carry on its role as disputed territory between France and Germany. In 1870, after the Franco-Prussian War, the new German Empire annexed Alsace and the northeastern part of Lorraine (*Alsace-Lorraine*) and that has oscillated since: back to France in 1918, then to Germany in 1940, and to France again in 1945.

Los Angeles

In 1498, Christopher Columbus spied an island off the coast of South America marked by three mountain peaks. To Columbus, they seemed to symbolize the three members of the Trinity and so he named the island *Trinidad*. It became British in 1797. Northeast of Trinidad, Columbus discovered a smaller island he named "Assumption," in honor of the Virgin Mary. It is now known as *Tobago*, a corruption of the native word "Tapuago." It became British in 1814. In 1962 the two islands gained independence as *Trinidad-Tobago*.

However, Spanish explorers have not always made their religious names short ones. For instance, in 1769, a Spanish explorer named Gaspar de Portola landed on the shores of a small river in what is now southern California. He named it El Rio de Nuestra Señora La Reina de Los Angeles de Porciuncula, which means "The River of our Lady, the Queen of the Angels of the Little Portion."

A city was finally established near that spot in 1871 which eventually became the third largest in the United States. For all its size, though, it could not use the entire name, but chose a small portion of it and so it is *Los Angeles*. But there are Indian names, too, in California. Ten miles north of Los Angeles is *Pasadena* named from an Indian word meaning "Valley between the hills."

The Portuguese were as apt as the Spaniards to place religious names on the map. One large tract of Portuguese territory in southwestern Africa is *Portuguese West Africa* and one of the important towns of the area is *São Salvador*, meaning "Holy Savior." (A town in the same territory is *Nova Lisboa*, meaning "New Lisbon.")

The more common name for Portuguese West Africa is *Angola* and it would be natural to wonder if this, like *Los Angeles*, has something to do with angels. Alas, it has not. The Bantu languages of the African Negroes make use of several sounds unfamiliar to Europeans. One of them is a nasal sound used at the beginning of words. This sound is usually written *ng* because it resembles the nasal sound in our word "long." To the natives the region was named Ngola. The Portuguese found they had to put a vowel first in order to get the *ng* sound pronounced and it became *Angola*.

120

Louisiana

THE LOWER Mississippi River was first discovered in 1541 and the upper Mississippi was explored in the 1670's. However, the man who really opened up the Mississippi Valley to European colonization was the French explorer Robert Cavelier de la Salle who, in the 1680's sailed down the entire length of the river. (The city of *La Salle*, in northern Illinois, which, however, is not on the river, is named for the explorer.)

La Salle claimed all the land drained by the Mississippi River and its tributaries for France and this was a generous slice of territory, for it makes up the central half of what is now the United States. He named it *Louisiana*, after the then-reigning French king, Louis XIV.

The territory remained French until 1763 and the British victory in the French and Indian War. That portion of Louisiana east of the Mississippi then went to Great Britain, while the western portion went to Spain. After the Revolutionary War, the eastern portion became part of the United States. Later, Napoleon seized the western portion from Spain and, in 1803, the United States bought it from him.

In 1812, the southernmost portion of the new territory, the region about the mouth of the Mississippi, was admitted to the Union as the 18th state. It bore the name *Louisiana*, which thus covers only one-thirtieth the territory to which La Salle had originally given the name.

In 1763, just before Louisiana was lost to the French, a party of French settlers established a town about twenty miles south of the point where the Missouri enters the Mississippi. The town was named *Saint Louis* in honor of Louis IX, who had been king of France from 1226 to 1270 and had been canonized in 1297. It also served to honor Louis XV, who was then king of France and who was the great-grandson of the Louis XIV who had given his name to Louisiana. It was a queer coupling of names, however, for although Louis IX was as close to sainthood as a medieval king could be, Louis XV was anything but.

Louisville

THE WORD "ville" in French means "town" and it is therefore sometimes used as a suffix in the names of French towns, though not, for some reason, among the larger ones. One of the more familiar French towns bearing the suffix is *Abbéville* (abbay-veel') in northern France. Its name means "abbey-town" since, in the 800's, the town belonged to the Abbey of St. Riquier.

The suffix was adopted in the United States during the Revolutionary War when the French alliance made all things French temporarily popular. Thus, in 1778, when George Rogers Clark was making his way up the Ohio in his victorious northwestern campaign, some families of prospective settlers accompanied him and settled down at a site on the south bank of the Ohio. This they decided to name after Louis XVI, then king of France. They felt a French suffix would be appropriate so the town became *Louisville*.

Louisville is now the largest city in *Kentucky*, a state that gets its name from Indian words that have been translated in a variety of ways. The best guess seems to be that it means "meadowland." Kentucky was admitted to the Union in 1792 as the 15th state.

In time, the suffix "-ville" became smart and fashionable and was used where French names were not involved; in fact, it was used in very English names. For instance, in 1822, Andrew Jackson was appointed first territorial governor of the newly purchased Florida. A new city was being built in northeastern Florida at the time and it was named *Jacksonville*, although there isn't a name you can imagine that is more English than Jackson.

In the same way a town on the Cumberland River was named Fort Nashborough after Francis Nash, an American general who died in the Revolutionary war. The suffix "-borough" is eminently English, but in 1784 the tide of French popularity changed the name to *Nashville*. This city is now the capital of the state of Tennessee.

122

Mackenzie River

In the late eighteenth century, explorers were still searching for water routes around the Arctic shores of North America. A Scottish explorer, Alexander Mackenzie, suspected that the great lakes in northern Canada drained westward and set out to search for the river that did so. In 1789, he located the river, but instead of flowing toward the Pacific, it flowed into the Arctic and, eventually, ice stopped his boats. He called it River of Disappointment but others felt the appropriate name to be *Mackenzie River* and that is what appears on the maps.

The portion of northern Canada that includes the lakes and the Mackenzie River is the *District of Mackenzie*. It is virtually uninhabited, but in one section pitchblende, a uranium ore, was located. This was in the days when uranium itself was of little value and only the radium that accompanied it in traces was sought for. The town founded at the site was given the unusually chemical name of *Port Radium*.

A somewhat later explorer of the Arctic was Ferdinand Petrovich von Wrangel, a Russian who traveled through eastern Siberia and Alaska. Native Siberians reported an island off the northern coast and in 1823, Wrangel searched for it diligently and long, but failed to find it. Forty-five years later, the American explorer George Washington De Long discovered it, but it received the name of the earlier man and is known as *Wrangel Island*.

Wrangel Island is part of the Soviet Union now, but not so with another portion of the earth's surface which bears the explorer's name. From 1829 on, he was intimately connected with the Russian dominions in Alaska, serving as governor for several years. A mountain range in the southeast, containing some of the highest peaks in North America were first observed by him and are known in his honor as the *Wrangell Mountains*. (It is spelled with two *l*'s.)

Wrangel, in his old age, bitterly opposed the sale of Alaska to the United States but it was carried through and the mountains named for him are now on American soil.

Madagascar

OFF THE southeastern coast of Africa is a large island that seems to be a piece of the East Indies broken loose and moved four thousand miles westward. For one thing it is a very large island, larger than Sumatra and, by coincidence, much the same shape.

Secondly, it is populated by people of the Malayan group, as the East Indies are, and represents, in fact, the westernmost extension of that racial group. The Malayan origin of the people shows up in the name they apply to themselves, "Malagasy," in which the first two syllables mark the fact.

In Marco Polo's book of travels, written in the thirteenth century, a land is described which is called Madeigascar, which may refer to this island or to the near-by mainland (for he could speak only through hearsay with respect to Africa). This name seems to be a distortion of "Malagasy" and when Europeans reached the island they naturally called it *Madagascar*.

Although the Portuguese reached it in the sixteenth century, it was not until the late nineteenth century that European influence became paramount. By 1896, France had firm control of the whole island and it remained French till after World War II. In 1947, rebellion broke out and, although this was held in check, the end was inevitable. In 1960, the island gained complete independence as the *Malagasy Republic*.

At the extreme southern tip of the island is the city of *Fort Dauphin*, which is a reminder not of the recent French occupation of the island but of French explorations and settlements that were far older. In 1637, the French king, Louis XIII, was given a son after twenty-two years of childless marriage. There was naturally great rejoicing over this. Consequently, in the early 1640's, the French explorer Jacques Prony named one of his settlements on that island for the new prince, since in royalist France, the King's oldest son was always referred to as the "Dauphin." (This Dauphin became king in 1643 and reigned for seventy-two years as Louis XIV.)

Maine

In Roman times there was a town in what is now northwestern France called Cenomani after a Gallic tribe living in the region. The first half of the name vanished during the unsettled period of barbarian invasions and it is now known as *Le Mans* (luh-mahng'). The name of the district about it underwent another slight change in spelling and became the old French province of *Le Maine* or, simply, *Maine*. This was sometimes spelled *Mayenne* and there is a town by that name to the northwest of Le Mans.

Henrietta Maria, the daughter of Henry IV of France, was Duchess of Maine and, as the wife of Charles I of England, she was the English queen after 1625. In 1639, two Englishmen, Ferdinando Gorges and John Mason, were granted territory north of Massachusetts and supervised the settlement of a new colony which they called *Maine*. This may have been after the French title of the Queen. Another story, much less romantic, but more likely to be true, is simply that the numerous islands of the coast of that region were first settled and that the coast itself, or mainland, was referred to as "the maine."

Massachusetts bought the province from the heirs of Gorges in 1677, but in 1820 it was admitted to the Union as a separate state, the 23rd.

The northwestern portion of New England, east of Lake Champlain, is noted for its low, forest-crowned hills which are therefore called the *Green Mountains*. The region was first explored by Frenchmen pushing down from Canada and they, too, noticed this, and referred to the Green Mountains as "les monts verts."

The later colonists, knowing little of French word order, put the adjective first, and "verts monts" became *Vermont*. This entered the Union in 1791 as the 14th state, the first new state to be admitted after the original thirteen. Since New England is the longest-settled region of the United States, it is always surprising to remember that neither Maine nor Vermont was among the thirteen original states.

Manchuria

TWICE CHINA was under the domination of Tatar tribesmen. The first time was in the thirteenth century, when the Mongols conquered China along with most of Asia and eastern Europe. That was the time of Kublai Khan and Marco Polo.

Four centuries later, in 1644, a group of Tatar tribesmen from China's northeast repeated the process. They call themselves Niuchi, which may have meant simply "people," and that name has become "Manchu" to us. The region in which they dwelt at the time they began their conquest of China is still called *Manchuria*, although to the Chinese it is known as "Tungpei," meaning "the northeast." In time, the Manchus were completely absorbed by the Chinese, and Manchuria today is as Chinese as the rest of China.

In the 1890's, Russia and Japan both began to maneuver for control of Manchuria and for forty years, Japan had the upper hand. First, in outright war, Russia was defeated by Japan in 1904. Russia's revolution in 1917 weakened her further. Finally, in 1931, Japan invaded Manchuria and took over complete control. They renamed the area *Manchukuo*, meaning "the nation of Manchu," thus attempting to emphasize the fact that it was a separate nation independent of China; though, in actual fact, it had become a mere Japanese colony. They placed Henry Pu-Yi, the last of the Manchu emperors of China (he had been dethroned in 1912 when he was only five years old) on the throne and named his capital city *Hsinking* ("new capital").

However, few nations recognized Manchukuo and, after World War II, the region was restored to China and is once more known to the western world as Manchuria.

One famous city of Manchuria is known to the western world by a name that is neither Chinese, Japanese, nor Russian, but English. In 1861, English ships arrived at the Manchurian coast and a Lieutenant Arthur headed a surveying party. The town at that point is still called *Port Arthur* in his honor — at least by Westerners.

126

Manhattan

NEW YORK CITY (under the original name of New Amsterdam) was founded on the southern tip of a small island at the mouth of the Hudson River, which had been inhabited by an Indian tribe that called itself Manna-hata or Manahatin, meaning "hilly island" perhaps. The island is now called *Manhattan*. The city expanded northward up the island and, by the end of the nineteenth century, occupied all of it.

Beginning in 1873, the city began to spread beyond the confines of Manhattan, first to adjacent areas on the mainland. This region is the *Bronx*, so-called from Jonas Bronck, a Dane who had been one of the early settlers in the region. The originial New York became the *Borough of Manhattan* to which was now joined the *Borough of Bronx*. (The word "borough" is from the Anglo-Saxon word for "city.")

By 1898, Manhattan plus outlying districts became known as *Greater New York*. This included the two westernmost counties of the much larger island to its east. This island had first been explored by the Dutch navigator Adriaen Block in 1614. After circumnavigating it, he gave it the logical name of *Long Island*. *Block Island*, northeast of Long Island, and discovered by Block that same year, was named for the explorer.

When the English took over the colony from the Dutch, they named the westernmost county of the island *Kings* and the one to its east *Queens* for Charles II and his queen, Catherine of Braganza, and these names survived the republican fervor of the Revolutionary war. Queens is still the *Borough of Queens*, but Kings County is the *Borough of Brooklyn*. The latter name is a version of the Dutch "Breukelen," a village they had established just across the water from Manhattan and which they had named after a village of the same name (Dutch for "broken land") in the Netherlands.

The fifth borough of New York (the *Borough of Richmond*, after an English city of that name) makes up all of an island south of Manhattan and somewhat larger. This island was bought from the Indians in 1630 by a Dutchman, Michael Pauw. The Netherlands was a republic at the time with its affairs being conducted by a legislative body called the States General. In honor of that body, the island was named *Staten Island*.

127

Manitoba

ALTHOUGH MANY places in the western hemisphere were named for saints by the pious Catholic explorers of the early days, there are few places named for the heathen gods of the natives who lived there before the coming of the white settlers. An example of the latter is to be found in Canada.

In 1870, the region west of Ontario was admitted into the Dominion of Canada as a fifth province. It took the name of *Manitoba* from "Manitou," the Indian word meaning "great spirit," this being their name of the god who ruled the universe.

The largest city in Manitoba is *Winnipeg*, which comes from Indian words, "win nippee," meaning "muddy water." The muddiness of the river on whose banks Winnipeg stands is borne out by its name of *Red River* (which flows into *Lake Winnipeg*).

(Sometimes Winnipeg's river is called *Red River of the North* to distinguish it from another and longer *Red River* that, far to the south, crosses Texas, Oklahoma, and Louisiana to flow into the Mississippi.)

A Canadian province whose name derives from the characteristics of another river is *Saskatchewan*. This comes from Indian words meaning "swift flowing" and is a reference to the *Saskatchewan River*, the name of which was taken by this region (just to the west of Manitoba) when it entered Canada as a province in 1905.

The city of *Saskatoon*, which is on the river, does not, apparently take its name from it, but from Indian words for an edible berry found in the vicinity.

The capital city of Saskatchewan was once known as *Pile o'Bones* because it was first settled near a giant heap of buffalo bones awaiting shipment to the United States as fertilizer. When it became the capital of the area in the 1880's, however, a more dignified name was necessary. It got as dignified as possible by adopting the name of *Regina* (ri-jie'nuh), meaning "queen," after the then-reigning Queen Victoria.

Mariana Islands

WHEN Ferdinand Magellan, in his circumnavigation of the globe, had skirted South America and entered the Pacific Ocean, the hardest part of his task lay before him. Although he didn't know it, he was going to be crossing the largest ocean of the world at its point of greatest width. For four months, through the winter of 1520–21, he traveled across 7000 miles of open water with supplies running so low the crew had to chew leather. Finally, he reached a group of islands about 1200 miles south of Japan.

There he obtained fresh supplies, but was irritated by the thievery of the natives (who, seeing European objects they had never seen before, could not resist appropriating some). He called them the *Ladrone Islands*, meaning "Thieves Islands."

In 1667, a band of missionaries were sent to these same islands by the queen of Spain who was then acting as regent for her infant son, the king. Her name was Mariana and on reaching the islands, the missionaries renamed them for the queen. They have been the *Mariana Islands* ever since.

In 1898, after the Spanish-American War, Spain ceded the island on which Magellan had landed (*Guam*), which was the largest and most southerly of the group, to the United States. The next year they sold the rest to Germany. After World War I, defeated Germany ceded them to Japan, and after World War II, defeated Japan ceded them to the United States.

South of the Mariana Islands are a group of nearly a thousand tiny islands spread over a vast area of the Pacific. These were first discovered by the Portuguese but, in 1686, they were annexed to Spain by the Spanish navigator Francisco Lazeano, who named them the *Caroline Islands* after Charles II of Spain ("Carlo" in Spanish, and "Carolus" in Latin) who was Queen Mariana's son now grown to mentally and physically retarded manhood. The Carolines, too, passed to Germany, then Japan, then the United States.

129

Maryland

In 1532, the English king, Henry VIII, established a form of Protestantism in England and for three hundred years after that, Englishmen who remained Catholic suffered discrimination.

When England began colonizing the American coast, Protestants of sects more extreme than the official English church found refuge there, and it occurred to some that English Catholics might do well to follow their example. In 1629, therefore, Sir George Calvert, an English statesman who had just been converted to Catholicism, persuaded the English king, Charles I (who was sympathetic to Catholicism), to grant territory north of Virginia for the purpose.

The first settlers arrived in the new colony in 1634 and, in accordance with the King's own suggestion, it was named in honor of his Catholic queen, Henrietta Maria. Thus, the colony of *Maryland* was established. George Calvert had been forced to resign his government offices after his conversion but he was raised to the peerage and assumed the title of Lord Baltimore. In 1729, a town was founded that was named for him and *Baltimore* is now the largest city in Maryland.

Well to the south of Maryland, a humanitarian project of another sort founded another colony and honored another monarch. In 1732, an idealistic Englishman, James Oglethorpe, got the idea of setting up a colony to which debtors and destitute men could migrate. He obtained a grant for the region south of the Carolinas from the king of England, who was then George II, and the new colony, the last of the thirteen, was consequently named *Georgia*. In honor of the founder, one of Georgia's counties is named *Oglethorpe* as well as one of its towns (which is not in the county). Georgia also boasts a *Mount Oglethorpe*.

Both Maryland and Georgia were among the thirteen original states of the United States. Georgia was the fourth and Maryland the seventh state to ratify the Constitution.

Mauna Loa

THE GREAT mountain ranges of the world are, as is to be expected, on the continents. Really tall mountain ranges are usually absent from islands, although individual mountain peaks may exist. For instance, the island of Hawaii has *Mauna Kea*, meaning "white mountain," and *Mauna Loa*, meaning "long mountain." These are lower than some of the mountains in the American Rockies, if one measures the height of their peaks above sea level. If their height were measured from the land base upon which they stand (which is several miles below sea level), they would be the highest mountains in the world.

Nevertheless, there is one island that has a mountain range along its length that can rival in height and ruggedness almost any of the continental ranges. The island is New Guinea. The highest mountains in the British eastern half of the island are the *Bismarck Mountains*, named for Otto von Bismarck, of course, the name dating back to the days before World War I when Germany occupied that portion of the island. The highest individual peak of the range is *Mount Wilhelm*, after the German Kaiser Wilhelm (William) I.

In the Dutch western half of the island are ranges that are even higher. These are called the *Snow Mountains* and in them are actually found glaciers, although the island is just south of the equator. Higher than Mount Wilhelm by nearly 1500 feet and as high as almost anything in the Alps is *Mount Wilhelmina*, named for Queen Wilhelmina, who ruled the Netherlands from 1890 to 1948. Included also are the somewhat lower peaks of *Mount Juliana*, named for Wilhelmina's daughter, the present Queen of the Netherlands, and *Mount Willem III* after Wilhelmina's father.

The House of Orange, to which the Dutch royal family belongs, became known as Orange-Nassau after 1702, when a collateral line succeeded to the throne, so that it is appropriate that this range be known by the alternate name of *Nassau Mountains*.

131

Mauritania

EUROPEANS, on first meeting Africans (even North Africans), are always struck by their dark, swarthy complexions (see ETHIOPIA). A Greek word for "dark" is "mauros" and the inhabitants of the northwest corner of Africa came to be known as "Maurus" to the Romans (from which comes the Spanish word "Moro" and our word "Moor"). The land of the Maurus was *Mauretania*.

Mauretania was conquered by the Moslem armies about 700 and from it as a base, they invaded and conquered Spain in 711. In 1062, a Moslem ruler, Yussuf ibn-Tashfin, founded the city of *Marrakech* (muh-rah′kesh), which served as capital of the entire region, including southern Spain. To the Spaniards the land of Marrakech became "Marruecos," from which we get *Morocco*.

Eventually, the tide of conquest turned full circle and Europeans began to invade Morocco. The first landings were made in 1415 by the Portuguese and for four centuries Spain, Portugal, and England kept nibbling away — without making permanent dents, however. Finally, in the late nineteenth century, when all Africa was being partitioned, Morocco was absorbed. By 1911 it was quite settled that all of Morocco but the northern shore was to be French territory and it came to be known as *French Morocco*. The northern shore was *Spanish Morocco*. This lasted less than half a century. In 1956, both French and Spanish Morocco received their independence and Morocco is again a sovereign nation.

Meanwhile the region to the south of Morocco bore the name *Mauritania* (with an *i* rather than an *e*). The French had penetrated that area in the nineteenth century and it was made part of *French West Africa* (a stretch of territory taking up most of the western Sahara) in 1904. In 1960, the constituent regions of French West Africa, among them Mauritania, gained their independence so that name, too, slightly misspelled, found itself back on the map, slightly misplaced.

132

Mauritius Island

SOMETIMES ISLANDS, small, isolated, and unimportant, become world-famous because of some biological curiosity upon them. Two examples are to be found in the Indian Ocean.

East of Madagascar are a group of islands discovered by the Portuguese navigator Pedro Mascarenhas, in 1513. They are called the *Mascarene Islands* (mas'kuh-reen) in his honor. Portugal, however, made no attempt to occupy the islands.

The Dutch in 1598 claimed one of the islands and named it *Mauritius Island* (maw-rish'us) in honor of Maurice of Nassau, who then ruled the Netherlands. They abandoned the island in 1710 and it came under the control of the French, who renamed it *Ile de France*. The British took it during the Napoleonic Wars and restored the old Dutch name. It is still British.

Mauritius is famous because, when first discovered, it was the home of the large flightless dodo. The bird was worthless as food, but, by 1681, it was exterminated by man and the domesticated animals he brought with him to the everlasting regret of zoologists.

Mascarenhas had also discovered a group of islands about a thousand miles north of the Mascarenes. These, too, were untouched by the Portuguese and it wasn't till 1742 that the French navigator Lazare Picault landed there. He was being sponsored by the governor of Mauritius (which was in its French interval at the time), who was named Mahé de la Bourdonnais, so the largest island in the group was named *Mahé* (ma-hay') in his honor. The group as a whole was afterward named the *Seychelles Islands* (say-shel') after Morau de Seychelles, who was finance minister under Louis XV at the time. The British took these islands in 1794 and they have remained British since.

The Seychelles are noted for palms producing giant double coconuts that were once considered valuable and wonder-working when they were only occasionally found floating in the sea, but which became worthless (they are not good to eat) when the source was discovered.

Mecklenburg

THAT PART of Germany which lies east of the Elbe was taken by the Germans from Slavic peoples during the Middle Ages. (The Germans refer to this period of their history as the "Drang Nach Osten" meaning "the push to the east.") The Slavic origins of eastern Germany are still to be found in the names of the provinces (see BRANDENBURG).

Pomerania (in German, "Pommern"), lying on the shores of the Baltic Sea just west of prewar Poland, derives its name from the Slavic word "pomorze," meaning "on the sea" (see KALININGRAD). Again, *Mecklenburg*, the name of the province to the west of Pomerania, is a form of "Michilen-burg," from "Michilen," the name of the chief Slavic town of the area before the coming of the Germans in the twelfth century.

After World War II, Pomerania was annexed by Poland and the area is now called *Szczecin* (shche'tseen), which is the Polish version of "Stettin," which had been the German name of the chief city of Pomerania. The city itself is now also Polish. Pomerania has not entirely disappeared from the map, for the Mecklenburg area, now making up the northernmost part of East Germany, is called Mecklenburg-Vorpommern; that is, "Mecklenburg and Hither Pomerania," the "Hither" referring to the fact that it is that portion of Pomerania nearer the center of Germany.

Mecklenburg plays its role on the map of the United States, too. In 1761, the new British king, George III, married a girl of one of the princely houses of eastern Germany. She was Charlotte of Mecklenburg. In honor of the new queen, a town founded in western North Carolina in 1768 was named *Charlotte*, and it is now the largest city in the state. The county in which it is located, to make the honor double, was named *Mecklenburg*. As it happened, citizens of Mecklenburg County adopted a resolution of independence from England more than a year before the national Declaration of Independence. So it is that the "Mecklenburg Declaration," a curious piece of Americana, bears a German name.

Medina

THERE ARE very few cities that are so important as to be known simply as "The City." The financial center of London is called that (see LONDON) but that is only a colloquialism. But there is a true example of a town named just that — in Arabic.

Mohammed, the Arabian prophet who founded the religion of Islam, was born in *Mecca* (a name of uncertain origin) which, for the very reason of his birth there, is considered the most holy city in the world by Moslems. However, the inhabitants of Mecca were not at all willing to accept Mohammed's new religion, and in 622 they drove him out, together with his few followers.

He fled 250 miles northward to the welcoming city of Yathrib and safety. This flight is called the Hegira, from the Arabic word for "flight," and Moslems count their years from that time as Christians count theirs from the birth of Christ. In Yathrib, Mohammed made converts, established an army, set up a base for raiding parties and, seven years after the flight, returned to Mecca in triumph as conqueror.

Yathrib, because of this, is called "The City of the Prophet," or just "The City," which in Arabic is "al-Medina." It is as *Medina* that it now appears on the map. And yet Mecca remains holiest, Medina only second.

Arabia had some decades of glory, but leadership of the Moslem world quickly passed to Persians, Egyptians, and Turks. Arabia sank back into long centuries of vegetation. Nevertheless, the main body of the Arabian peninsula has remained secure against European control ever since.

Only on its coasts could the Europeans take over. In the southwest corner was a city called Attanae by the Romans. This is now *Aden* (no connection with "Eden" since Aden's climate is closer to that of Hades). The British took it over in 1839 and have held it since. The ill-defined strip of Arabian coast to its east is the *Aden Protectorate*, and the ocean inlet between it and Africa is the *Gulf of Aden*.

135

Mesopotamia

ONE OF the earliest seats of civilization on the planet is in the land watered and made fertile by the rivers *Euphrates* and *Tigris*. Both these names are of Greek origin. *Euphrates* is from a Greek word meaning "delight," perhaps because to wanderers from the surrounding desert the site of the region, well irrigated by the river, fertile and flourishing, was delightful. (According to the Bible, the Euphrates was one of the rivers in the Garden of Eden.) A more prosaic reason for the name is that it is a corruption of an old Persian name "Ufratu" meaning "broad river." *Tigris*, of course, means "tiger," perhaps because the water of the river is tiger-swift as it shoots through the rapids that make it unnavigable. Again it may be a corruption of an old Persian word for "arrow" which also emphasizes the swift current.

The first civilization in the region was that of the Sumerians, and the plain between the rivers was called *Sumer*, a name of unknown origin. (In the Bible, it occurs as "Shinar.") The Sumerians flourished between 4000 and 2000 B.C., then gradually vanished from the map and from history. About 2000 B.C., a city called Bab-ili (meaning "gate of god" in the local language) became important, and people speaking Semitic languages took over the area. To the Hebrews, the name of the city became "Babel" and to the Greeks, *Babylon*. The city gave the name to the region, which became *Babylonia*. The city of Babylon remained important for 2500 years, then, under the successors of Alexander the Great, it faded out.

When the Greeks first traveled to the region, they were impressed by the position of the valley between two large rivers and they called the region *Mesopotamia* ("between the rivers" in Greek). This was by no means the native name. In Greek times, the Babylonian region was ruled by Persia and in the Persian language, the word for Persia was "Iran"; while in a later dialect it was "Iraq." And so it happens that nowadays, the nation that rules the core regions of the old Persian Empire is named *Iran*, while the nation that rules the once Persian-controlled region of Mesopotamia is called *Iraq*. These are but different versions of the same name.

Middle East

NATIONS VERY naturally consider themselves as centrally located and define other regions of the earth as being "east" or "west." Certainly, if any nation ever had some justification for such self-absorption it was nineteenth-century Great Britain whose forces controlled one quarter of the world's land areas and dominated all the oceans.

During that time, the British got into the habit of dividing up the non-European east into three areas based on closeness to the west (and themselves). These were the *Near East*, the *Middle East*, and the *Far East*.

Near East was originally applied to the areas that, in 1800, were part of the Turkish Empire. This included Arabia, Egypt, and the Balkan peninsula. It was also called the *Levant*, a French expression meaning "the rising," since the lands were in the direction of the sunrise.

The Far East included China, Japan, and Southeast Asia. The Middle East included what was between Near and Far; that is, Iran, Afghanistan, and India. The Far and Middle, but particularly the Far, are often termed the *Orient*, from a Latin word meaning "to rise." Europe and the Americas on the other hand are the *Occident*, from a Latin word meaning "to go down."

After World War I, the states of southeastern Europe, proud of being independent and European, objected to the term "Near East" as applied to themselves. They did not want to be lumped with the colonial Asians. For that reason, the term "Near East" fell out of use.

In World War II, the term "Middle East" became increasingly popular and came to include part of what had formerly been the "Near East." Turkey, Syria, Egypt, the Sudan, all were lumped with old Middle Eastern states such as Iran. In fact, "Middle East" began to be applied to the whole Arab world, so that newspaper articles will sometimes refer to North African states as Middle Eastern — even Morocco, which is farther west than any nation of Europe. This, obviously, is going too far.

Minneapolis

THE GREEK word for "city" is "polis" and there are various towns which were under Greek influence in ancient times and which still retain such names, more or less distorted. There is the case of Istanbul (see CONSTANTINOPLE) and Sevastopol (see CRIMEA) where the "-bul" and "-pol" are twisted forms of "-polis."

In the United States, however, there are several cases of names in which the "-polis" stands full and untouched. One such is in the region of the Midwest where the Mississippi has its source, a region named *Minnesota*, from Indian words that mean "clear water" or "cloudy water" but which many people romantically translate as "sky-blue water." It entered the Union in 1858 as the 32nd state. Some years before that, in 1852, a settlement growing up on the western bank of the upper Mississippi was named *Minneapolis*, which may be considered to mean "water city" or "Minnesota city."

The use of such a name followed the precedent established a generation earlier by the state of *Indiana*. In 1816, Indiana entered the union as the 19th state (having been named, obviously, for the Indians). In 1820, a commission selected a site for the state capital, which was built and named *Indianapolis* ("Indiana city").

The earliest case, however, involved a city that was not named after a state because it was founded before the United States existed. In 1694, a town in Maryland that had had a number of names was finally selected as capital of the colony and, in 1708, it was formally chartered as a city. Anne was at that time Queen of England and so the city was named *Annapolis* ("Anne's city"). Thus a state named after one queen of England (see MARYLAND) had a capital named after another.

Minneapolis, although the largest of the three "polis cities," is the only one not a state capital. The capital of Minnesota, St. Paul, is, however, located just across the river from Minneapolis and, together, the two towns are frequently referred to as the *Twin Cities*.

Mississippi

In 1539, the Spanish explorer Hernando de Soto landed in Florida on the first leg of a search for treasure that was to carry him through much of what is now the southeastern United States. Two years later, he was the first white man to look upon the *Mississippi River*. The next year, he died on its banks and was buried in its waters. A town in eastern Missouri and a county in Louisiana are named *De Soto*. Those are the chief geographic memorials to the explorer and neither town nor county is on the banks of the Mississippi.

Over a century later, French explorers came across a huge river flowing into the Mississippi from the west. The name *Mississippi* was applied by them to the main river, from Indian words, "mici sepe," meaning "great river." The tributary was called the *Missouri River* from an Indian tribe living on its banks.

The part of the Mississippi north of the Missouri is called the *Upper Mississippi*. Actually, the Missouri is much longer than the Upper Mississippi, a fact not discovered until explorations of the early nineteenth century. It is customary to consider the longest stream the main river so that the Missouri plus the *Lower Mississippi* is used by geographers as the longest river of the continent. In fact, the *Missouri-Mississippi* (as it is frequently called) is rivaled in length only by the Nile and the Amazon.

Both rivers have given their names to states. Along the eastern bank of the lower reaches of the Mississippi is the state of *Mississippi*, which entered the union in 1817 as the 20th state.

On the western banks of the central Mississippi is the state of *Missouri* (through which the Missouri runs to its union with the Mississippi). It entered the Union in 1821 as the 24th state. A county in southeastern Missouri is named *Mississippi* and so is one in Arkansas, the state to the south of Missouri. Both counties are on the banks of the river, naturally.

Moluccas

THE EUROPEANS of the Middle Ages were intensely interested in the *Spice Islands* (see EAST INDIES) from which valuable spices were obtained (hence the name, of course). To begin with, these islands were but vaguely located somewhere in the Far East. As knowledge of the East increased during the age of the great explorations, the Spice Islands were pinned down to a definite group between Celebes and New Guinea in the East Indies.

These are still called the Spice Islands sometimes but they appear on the map as the *Molucca Islands* (mo-luk'uh). The value of their products to others than Europeans is shown by the fact that this name may come from the Arabic word for "king," dating back to the days when Arabic traders conducted the traffic in the kingly commodity of spices. The largest island of the group is *Halmahera* (hal-muh-her'uh), which is almost as large as Massachusetts. The name comes from a native word meaning "great land."

Among the smaller East Indian islands, the one that is perhaps the most "romantic" is *Bali*, a name that comes, possibly, from a Sanskrit word meaning "strong," so that it is another one of the self-praising names common among tribes of human beings. Bali recalls the East Indies of an older day, for before the Moslem traders came with their Mohammedan religion, Indian invasions had spread Hinduism. Bali remains a land of Hinduism surrounded by Moslems.

Another kind of older day is preserved in another island about 700 miles east of Bali, one named Timor. Before the Dutch came to the islands in the seventeenth century, the Portuguese had had trading posts and controlled many of the island coasts. Slowly they lost out to the Dutch. One place only they retained and that was the eastern half of Timor, which is consequently called *Portuguese Timor*. When the East Indies gained their independence from the Netherlands, Portuguese Timor remained Portuguese, an island of colonialism in the midst of Indonesia.

Monaco

ON THE Mediterranean shore, just at the point where nowadays France and Italy meet, the Phoenicians built a temple. The Greeks took it over and dedicated to Heracles, calling it Heracles Monoikos, meaning "Heracles One-House," perhaps because there was this single temple on the headland. The region is now known as *Monaco*, from "Monoikos."

Monaco has managed to remain independent ever since, although it was temporarily annexed by France in Napoleon's time. It is now under the protection of France, but its area of 0.6 square mile (less than half the size of Central Park) forms a sovereign state under a prince who some years ago achieved fame by marrying the American actress Grace Kelly. It is also famous for its town of *Monte Carlo* ("Charles Mountain") and the gambling casinos located there — which support the small nation on a tax-free basis.

The Mediterranean coast along France and Italy is known as the *Riviera*, from a Latin word meaning "bank." To be sure, "banks" are usually associated with streams, which is how we get our word "river," but in this case it is the bank of a sea that is involved. Naturally, there are the *French Riviera* and the *Italian Riviera*. The chief town on the Italian Riviera is *Genoa*, a city with a name of obscure origin, which was referred to in early Roman terms as "Genua."

A well-known town on the French Riviera, to the west of Monaco, is *Nice* (nees). This was "Nicaea" in ancient times, a name derived from the Greek "nike," meaning "victory" — a good-luck name to give a town.

Another *Nicaea* (nigh-see'uh) existed in ancient and medieval times in what is now northwestern Turkey. (The present Turkish name is "Iznik.") In 1204, when western Crusaders captured Constantinople, the defeated Greeks fled across the straits to Asia Minor, forming the Greek kingdom of Nicaea about the city and waiting for their chance to return. This they did in 1261, so that there the name "Nicaea" seemed prophetic.

141

Mongolia

THE MONGOL nomads conquered the largest continuous land empire the world has ever seen, but nothing of that thirteenth-century empire remains to them today outside the vast mid-Asian steppes from which they originally came. That region is still called *Mongolia*.

In modern times, Mongolia has been divided into two main regions, *Outer Mongolia* and *Inner Mongolia*. These names originate from a Chinese point of view since the "inner" section is closer to China. Inner Mongolia has been heavily peopled by Chinese and is now an integral part of China, as the *Inner Mongolian Autonomous Region*.

Outer Mongolia maintained only weak ties with China. The northernmost portion of Outer Mongolia declared itself independent in 1911 after the Chinese Revolution had overthrown the Manchu Dynasty. It was known as *Tuva* and later as *Tannu-Tuva*, which were tribal names. In 1945, it was annexed by the Soviet Union as the *Tuva Autonomous Region*.

The rest of Outer Mongolia came under Soviet influence in 1924 and the *Mongolian People's Republic* was then established.

Directly north of Tuva are regions of Siberia which are inhabited by Mongol tribes and this was organized into the *Buriat-Mongolian Autonomous Soviet Socialist Republic*.

In the southwestern sections of the Asiatic portions of the Soviet Union (*Soviet Central Asia* is a common name for the region) there are tribes of Turkish-Mongol heritage. Under their tribal names, they have been organized into Soviet Socialist Republics, too. There is the *Kirgiz S.S.R.* (kir-geez') and to the north of it, over a vast area of semidesert, the *Kazakh S.S.R.* (kah-zahk'). The former is sometimes called *Kirgizia*, the latter *Kazakhstan*.

The word "Kazakh" means "rider" in the native language and points up the fact that the Mongol virtually lived on horseback. The Russians borrowed the word for their own hard-riding frontiersmen and it comes down to us as "Cossack."

Montpelier

THE FRENCH, who first explored the St. Lawrence Valley and Lake Champlain, left their mark on the map of Vermont not so much directly as because the English settlers who came afterward seemed rather proud of the French tradition and showed it in the very name of the state (see MAINE). They also showed it in the name of the state capital. When it was founded in north-central Vermont, one of the founders, Jacob Davis, named it after the French town of Montpellier for no reason, perhaps, than that it sounded high-toned. One of the *l*'s dropped out, but *Montpelier* it remained ever since. However, its name is pronounced "mont-peel'yur" in strictly English fashion.

However, France was not the only inspiration for names by any means. The town of *Rutland* in southern Vermont, founded in 1714, was named for the smallest of the English counties.

The largest city in the state, on the eastern shore of Lake Champlain, is *Burlington*, and that apparently derives its name from a family named Burling that lived on the site at the time the town was founded in 1763. That same obscure family made its mark in the Midwest, for, in 1834, some Vermonters settled in Iowa and named the new town they had founded Burlington, after their old home.

There is also a Burlington in New Jersey that has nothing to do with the Burling family. It was originally named after a town in Yorkshire called Bridlington when it was founded in 1677, but misspelling froze its name to Burlington.

Before Vermont became a state, its territory was claimed by both New York and New Hampshire (and after the Revolutionary war, the bellicose Vermonter Ethan Allen offered to declare war on the whole universe rather than to submit to either). The old days are marked by the town of *Bennington* in the extreme southwest of the state. It was settled in 1761 and was named for Benning Wentworth, who, at the time, was royal governor — of New Hampshire.

143

Murmansk

THERE IS this difference between the Arctic and the Antarctic oceans — the land bordering the latter is uninhabited while that bordering the former contains men and cities. In the northern reaches of the Soviet Union is located the largest of all Arctic cities. Its harbor is choked by ice for more than half the year, but in the days of Ivan the Terrible it became Russia's seaport (and its only seaport at the time, too) when an English navigator, Richard Chancellor, built a trading post in the region in 1553. Before that the site had been occupied only by a monastery dedicated to the Archangel Michael and the name of the town is, for that reason, *Archangel*. (In Russian, it is "Arkhangelsk.")

Farther north and to the west is a section of shore that was once called the *Norman Coast* because of the incursions of Northmen from Norway, which lies to its west. In Russian, this has been twisted to "Murman" Coast and on that coast the Russians built the city of *Murmansk* (moor-mansk'). Although farther north than Archangel, Murmansk gets the final dregs of the Gulf Stream and is ice-free all year round. It has become the most important Arctic port of the Soviet Union, although it is not as populous as Archangel.

The American Arctic, without the Gulf Stream, can boast nothing like this. The most northerly point of Alaska is *Point Barrow*, named for the English traveler and geographer John Barrow, who in the mid-nineteenth century sponsored explorations in the region. Just south of Point Barrow is *Barrow*, the most northerly town in the United States.

The most northerly portion of the Canadian mainland is *Boothia Peninsula*. It was discovered by John Ross in 1830 and was named for Felix Booth, who had financed the expedition. On the east of the peninsula, between it and Baffin Island, is the *Gulf of Boothia*, while on its west is *John Ross Strait*, separating it from other islands. Just off Boothia Peninsula is the "North Magnetic Pole."

Naples

THE SIMPLEST name for a new town is "New Town" and examples of this were present in ancient times. About 600 B.C. the oldest Greek settlement in Italy established a new town a few miles away, on the abandoned site of an older one called *Parthenope* (pahr-then'o-pee), which, in Greek, means "maiden's face." The new town was named *Neapolis* (nee-a'po-lis), meaning "new town."

The old town has faded out and no longer exists but Neapolis is now a great city. To the Italians the name has been shortened by the loss of two letters and become "Napoli" and, to us, it is *Naples*. Through the Middle Ages and early modern times, Naples ruled the southern half of Italy and, most of the time, Sicily as well. In 1799, French armies captured the kingdom of Naples and established a republic that lasted a few months. Napoleon was in charge and since he was a great lover of the past, he named it the *Parthenopean Republic*, harking back to the old, old name.

Even before the days of the Greek settlements, Phoenicians (who, like the Greeks, settled the coasts of the Mediterranean) founded a city in northern Africa near an older settlement. The older settlement was known to the later Romans as *Utica* while the newer was *Carthage*, these being versions of the Phoenician names that meant "old town" and "new town" respectively.

Carthage grew powerful with time and in 225 B.C. conquered parts of the Spanish peninsula. There she founded a town which, in Latin, was known as "Carthago Nova" or "New Carthage" (a kind of "new new town"). That city still exists on the Spanish coast and is now known as *Cartagena*.

Thirteen hundred years later it was the Spaniards who were settling coasts the Phoenicians never knew. In 1533, a town was founded on the northern shores of South America and named for the Spanish city so that now there is a *Cartagena* in Colombia as well as in Spain.

Nebraska

FLOWING EASTWARD toward the Missouri are two streams, one starting in Wyoming and one in the state to its south, Colorado. To the east of these two states, the rivers join and flow the remaining 400 miles to the Missouri. The combined river is unusually wide but very shallow. The Indians of the region call it Ni-brathka, meaning "flat water," which is an excellent description.

In 1714, a French explorer made his way up this river and translated the Indian name into what is now *Platte River*. (The Latin word "plattus" means "flat.") Of the two branches, the northern or Wyoming branch is the *North Platte River*, while the other is the *South Platte River*. When the region was organized as a territory in 1854, the American army officer, John Charles Frémont, a noted Western explorer, suggested that the old Indian name be revived. The territory entered the Union as *Nebraska* in 1867, the 37th state to be admitted.

On the Missouri River, a little to the north of the point where the Platte River enters, settlers obtained land by peaceful negotiation with a tribe of Indians living there. The tribe called itself Omaha, from a word that seems to mean "those who go upstream." The city was named for the tribe and *Omaha* is now the largest city of Nebraska.

The colorful Frémont was making his mark on the west in a number of ways. In 1848, he had had an epic feud with his superior officer, Stephen Watts Kearny, and was convicted at a court-martial and forced to resign from the army temporarily. Eight years later, he was running for the office of the presidency as candidate of the brand-new Republican party. (He was defeated.) In the latter year, 1856, a town on the Platte River, about fifty miles west of Omaha, was founded and named *Fremont* in his honor.

Oddly enough, about 150 miles farther up the river a "Fort Kearny" had been established in 1848, named for Frémont's enemy. It is now the city of *Kearney* (kahr'nee) with an extra *e* added, so that Nebraska stands neutral in that old feud.

Netherlands

THAT PART of the European shoreline directly east of southern England is quite low-lying. Large areas are beneath the high-tide level. The inhabitants, however, have made additional land for farming by building dikes to hold the water back. They refer to their land, naturally enough, as "Nederland" ("low-lying land") and this becomes, in English, the equally straightforward *Netherlands*.

In 1555, the flourishing cities of the Netherlands passed under the control of Philip II of Spain, who was determined to exterminate the Protestantism toward which a number of the Netherlanders had turned. After a long series of wars, the northern part of the Netherlands gained their independence and it is to that portion only that the term "Netherlands" is applied today.

The southern portion (mainly Catholic) remained under Spanish control and was known, during the seventeenth century, as the *Spanish Netherlands*. In 1701, there was a change in dynasty in Spain, however, and after the war that resulted, the Spanish Netherlands were ceded to Austria and became the *Austrian Netherlands*. Eventually, they, too, gained their independence (see BELGIUM).

In ancient times, a Germanic tribe called the Frisii by the Romans dwelt in the region that is now the Netherlands. (The tribal name may come from an old native word meaning "brave.") As a result, the whole area was called *Frisia* in early medieval times. The name persists today in the form of the Netherlands' northern province of *Friesland* ("land of the Frisians").

There are a group of islands lining the North Sea coast from the Netherlands to Denmark that are lumped together as the *Frisian Islands*. Those islands north of the Netherlands are the *West Frisian Islands*. East of these are islands just north of western Germany, and belonging to Germany, called the *East Frisian Islands*. Those lining the Danish shore are the *North Frisian Islands*.

Nevada

THE FACT that the American Southwest was first Spanish and then Mexican until 1848 shows up on the map very clearly. For instance, the word for "mountain range" in Spanish is "sierra," this being also the word for "saw," since the successive peaks of a mountain range make, at a distance, a jagged, sawlike profile against the sky. The highest mountain range in Spain is in its extreme south. The mountain peaks of that range are snow-covered and so it is termed the *Sierra Nevada* or "snowy mountains."

In 1772, two Spanish explorers, Pedro Fages and Father Juan Crespit, sighted a high mountain range near the Pacific coast of what is now the United States. It, too, was snow-covered and it also received the name *Sierra Nevada*.

After the Mexican War, when the entire area became American, gold strikes populated California with miners and, to a somewhat lesser extent, silver strikes did the same for the region east of California. In 1864, this eastern region was brought into the Union as the 36th state and it chose to be known as *Nevada* from the mountain range, although virtually none of the range is in Nevada. It is in California.

However, Spanish names were the rage at the time and if none existed, some were made up. A mountain state in the north was admitted into the Union in 1889 as the 41st state and it adopted the name *Montana*, which was the Spanish word for "mountains." The Spaniards had never been that far north, but the word was showy.

The *Colorado River* cuts its canyon through garishly colored rocks and is named from the Spanish word for "red" either because of those rocks or of the muddiness of its water at times. The area containing the source of the river entered the Union in 1876 as the 38th state and is known as *Colorado*. The *Grand Canyon* itself ("large gorge" in Spanish) is mostly in *Arizona*, which is a slightly shortened version of "arida zona," meaning "dry belt." Arizona, which is dry indeed, entered the Union in 1912 as the 48th state.

Newark

WE LIKE to think fondly of brave pioneers coming to America in search of a new home where they might find religious freedom and live according to their own consciences. The trouble is that they were not always ready to allow others the same freedom they demanded for themselves so that it was often necessary for groups to split off and search for still newer lands of freedom.

For instance, some colonists in the town of New Haven found it an insufficient haven and decided to try again. In 1666, a group of them under Robert Treat migrated to the new colony of New Jersey and founded a town which they called *Newark*. This may have been named after an English town of that name. Or it may have meant "new ark," a vessel in which their freedom might be saved from the flood after the "new haven" had failed. Or it might even have meant "new work," meaning that they were starting all over again.

About the same time, the neighboring town of *Elizabeth* was founded and there is no ambiguity about its name. It was named in honor of the wife of George Carteret, to whom the colony had been granted by King Charles II.

These towns are both in eastern New Jersey. The capital of the state is in its west and received its name in more straightforward fashion still. In 1714, a Philadelphian named William Trent bought land on the New Jersey side of the Delaware River and laid out a town which became known first as "Trent's town" and then as *Trenton*.

Farther down the Delaware River, directly opposite Philadelphia, in a New Jersey town whose name memorializes the rising tide of ill-feeling toward England. It was founded in 1773 at a time when the question of "taxation without representation" was beginning to rack the colonies. There were English statesmen who were completely on the colonial side in this matter and one of them was the Lord Chancellor, Charles Pratt, Earl of Camden. In his honor, the new town was named *Camden*.

149

New Brunswick

MOST OF the provinces of Canada are huge slices of land compared to the states of the United States (although Alaska can hold its own). However, in Canada's far eastern sections are three small provinces no larger than some of our smaller states.

The most easterly is Nova Scotia ("New Scotland"). Adjoining it to the west is a slightly larger province that was once part of Nova Scotia but, in 1784, was made a separate province. At that time, George III was king of Great Britain, third in the line of the "House of Hanover," who were Electors of Hanover and Dukes of Brunswick (see HANOVER) as well as being British monarchs. With the colonies having revolted and become independent, it seemed a mark of loyalty to name the new Canadian province after the king and so it was named New Brunswick.

(In the days when the American colonies were still safely loyal to the British crown, a similar motive led to the naming of a town in New Jersey. That was in 1724 and it was George I, great-grandfather of George III, who was being honored, so there is now a New Brunswick in New Jersey, too.)

New Brunswick's capital has a name that dates back to the time when France owned Canada. The French explorer Samuel Champlain entered its harbor in 1604 on the day dedicated to John the Baptist. He named it for the Baptist and the town established there is now *Saint John*.

East of New Brunswick is an island that forms a province all by itself though it is scarcely larger than Rhode Island. The French had called it St. John's Isle but, in 1798, the British renamed it in honor of Prince Edward, fourth son of George III, and it became *Prince Edward Island*. (No one knew it at the time, of course, but Edward was fated to be the father of none other than Queen Victoria.) The capital of the province, *Charlottetown*, was named for George III's queen, as Charlotte, North Carolina, had been.

New Caledonia

ONE OF the names given the northern part of Britain by Roman writers was *Caledonia*, a name of obscure origin that may stem from some Celtic word for "forest." Ever since, *Caledonia* has served as a poetic synonym for Scotland.

In 1774, Captain Cook came upon an island about halfway between the Solomons and New Zealand. In its coastline, he fancied he saw a resemblance to that of Scotland and it was therefore the work of an instant for him to name it *New Caledonia* and place the old term on the map once more. It was the French, though, who first settled the island. They annexed it in 1853, but did not change the name except to translate it into the French equivalent, "Nouvelle Calédonie."

Cook had reached the island just after passing through a group of islands to the northeast. Concerning those, the same Scottish fancy must have struck him, for he named them the *New Hebrides* after the islands off the west Scottish shore (see HEBRIDES). Both Great Britain and France share dominion over these islands.

Captain Cook was not the real discoverer of either the New Hebrides or New Caledonia since French and Portuguese navigators had preceded him. Nevertheless, it was Cook's names that stuck. This was not always the case. North of the New Hebrides are a group of islands discovered by the Spanish explorer Alvaro de Mendana de Neyra in 1595. These he named the *Santa Cruz Islands* (meaning "Holy Cross"). Far to the east, he had also discovered, that same year, the *Marquesas Islands* (mahr-kay'zas), meaning "Marquise" and named after the Marquise de Mendoza, wife of the man who was sponsoring his voyage. Captain Cook came across these islands, too, but here the older names stuck.

Usually, sponsors, politicians or, at the very least, leaders of expeditions get their names attached to new islands. One unusual case took place in 1767, when a British navigator, Philip Carteret, came across an island 1500 miles southeast of the Marquesas which he named *Pitcairn Island* after the sailor who actually sighted it first.

New England

WHEN THE European colonists first came west to the New World, they naturally tried to set up a culture that was just like the old one they were used to. They even named the regions they settled after the "old country." For three hundred years, for instance, from 1521 to 1821, the Spanish settlements in Mexico, Central America, the West Indies and the Philippine Islands were lumped under the name of *New Spain.*

In the same way, the French possessions in Canada and the Mississippi Valley during the seventeenth and early eighteenth centuries were known as *New France.* Swedish settlements were made in 1638 in what is now Delaware and were known as *New Sweden.*

The best-known example to Americans is that of the Dutch who settled along the Hudson River in the early seventeenth century and called the area *New Netherlands,* naming the most important town, one at the mouth of the Hudson, *New Amsterdam,* after old Amsterdam, the most important town in old Netherlands.

None of these names survived. The territories of New Sweden were lost to the Dutch in 1655 and added to New Netherlands, all of which were in turn lost to the English in 1664. New France was lost to Great Britain in 1763. Finally, in 1821, the greater portion of New Spain broke away and declared its independence.

With England the big winner of the colonial era, it is natural that there be a section of the New World named for it, too. John Smith, the English pioneer who made the Virginian settlements of 1607 a success, saw to that. In 1614, he went exploring northward along the coast. In the case of one section, he was so struck by the resemblance of the countryside to that of England that he named it *New England* and labeled it so on the map he drew.

That name survives, not as a specific place name but as a familiar name for the six northeastern states of the United States. In one of them, Connecticut, the city of *New Britain* is also to be found.

Newfoundland

ENGLAND MADE an early start in the race to explore the western hemisphere. In 1497, King Henry VII commissioned an Italian navigator,
Giovanni Caboto (who anglicized his name to John Cabot), to sail
westward. Cabot did so and landed on an island which received a very
literal name. It was new-found land and it was named *Newfoundland*. It is pronounced on the first syllable, "nyoo'fund-land," which
obscures the meaning somewhat.

It took almost a century before any English settlement was made
on the island, but in 1583, when one was placed there, Newfoundland
became England's first colony outside the British Isles, and was the
beginning of her Empire.

From 1855 to 1933, Newfoundland was a self-governing dominion
of the British Commonwealth but in 1933 it voluntarily gave up self-
government because of the economic difficulties brought on by the
Great Depression and became a colony again. In 1948, however, it
voted to become a province of Canada (the tenth).

The province of Newfoundland is more than just the island. A
large section of the mainland coast to the northwest is also a part of
it. The mainland area bears a Portuguese name, however, which is
unusual for that part of the hemisphere. It seems that, in 1500, a
Portuguese navigator, Gaspar Cortereal, sailed along that coast and
picked up a group of Eskimos whom he took back for slaves. He
called the coast Terra del Laboratore ("Land of Slaves") and this
became *Labrador*.

Labrador and the province of Quebec to its west make up a huge
peninsula that is frigid because of the Arctic waters of the Labrador
Current that bathes it, although it is in the same latitude as Great
Britain (which, for its part, has the warm Gulf Stream). On the west
of the peninsula is Hudson Bay, with a final indentation at its south
called *James Bay*. This is not named for any King James but for the
explorer Thomas James, who first sailed into its waters in 1631.

New Hampshire

In 1622, territory in New England was granted by King James I of England to Ferdinando Gorges and John Mason. Mason, who had earlier been the governor of Newfoundland, had been born in the county of Hampshire in south-central England. He named the new colony in honor of his birthplace and it is *New Hampshire* now.

Hampshire is on the channel coast and its chief coastal city is *Portsmouth* (a port at the mouth of a river, obviously). In this, New Hampshire keeps it company, for in 1653, a settlement was founded on the very short stretch of seacoast to which that colony fell heir and that, too, was named *Portsmouth*. The capital of New Hampshire bears the typical Puritan name of *Concord*, for the Puritans named towns for the virtues and the pleasant gifts of God almost as the Catholics named them for saints.

In southwestern New Hampshire is *Mount Monadnock*, a solitary knob of rock which dominates the flat countryside, as the name itself indicates, for it comes from an Indian word meaning "prominent mountain." Nowadays any mountain anywhere on the planet that stands by itself and is not part of a range is called a monadnock.

The western boundary of New Hampshire runs along the *Connecticut River*, which is another Indian-derived name from a word meaning "beside the long, tidal river." The Connecticut River flows through Massachusetts and continues south to the Atlantic. Its lowermost regions pass through *Connecticut*, named for the river.

In 1636, a city in the Connecticut interior was founded and named *Hartford* because the home town of one of the leading settlers was Hertford, England. (The spelling is different for some reason.) Hartford has been capital of Connecticut since 1662.

Connecticut and New Hampshire are both among the original thirteen states. Connecticut was the fifth state to ratify the Constitution while New Hampshire was the ninth.

New Jersey

IN 1066, William II, Duke of Normandy, set sail for England, defeated and killed the English king, Harold, and became William I, King of England. His descendants ruled both England and Normandy, plus other sections of France from time to time. Gradually, over the centuries, however, the English-ruled portions of France were taken by the French armies. Finally in 1558, the English lost their last foothold in continental France.

Of the Norman inheritance, however, they retained one last remnant, a few islands off the coast of France. Because they are in the English Channel, they are called the *Channel Islands*.

The largest of these islands was called, in Roman times, "Caesaria insula" ("Caesar's island"). During the Middle Ages, when the Latin language was garbled by barbarians, "Caesaria" became tongue-twisted to *Jersey*.

A successful British naval officer of the seventeenth century, George Carteret, was born on the island of Jersey. During the English Civil War, Carteret was a Royalist fighting for the king. When Charles I was beheaded in 1649, Carteret held out in Jersey for two years before he was forced to retreat to France.

The son of Charles I visited Jersey before the surrender and, in gratitude, granted Carteret land in America. In 1660, this son regained the throne as Charles II and when, in 1664, the Dutch possessions in America were captured, part were given to Carteret in fulfillment of the promise.

Carteret named his territories after the island of his birth which he had so well defended and it is still known as *New Jersey*, though before 1702 it existed in two sections, *West Jersey* and *East Jersey*.

New Jersey was one of the thirteen original states of the United States and was the third to ratify the Constitution.

New Orleans

IN THE third century, the Roman Empire seemed on the point of disintegration as a result of barbarian invasions and civil wars. In 270, however, Lucius Domitian Aurelianus became Roman Emperor and, in an energetic reign of five years, defeated the barbarians, reconquered sections of the Empire which had broken away, and left it all whole and ready for two more centuries of existence. In his honor, a city in Gaul was renamed Aurelianum. With time, this was distorted to *Orléans* (awr-lay-ahn').

In the late Middle Ages, the French kings took to conferring the title "Duke of Orléans" on their brothers or other close relatives. When Louis XIV died in 1715, his nephew, Philippe, who was Duke of Orléans at the time, became regent for Louis XV, the old king's five-year-old great grandson.

In 1718, a French explorer, Jean Baptiste Lemoyne, founded a city in the lower reaches of the Mississippi, in what was then the extreme south of the vast French territory of Louisiana. He named it in honor of the regent as "La Nouvelle Orléans." In 1763, the French, defeated by the British, turned the western section of Louisiana, including the southern city, over to the Spaniards. In 1803, however, all of Louisiana became American and the city's name was translated into the English *New Orleans*. It is pronounced English-fashion also, the natives saying "awr'lee-inz" and others saying "awr-leenz'."

Other cities of the area retained their original French names untranslated. For instance, farther up the Mississippi was a settlement founded in 1719. The site had first been noted by French explorers in 1699 and had been named Baton Rouge ("red stick") because of a red stick or marker placed in the ground there by the Indians to mark a boundary line. The settlement took the name of the site. It is now the capital of the state of Louisiana and is still *Baton Rouge*. It is pronounced in mixed English-French fashion as "bat'n-roozh'."

New York

WHEN BRITAIN was a Roman province, its most important town was Eboracum in the north. Its name has been traced to a Celtic word for "yew tree," for which the site may have been noted in early days. After the departure of the Romans and the coming of the Anglo-Saxons, the name was twisted first to "Eoforwic" and then to *York*.

York is only a rather small town now but there are still signs of its ancient greatness. For instance, the king's brother or his second son is often given the title of "Duke of York."

The Scottish kings also had a title they reserved for important relatives and that was "Duke of Albany," for Albany (or "Albania" in Latin) was a name given to the Scottish Highlands (see ALBANIA). After 1603, when the Scottish kings came to rule England also, the titles were combined. For instance, Charles II, who ruled from 1660 to 1685, made his brother James Duke of York and Albany.

During the mid-seventeenth century, Great Britain and the Netherlands had been fighting naval wars. In 1664, Great Britain was victorious, making a notable conquest of the Dutch colony of New Netherland. Charles II had granted the land to his brother and the colony was therefore named *New York* in honor of his dukedom, while the city of New Amsterdam became *New York City*.

A Dutch town about 150 miles up the Hudson was called Fort Orange in honor of the Dutch royal house of Orange. This, too, was captured, and named in honor of James's other dukedom, becoming *Albany*. It is now the capital of New York State, which was one of the original thirteen states of the Union and the eleventh state to ratify the Constitution.

In 1685, Charles II died and his brother succeeded as James II. James was a poor king, ruling for only three years before being exiled by his rebellious subjects. So it happens that the largest and wealthiest city and state of the United States are named for one of England's least successful kings.

Nigeria

IF EUROPEANS were impressed with the swarthiness of the peoples of North Africa (see MAURITANIA), they were impressed even more by the dark skins of the population south of the Sahara. The Berbers of North Africa sent out trading caravans across the desert and came back, apparently, with tales of a large river to the south along whose banks lived people with very dark skins. The Berber word for "river" is "n'eghirren" and because of that, the Romans may have termed the river "Nigris." However, the Roman word for "black" is "niger" and it is quite reasonable to suppose it was the skin color of the natives that did most to form the word. The modern name of the river that drains the region south of the Sahara and enters the Gulf of Guinea is the *Niger River*.

The British began to take over the section of the coast about the Niger in 1879 and gradually expanded their holdings inland through the following decades. The region was first the *Niger Coast Protectorate*, and, eventually, *Nigeria*. In 1960, Nigeria gained its independence and joined the company of sovereign nations.

North of Nigeria is a section of territory called *Niger*, which was part of the French holdings in the west Sahara region, these holdings being lumped together under the self-descriptive name of *French West Africa*. In 1960, it, too, obtained its independence. Its name, pronounced French-fashion, is "nee-zhair'," but English-speaking people are almost certain to refer to it exclusively as "ni'jer."

West of the Niger is the *Volta River*. It was discovered in the fifteenth century by the Portuguese, who gave it the name from a Portuguese word meaning "turn," because of its turning, winding course. Another section of French West Africa lying along the upper reaches of the Volta River obtained its independence in 1960 and adopted the name (straightforwardly enough) of *Upper Volta*. In French, this is "Haute-Volta."

Norfolk

WHEN THE Angles, Saxons, and Jutes invaded Britain after the departure of Roman troops, the Angles set up a kingdom in the southeast which was called *East Anglia*. In the end, it gave its name to all of England (see ENGLAND) but it was not really successful as a kingdom. It was absorbed by Mercia, another Anglian kingdom, in the seventh century, and its name disappeared from the map. Where the kingdom was, however, there now stand two English counties, *Norfolk* (the "northern people" of the kingdom) and *Suffolk* (the "southern people"). The capital of Norfolk is the town of *Norwich*, which is pronounced "nor'ij" by the British and which means "northern district."

The settlers of Massachusetts likewise inserted a Norfolk and a Suffolk among the counties of the colony, but after several changes, the end result was that Suffolk found itself north of Norfolk. The county of Suffolk encompasses the city of Boston and a couple of northern suburbs, while the much larger Norfolk takes in the southern suburbs down to the Rhode Island border.

In New York State, there is a Suffolk County comprising the eastern two thirds of Long Island, but no Norfolk County. Virginia makes up for that by having a Norfolk County but no Suffolk. In fact, a city in Virginia's Norfolk County, likewise named *Norfolk,* is the second largest in the state.

South of East Anglia was the one kingdom of Anglo-Saxon times that was set up by the Jutes. It was named *Kent,* from "Cantii," the name of the British tribe dwelling in the region at the time of the coming of the Romans. The region, England's easternmost county, is still called by that name.

The capital city of Kent was named Cantwaraburh, or "town of the men of Kent." This was eventually twisted to *Canterbury.* It was here that Christianity first reached post-Roman England in 597 and the chief priest of the Church of England is still the Archbishop of Canterbury.

Norway

THE NORTHERNMOST peninsula of Europe extends southward nearly to the German coast. This southernmost portion was the first portion known to the people of the south and west. Its native name is "Skane," of uncertain origin. This was Latinized to *Scania* (skay'-nee-uh). It is common for the first-explored or first-encountered region of any land to give its name to the entire territory, so the whole peninsula became known as *Scandinavia*.

In the early Middle Ages, overpopulation on this northern, cold and mountainous region forced roving bands into piracy, emigration, and conquest. The people of Scandinavia called themselves Vikings (meaning "men of the bays," since the Atlantic coast of Scandinavia is riddled with bays) but to the people suffering their raids they were simply men of the north. They were therefore called Northmen, Norsemen, or Normans. This notion leaves its mark on the map, for the western portion of the peninsula now forms the nation of *Norway* (or "Norge" in the native tongue).

The eastern half of Scandinavia forms the nation of *Sweden* ("Sverige" in the native language). This name is derived from a tribe known as the "Sveare," who lived in the southern part of the country and who were known to the Roman geographers as the "Suinones." East of Sweden, across the Baltic Sea, live a group of people called "Finns," a name of obscure origin dating back to ancient times. We call the nation *Finland* ("land of the Finns" obviously), but the Finnish name of the country is "Suomi."

Beginning in 1787, the Northmen raided Scotland, England, France, and Germany, killing and looting. In 911, the French King, Charles III, unworthy great-great-grandson of Charlemagne, bribed the Northmen with a section of northern France to stop their raids, giving them some to save the rest. That section, in which the "Normans" settled has been known as *Normandy* ever since.

Nova Scotia

THERE IS a peninsula in southeastern Canada, to the east of Maine, which was first settled by the French in 1605. It was called Acadie by them, a word usually presented as *Acadia* in English. This is from a local Indian word meaning "plenty," so that it was a good-luck name intended to bring prosperity.

Oddly, there is a district in Greece called *Arcadia* (which, according to the ancient Greeks, was named for an ancestral dweller in the region, who was named Arcas). Arcadia remained a countrified, backward section to which the more citified Greek areas looked back as a home of unspoiled happiness, a kind of country Utopia.

However, the French Acadia proved to be no Arcadia nor did good luck come to it. It was constantly under dispute between the French and the English (who owned the near-by island of Newfoundland and had settled the American coast to the south).

In 1713, after the War of the Spanish Succession (called Queen Anne's War in the colonies) Acadia was ceded to victorious Great Britain. The Acadian population would not take an oath of allegiance to Great Britain, however, and in 1775, they were deported and scattered through the British colonies. Some settled in Louisiana and a section of the coast of that state, west of the Mississippi River, is still called the *Acadian Coast* as a result.

Both before and after the deportation of the Acadians, new settlers swarmed in from New England and from Great Britain. Since the land was to the north of New England it seemed logical to name it New Scotland after the land that was to the north of old England. This was done, in Latinized fashion, by use of the name *Nova Scotia*.

The capital of Nova Scotia is *Halifax*. It was founded in 1749 and was named for George Montague Dunk, Second Earl of Halifax, who was president of the Board of Trade at the time and who had been active in promoting the settlement of the town.

Novgorod

WHEN NEW towns are being founded, there is always a great temptation to name them "New Town" (see NAPLES). For instance, in 1630, when Boston was founded, another city was settled across the *Charles River* (which was named for the then-reigning king of England, Charles I). This new settlement was named *New Towne*.

In 1636, the first institution of higher learning was established in the English colonies with the help of a bequest from a young clergyman named John Harvard. This institution (which became Harvard University, of course) was established in New Towne, which promptly renamed itself *Cambridge* after the English university town where John Harvard had studied.

New Towne was not entirely lost, for its original area was huge and other towns were split off. One of them, now a western suburb of Boston is *Newton*, which is "New Towne" said rapidly.

English is not the only language in which this takes place. There are a few places called "Nieuville" and "Neustadt," which are "New Town" in French and German respectively. For instance, a southern suburb of Vienna is *Wiener Neustadt* (vee'ner-noi'shtaht), the "new town of Vienna."

The Russians do the same. When Swedish tribes first penetrated Russia in the ninth century they founded (or took over) a city in Russia's northwest which was called *Novgorod*. This is Russian for "New Town." During the next 500 years, Novgorod grew rich and powerful on the fur trade and controlled the whole northern half of European Russia. For a while it rivaled Muscovy, but in the fifteenth century, Muscovy, under Ivan III, defeated and annexed Novgorod and the Russian kingdom was born.

There are other Novgorods in Russia, particularly one which is about 500 miles to the east of the first one. This other Novgorod was founded in 1221 and is distinguished from the first by being called *Nizhnii Novgorod* ("lower Novgorod"). In 1932, it was renamed *Gorki* after the Russian writer, Maxim Gorki, who had been born there in 1868.

Oceania

THE REMARKABLE thing about the Pacific Ocean is its emptiness. It is a waste of waters covering an area about twenty times the size of the United States. What land it possesses is in the form of numerous islands, most of them quite small. The Caroline Islands, for instance (see MARIANA ISLANDS), are made up of nearly a thousand separate pieces of land, spread out over a width of fifteen hundred miles, yet the entire land area put together is no larger than Greater New York. It is no wonder that this world of islands is referred to as *Oceania*.

On the eastern edge of this region are a group of islands which were first visited by the Englishman Samuel Wallis, in 1767, and by the Frenchman Louis Antoine de Bougainville, in 1768. In 1769, the famous Captain Cook brought to those same islands a party of scientists from London's Royal Society. In honor of that organization, the island group is now known as the *Society Islands*.

The earlier explorers are not forgotten, however, for they encountered other bits of land in their voyagings. Fifteen hundred miles west of the Society Islands are a small group called the *Wallis Islands*, while fifteen hundred miles farther west still is *Bougainville Island*, which English-fashion, is pronounced "boo'gan-vil."

The Society Islands, Wallis Islands, and some others were eventually occupied by France and make up what is now known as *French Oceania*.

Oceania is divided into three parts. The Caroline Islands plus other groups of that area make up *Micronesia*, from Greek words meaning "small islands," which is an excellent description. The islands closer to Australia and New Guinea are inhabited by people with Negroid coloring and these (including Bougainville) are included in *Melanesia* ("black islands"). Finally, a wide scattering of islands from French Oceania north are lumped together as *Polynesia* ("many islands"). All Oceania is sometimes lumped with the islands of the Indian Ocean, west to Madagascar, as *Austronesia* ("southern islands").

163

Ohio

IN WESTERN Pennsylvania, the *Allegheny River* (al'uh-gay'nee) flows southward. Its name comes from Indian words meaning "fine river" and that name is also applied to the *Allegheny Mountains* of that area. Flowing north to meet the Allegheny is the Monongahela River (mon-non-guh-hee'luh), another Indian name, but one of uncertain meaning.

The two rivers join and a combined stream, larger than either of its tributaries, flows westward. This combined stream was called the Great River by the Indians and their word for this was written "Ohio" by the French so that we now speak of the *Ohio River*.

After the Revolutionary war, the entire territory north of the Ohio River was known as the *Northwest Territory*. Various eastern states claimed all or part of it because their original charters from the British kings had given them title to land indefinitely westward, to the Pacific Ocean in some cases. Even little Connecticut had claims to a strip of land across the territory.

This threatened to make trouble for the new nation, but under pressure from those states that did not have claims to the area, the Northwest Territory was ceded to the central government in 1786. Connecticut didn't quite abandon all her claims, however, reserving a section south of Lake Erie and west of Pennsylvania and calling it the *Western Reserve*.

In 1796, Connecticut sent out a surveyor named Moses Cleaveland to survey the land and establish a "New Connecticut." As a result of his surveying, a capital city of the area was laid out on the shores of Lake Erie and was named for him. The *a* in his name dropped out, because the whole name was one letter too long for a newspaper masthead, so that the city became *Cleveland*.

But Connecticut's plan came to naught. The entire territory was carved into five new states with no additions to the old ones. The southwestern portion, including Cleveland, became the state of Ohio, which entered the union in 1803 as the 17th state.

Oklahoma

WHEN THE English colonized what is now the Atlantic seaboard of the United States, they did not find an empty land. It was already occupied by Indians. However, most settlers did not really consider they had to worry about the rights of "savages."

Many settlers, therefore, simply took the land they wanted, or went through the formality of buying it for a few trinkets after getting the Indians drunk. The Indians, in turn, fought and killed the settlers whenever they could. Little by little, however, the settlers pushed the Indians westward.

As the nineteenth century progressed, it came to be felt that it was wrong to kill Indians for no reason other than to take their land, that some land ought to be reserved for the Indians and, in 1834, the *Indian Territory* was established.

At first this covered a large section of prairie, but as the population of the United States continued to rise and as new land was desired, more and more of the Indian Territory was opened to settlement and the area reserved for Indians shrank continually. Indian tribes were made to move, either by agreement or by force, and by the 1890's, the Indian Territory had shrunk to an area lying between Texas and Kansas.

Finally, even this was opened to white settlement in the last "land rush" of the West, as hordes of settlers dashed in at the deadline to stake their claims. In 1907, the territory entered the Union as the 46th state. It took the name of *Oklahoma* from the Indian words "okla" ("people") and "humma" ("red") so that Oklahoma means "red people." Thus, the name still stands for the dispossessed Indians. The capital city is *Oklahoma City*.

The city of *Tulsa* in the northwestern portion of the state also recalls the sad Indian history. Its name comes from an Indian word meaning "town" and it was established in 1828, not by white men, but by Creek Indians who had been moved into the Indian territory from their old homes.

Omsk

THE GERMANS drove eastward across the Elbe in the tenth century, pushing the Slavs ahead of them. Those Slavs called themselves Poliane, meaning "dwellers of the field" and the land they lived in they called Polska. We call the people Poles and their nation, *Poland*.

Poland brought the German advance to a halt eventually and in its turn advanced eastward. After Russia had been laid in ruins by the Mongol invasion of the thirteenth century, Poland took over the western portions of that nation, including much of the Ukraine. In 1609, at the height of their power, the Poles even occupied Moscow for a short while.

It was the Polish influence that probably spread the suffix "-sk" into Russia in the naming of towns and the Russians carried it into Siberia. In Siberia, for instance, a city founded at the point where the Om River flows into the Irtish was naturally called *Omsk*, while another city 500 miles east, located where the Tom River flows into the Ob, is called *Tomsk*.

But Russians name for people as well as for rivers. In 1896, a town was founded 400 miles east of Omsk, and was named *Novonikolaevsk* (no-vo-ni-ko-lah'yevsk) after the new young Czar, Nicholas II. It was "new-Nicholas-town." After the Russian Revolution in which the Czar was executed, the name was changed to *Novosibirsk* (no-vo-si-birsk') or "new-Siberia-town."

Again about 400 miles west of Omsk, Peter the Great founded a city in 1721 and named it for his wife Catherine ("Ekaterina" in Russian). It was *Ekaterinburg* (ye-kat'er-in-burg'). After the Revolution, it was renamed *Sverdlovsk* (sverd-lufsk') after one of the Revolutionary leaders. In the same way, a city at the bend of the Dnieper River in European Russia lost its name. It was founded in 1786 and named *Ekaterinoslav* (ye-kat'er-in-o-slahv') after the reigning queen, Catherine II. After the Revolution, the Czarina's name was dropped for the river and the town became *Dniepropetrovsk* (nep'ro-pe-trufsk').

Ontario

Two of the five Great Lakes, *Lake Huron* and *Lake Erie*, are named after the Indian tribes that originally lived along their shores. The names are not the actual Indian words, however. "Erie" is a French mispronunciation of the actual name of the tribe which meant "wildcat," while "Huron" is a French word altogether, meaning any person with a bristly unkempt head of hair. The French applied that name to Indians living near Lake Huron but the Indians called themselves Wyandot. There is a city named *Wyandotte* on the waterway that connects Lake Huron and Erie, so the true name of the tribe does not go completely unnoticed.

"Huron" and "Erie" are names that are applied to counties and cities on their shores, the most important being the town of *Erie* in Pennsylvania, but two other Great Lakes have given their names to larger areas. The smallest and easternmost of the Great Lakes is *Lake Ontario* from an Indian word meaning "beautiful." When Canada became a dominion, the region north of that lake adopted its name and became the *Province of Ontario*. Thus the name now graces a stretch of land half again as large as Texas.

Between Lakes Huron and Superior, extending southward, is the one Great Lake that lies entirely within the borders of the United States. It is *Lake Michigan*, from Indian words meaning "great water." Along its eastern and northern shores is *Michigan*, which was admitted to the Union in 1837 as the 26th state.

The French called Lake Ontario "Lac Frontenac" after Louis de Buade de Frontenac, who governed French Canada very energetically for much of the time between 1672 and 1698. This name didn't last but another did. The French named the westernmost and largest of the Great Lakes *Lake Superior* ("Lac Supérieur"), because in addition to being the westernmost, it was the northernmost. "Superior" means "above" and north is always above on maps. The name was kept by the English-speaking Americans, who supposed it to mean that Lake Superior was superior to the rest of the Great Lakes in size — which it is.

Orkney Islands

NORTH OF Scotland are various groups of islands that might almost be thought of as a kind of British Arctic region. Immediately off Scotland's northern coast are the *Orkney Islands*. To the Romans, who had just barely heard of these far-off bits of land, they were the "Orcades," but the name is thought to have originated not with them, but from the Norwegian "orkn," meaning "seal," and "ey," meaning "island." They were the "seal islands."

Although the climate is rigorous, the largest island is named *Pomona*, which means "fruit tree" in Latin, a good promotional name.

The Orkney Islands were Danish until 1468, when they were ceded to Scotland along with a group of islands still farther north, the *Shetland Islands*. The largest island of this group is *Zetland*, which may be an older form of the name, both being derived from the old Norse name for the islands, "Hjaltland," meaning, perhaps, "high land."

Still farther north, about 200 miles northwest of the Shetland Islands are a group of islands first discovered by the Vikings in the ninth century and in the possession of Denmark ever since 1380. (These she did not give up to Scotland.) These are the *Faeroe Islands* (fair-oh'), which in the old Norse means "Sheep Islands."

The chief town of the Faeroe Islands bears a name which is one of the few reminders of the old pagan days of Scandinavia, for it is *Thorshavn* ("Thor's harbor"), after the old Norse god of thunder and storm. (There is also a *Thorshöfn*, another form of the word, in northeastern Iceland.)

The largest Danish possession in these seas is Greenland (see GREENLAND) which bears the mark of modern rather than ancient Scandinavia. The southeastern shores of that island form *Frederick VI Coast*, while north of that is *King Christian IX Land*. In the far northeast is *King Frederick VIII Land*. These are all, as you might guess, Danish kings. Frederick VI ruled from 1808 to 1839, Christian IX from 1863 to 1906, and Frederick VIII from 1906 to 1912.

Ottoman Empire

BEGINNING IN the ninth century, Turkish (the name means "strong") peoples began drifting southward out of their Central Asia homeland into the Arabic world. They turned Moslem and were used by the Arab caliphs as bodyguards and as a kind of private army. This always has its dangers, however, for such an army tends to control the monarch, assassinating him when necessary. It was the uncontrollable Turkish bodyguard that helped break up the great Abbasid Empire of which Haroun-al-Raschid (of Arabian Nights fame) was the best-known monarch.

Eventually, the Turks formed the spearhead of the Moslem attack against the Byzantine Empire. A tribe of Turks whose leaders claimed descent from an ancestor named Saljuq (the "Seljuk Turks") defeated a Byzantine army in 1071 and quickly took over most of Asia Minor. But the Byzantine Empire, with the help of Crusaders from the west, clung tenaciously to life and the Seljuk Turks declined.

Another line of leaders, who claimed descent from someone named Othman (the "Ottoman Turks"), took over about 1350 and launched an attack into Europe. Constantinople itself fell in 1453 and the Byzantine Empire came to an end. The Turks went on to conquer large regions in Europe, in North Africa, and in the Middle East, but they reached their own peak between 1550 and 1650 and thereafter the tide started to recede. Little by little they gave up their conquests until, by 1920, they were back to their Asia Minor center.

The land they dominated was called *Turkey*, or, after the tribal name, the *Ottoman Empire*. At the height of the Empire, there was *Turkey in Europe* and *Turkey in Asia*, both large, but now Turkey in Europe is a small area about Constantinople and Turkey in Asia consists only of Asia Minor.

Nor can Turkey be spoken of any longer as the Ottoman Empire, for in 1923, the last Ottoman sultan, Abdul Mejid II, was dethroned and a republic established.

Pacific Ocean

AFTER THE Americas were discovered, it gradually dawned on Europeans that the wealth of India and the Far East was 10,000 miles farther westward. There began a search for some way to get past the Americas, which seemed to bar the way solidly north and south for many thousands of miles. Exploration inland in many parts of the New World showed no signs of any end to the land.

Then, in 1513, a Spanish explorer named Vasco Nuñez de Balboa moved inland into the land we now call Panama and suddenly came upon a huge body of salt water extending to the horizon. It was a new ocean. If you will look at the map, you will see that Panama is the narrow connecting link between North and South America and that it runs east and west. The Atlantic Ocean is to its north and the new body of water is to the south. Balboa therefore called it El Mar del Sur or, as we would say in English, the *South Sea*.

Six years later, Spanish ships, under the Portuguese navigator Ferdinand Magellan, were butting their way down the South American coast, looking for an all-water route from the Atlantic into the South Sea. They found none until they came nearly to the southern tip of South America, a region they named *Patagonia* ("big feet" in Spanish, because the Indian natives seemed to have them). There they finally reached a narrow water passage between the continent and another land (which later proved to be an island) that they called *Tierra del Fuego* (tee-er′uh-del-foo-ay′go), meaning "land of fire" because of campfires spied upon it. The passageway is still called the *Strait of Magellan*.

For five weeks, Magellan's men passed through the stormy strait and when they finally reached the South Sea, good weather dawned upon them at last. The grateful Magellan called the sea the *Pacific Ocean* ("peaceful ocean"). The Pacific Ocean it has remained ever since, though actually it is as stormy as the other oceans. Nevertheless, the older name is recalled whenever we speak of the islands of the Pacific as the *South Sea Islands*.

Pakistan

IN THE languages of southwestern Asia, the suffix "-stan" means "land of." Thus *Afghanistan* is "land of the Afghans" and *Baluchistan*, to its south, is "land of the Baluchis." Sometimes India is called *Hindustan* or "land of the Hindus."

After 1900, there was an increasing desire among the Indians for independence from Great Britain but one serious obstacle lay in the fact that Indians themselves were not united.

About A.D. 1000 Mohammedan invaders had entered from the northwest so that for a while India had been under Mohammedan rule and a large number of the population had become Moslem. The Moslems and Hindus were so far apart in religion and culture that it seemed impossible to get them to remain peaceably in a single government. The Moslems, who were in a minority, clamored for a separate state.

Now a Moslem poet had earlier drawn wonderful pictures of an ideal Moslem nation which he called Pakistan ("land of the pure"). It struck the Moslems that this was an excellent name because its letters stood for some of the Indian provinces that were most heavily Moslem. The *P* was for *Punjab* (from a native word meaning "five rivers," because the Indus and several tributaries passed through it). The *a* was for Afghanistan, because the *Northwest Frontier Province* (a self-explanatory name) bordered on it. The *k* was *Kashmir* (meaning "happy valley") and the *s* for *Sindh* (meaning "river"). The "-stan" suffix stood for Baluchistan.

In 1947, Great Britain granted independence to India, and the Moslems set up their own state of *Pakistan*. Most of the provinces mentioned above formed *West Pakistan*, but another heavily Moslem region in India's northeast (see BENGAL) was also included as *East Pakistan*. The two portions of the nation are separated by 1000 miles of India. Furthermore, Kashmir, although predominantly Moslem had a Hindu prince and India has managed to retain control of it, so the *k* of "Pakistan" is missing.

Palatinate

As WE all know, Rome was built on seven hills. The very first settlement was built on the "Mons Palatinus" or Palatine Hill. This name may be derived from the Latin word for "stake," for it may have originally been a stockaded fortress. Later on, Augustus, Rome's first emperor, had his official residence there. It was the "palatium" because of its location and ever since the residence of royalty has been known as a "palace."

During the Middle Ages, noblemen who served and functioned about the royal palace were "palatini," from which comes our word "paladin" for the heroic knights in attendance on Charlemagne. Such an official who also had lands of his own in which he could exercise dominion was a "count palatine."

The best-known of the count palatines were those who, beginning in the twelfth century, ruled over a section of the Rhine area that became known as the *Palatinate* (or, in German, "Pfalz"). In 1214, it came under the control of the Dukes of Bavaria who eventually formed two such states under two branches of the ducal line. The original palatinate was referred to as *Lower Palatinate*, because it was located along the lower courses of the Rhine River, or *Rhenish Palatinate*. A section of Bavaria near the source of the Rhine was *Upper Palatinate*.

The Rhenish Palatinate is one of the provinces of modern West Germany and its capital is at the site where the Moselle River flows into the Rhine. The Romans built a city there named Confluentes, meaning "flowing together" and that city is now known by the somewhat distorted version of that name, *Coblenz* (koh′blents).

About eighty miles southeast of Coblenz is a city with the nasty (in English) name of *Worms*, for which the German pronunciation is "vawrms." This arose in the usual mangling of Latin that followed the barbarian invasions. The Roman name for the town was "Borbetomagus." By changing the initial *B* to *W* (and the change from a *b* sound to a *v* sound is very common in all languages) and by leaving out half the remaining letters, it became first "Wormatia" and finally "Worms."

172

Paris

IN NORTHERN Gaul during Roman times and before, there was a tribe known to the Romans as the Parisii. They inhabited a section of the *Seine River* (a name which is a distortion of the Roman "Sequana"). On an island of the river they had a city named Lutetia. The Romans called it Lutetia Parisiorum ("Lutetia of the Parisians"). During the barbarian invasions of the third century it was destroyed, but when stability was restored (for Rome held off the barbarians for two more centuries), it was rebuilt and its name shifted from the first half to the second, becoming "Parisii" and, finally, *Paris*. This is pronounced "par'is" in English, but "pah-ree' " in French.

During the raids of the Northmen in the ninth century, the Parisian fortress on the island in the Seine held out in a long seige. That was the beginning of its importance as the key defense point of the French territories. The rulers of the city became the kings of France in 987 and Paris has been the capital of France ever since.

The oldest Roman settlement in Gaul, however, was in the south-west. As early as 59 B.C., just before Julius Caesar had begun his drive to conquer Gaul, some Greek refugees from the Mediterranean coast got permission from the Gallic tribes on the *Rhone River* (a distortion of the Greek "Rhodanus," meaning the "red" river) to establish a town which was given a Celtic name, "Lugdunum," meaning "hill of Lug," Lug being a local god. After the Romans had conquered the land, Roman settlers joined the Greeks and in the time of the Roman Empire, Lugdunum was the finest and largest city in Gaul.

It is still the third largest city in France but its name has been twisted more than most, for little is left but the initial. It has become "Lyon" in French, though in English an *s* is usually added, for some reason, making it *Lyons*. The French pronunciation is "lee-ohng' " but English-speaking people find the nasal *n* hard to handle and sometimes can't resist calling it "ly'unz."

173

Peking

MOST OF the successful invasions of China were from the north, so that there were periods during which southern China held out as a remnant of native-ruled country. As a result there developed two capitals. There was a northern one which often served as capital for the invading tribesmen, and a southern one that served for native Chinese. When the native elements were strong enough to control the north firmly, they often chose the northern capital because of its prestige and as a sign of strength.

Thus, the Mongol emperors, after conquering northern China, used the northern capital, while the Sung Dynasty, which was native, used the southern. When the Mongols captured southern China as well, the northern capital served for all of China, and for most of the rest of Asia as well.

In 1368, the Ming Dynasty, the last native dynasty of China, drove out the Mongols and established their capital in the south, giving it its modern name of *Nanking*, which means, straightforwardly enough, "southern capital." By 1421, the Ming Dynasty felt strong enough to move its capital to the old Mongol capital, which they now named *Peking* ("northern capital").

In 1644, the Manchus began their conquest of China and they established their capital as Peking, maintaining it there until the revolution of 1912 established China as a republic. Peking remained the capital till 1928, however. It was then that Chiang Kai-shek, marching from the south, united the nation under his leadership. Since Japan was strong in the north, Chiang re-established the capital at Nanking, and Peking was renamed *Peiping* ("northern peace") as a sign that its days as a capital were over.

But after World War II, the Communist armies, marching from the north, completely defeated Chiang. In 1949, they were in control. Peiping was renamed Peking and it is now the capital of the People's Republic of China.

Pennsylvania

In 1681, William Penn, a Quaker and idealist, decided to establish a haven of liberty in America. King Charles II was beholden to Penn's father (also a William Penn), who, when the king was in exile, had negotiated to restore him to the throne. Charles therefore gave the younger Penn a grant to American land.

Penn announced his intention of calling the colony Sylvania (the Latin word for "wooded land") instead of naming it for some member of the royal family as was then the custom. This was because, as a Quaker, Penn would not give that kind of honor to any man. King Charles, however, had a wry sense of humor and he changed the name to *Pennsylvania* ("Penn's wooded land") because he knew that Penn would, as a matter of principle, honor himself least of all. Penn objected very strenuously, but the king insisted and nothing could be done.

Penn's sons, Thomas and Richard Penn, were less humble. In 1748, they founded a town in southeastern Pennsylvania, which they named *Reading* (red'ing), after the English town in which the family estates were located.

Another colony took its name, indirectly, from the governor not of itself, but of a neighboring area. The first permanent English settlements in United States territory, established in 1607 in what is now Virginia, were going badly. After three years, those who survived decided to give up and try to sail home, when suddenly — literally in the nick of time — ships carrying new immigrants and plenty of supplies showed up under the leadership of Thomas West, Lord de la Warr, who then became first governor of Virginia.

When an English explorer, Samuel Argall, located a bay north of Virginia, he named it *Delaware Bay* in honor of the governor. Later, a British colony established there was named *Delaware*.

Both Delaware and Pennsylvania were among the thirteen original states, Delaware being the first to ratify the Constitution and Pennsylvania the second.

175

Persia

IN ANCIENT TIMES, there lived a group of people in southwest Asia who spoke a language related to those spoken in Europe today. We call such languages Aryan because one of the earliest of them was spoken by a tribe who called themselves Aryas and who invaded India from the northwest about 1500 B.C. (We also call the language family Indo-European as a result.) The people who remained west of India called themselves by a similar name, and in modern times, they have called their own land Iran (see MESOPOTAMIA), a name made official in 1935. You can see the relationship between "Iran" and "Aryan."

The territory west of India was called Persis by the Greeks (and the present name for that section is *Fars*). From "Persis," the Greeks came to call the large empire conquered by its inhabitants *Persia*, and the body of water bathing the coast of Persis became the *Persian Gulf*.

For two hundred years, from 550 B.C. to 331 B.C., the Persians ruled all the ancient world from India to Egypt. They conducted wars against the Greek cities of Europe, however, which ended disastrously, and in 331 B.C., the Greeks under the leadership of Alexander the Great counterattacked. They defeated the Persian armies, invaded almost every corner of the land, and destroyed the capital city, which the Greeks called *Persepolis* ("city of the Persians").

Persia revived to fight the Romans, was conquered by the Arabs and revived once more, Moslem this time. Modern Persia (now Iran) was established in 1502, and in 1788, the small town of *Tehran* (te-rahn') became its capital. The name is supposed to mean "the plains."

The second largest city in modern Iran was once called Tauris in ancient times, perhaps from the same tribe of "Tauri" which gave the name to the Crimean peninsula (see KHERSON) or perhaps from another tribe of similar name. The name has now been distorted to *Tabriz* (tuh-breez').

Philadelphia

AFTER THE time of Alexander the Great, there were lines of Macedonian monarchs over Egypt and Asia who kept largely to one or two names. For instance, all the Egyptian kings of the period were called Ptolemy, while the kings of western Asia were called, for the most part, Seleucus or Antiochus.

In order to distinguish one monarch from another, the kings would adopt a second name, which was usually very flattering. For instance the first Ptolemy was Ptolemy Soter ("preserver"). Next were Ptolemy Philadelphus ("loving his sister"), Ptolemy Euergetes ("benefactor"), Ptolemy Philopater ("loving his father") and so on.

About 260 B.C., Ptolemy Philadelphus rebuilt a city in Palestine that had suffered in recent wars and renamed it *Philadelphia* after himself. It is the modern *Amman*, the capital of Jordan.

In western Asia Minor, another line of Madedonian kings were called Attalus. Of these, the second was Attalus Philadelphus and, about 150 B.C., he founded a city which he called *Philadelphia* also. This Philadelphia is mentioned in the Bible, in Chapter 3 of Revelation, as a city that was faithful to Christianity under trying circumstances. Many centuries later, in 1390, it was the last city in Asia Minor to fall to the Turks. It is now called *Alasehir*, from Turkish words meaning "red city," because of the color of its soil.

The name of the old Macedonian kings traveled to the Americas in modern times. In 1681, a city was founded in the new colony of Pennsylvania by the pious William Penn. To him, *Philadelphia* seemed perfect on two counts. First, it reminded one of the old city of Asia Minor that was faithful to Christianity, and secondly, the word could be translated "brotherly love." So it is that the largest city in Pennsylvania and the fourth largest in the United States is called *Philadelphia*, and is sometimes referred to as the "City of Brotherly Love."

Philippine Islands

AFTER LEAVING Guam in 1521, in the course of his great voyage around the world, the Portuguese navigator Ferdinand Magellan, sailing in the service of Spain, traveled northward and reached larger islands, which he tried to conquer. He was killed in the effort, so he himself never completed the circumnavigation of the world. However, eighteen of his crew under Juan Sebastian del Cano finally completed the voyage in one last ship.

The islands on which Magellan was killed did come under Spanish domination, however. In 1565, a Spanish soldier, Miguel Lopez de Legaspi, founded the first Spanish settlement, which he named *San Miguel* (St. Michael) after his name-saint. The town is gone but *San Miguel Bay* is still to be found on the map on the southeastern coast of the largest island of the group. Legaspi named the islands the *Philippine Islands* after the then-reigning Spanish king, Philip II. One of the larger Philippine towns is named *Legaspi* in his honor.

The Philippines remained Spanish until after the Spanish-American war. Then, in 1898, they became American. The Japanese occupied them during World War II, but after their liberation, in 1946, they became the independent *Republic of the Philippines*. Its capital was at first *Manila*, "place of the nilads," the latter being the native word for a white flowering shrub that grows in the vicinity. In 1948 the capital was moved ten miles to the northeast to a new town, *Quezon City*, named for Manuel Luis Quezon, the first president of the Republic. He had died in 1944.

What astonished the Spaniards most about the Philippines was that the tribesmen in the south were Moslems. This indicated the far-penetrating voyages of Moslem traders throughout the Indian Ocean in late medieval times. The Philippines represented, in fact, their most easterly penetration. To the Spaniards all Mohammedans were "Moros," from the Greek word for "very dark" (see MAURITANIA), and so a large inlet in the southernmost island of the group (where the Moros are most numerous) is called *Moros Gulf*, and the name thus travels from northwest Africa to the South Seas.

Phoenicia

ALONG THE eastern shore of the Mediterranean Sea, there were a series of towns in ancient times that were great trading and shipping centers. The chief of these was *Tyre,* located on what was then a rocky island offshore, but that has now become a peninsula. The name is our version of the Greek form which is, in turn, a twisting of the native name "Sur," meaning "rock." (The Arabs still call the town Es Sur, while the ancient Hebrews called it Zor.)

The land which included Tyre and neighboring cities was called *Phoenicia* (fee-nish'ee-uh) by the Greeks, possibly from a word meaning "purple-red" because the Tyrians prepared a certain purple-red dye from snails. They had a monopoly on the process and grew wealthy on it in days when good dyes scarcely existed. Naturally, they would wear cloth dyed in this color often, whereas only the rich could afford to do so in other nations.

The city of Carthage (see NAPLES) was a Phoenician colony and the Romans called the Carthaginians Poeni for that reason. The great wars between Rome and Carthage are therefore termed the Punic Wars.

The Greeks also had a legend about a bird called the phoenix. After 500 years, the phoenix was supposed to consume itself in a fire. From the ashes of that fire, it emerged with its youth restored so that, in effect, it was immortal. From its name it is sometimes referred to as "the Phoenician bird" but it has nothing to do with the land of Phoenicia. More likely, the name comes from its supposed red-purple coloring or from the redness of the flames in which it regains its youth.

In any case, in 1867, a city was laid out in America's southwest on the site of an old village. The story of the phoenix restoring its youth had become a common metaphor and, sure enough, one of the founders predicted that the new town would emerge "phoenix-like" from the dead remnants of the old village. The name *Phoenix* (fee'-niks) was consequently given the town, which is now the capital of Arizona.

Pittsburgh

THE GERMAN word for "city" is "burg" and this naturally appears as the suffix in the names of a number of cities of that nation. The largest of these is *Hamburg*, near the mouth of the *Elbe River*. (The name of the river is a distortion of the Latin "albis," meaning "white.") The town was founded by Charlemagne about 810 and named Hammaburg because of the surrounding forest, so that its name means "Forest City."

The same suffix entered the British Isles through the Anglo-Saxon as "-burg," "-burgh," "-borough," and "-bury." Thus, among the Anglo-Saxon kingdoms set up in England was Northumbria (see ENGLAND). Its best-known king was Edwin, who, in 627, was converted to Christianity. He spread his dominions into what is now southern Scotland and founded a fortress at the northern limits of his land to guard against the savage Highlanders. This fortress became a town named *Edinburgh* or "Edwin's city." The longer version of the suffix shows up in the fact that it is pronounced "ed'in-bur-oh."

The suffix was carried over into the North American continent. The most important example starts with George Washington. In 1753, when Washington was only twenty-one, he was sent out with an expedition to save the western lands from encroachment by the French. At the point of land where the Allegheny River met the Monongahela River (see OHIO), Washington established a stockade he called Fort Necessity. He was quickly driven out by the French, who named their fortifications Fort Duquesne in honor of the man who was then governor of the French dominions in Canada. For several years, the British continued to lose until, in 1756, William Pitt became the British Prime Minister.

With energy and decision, Pitt drove Great Britain to victories over France in North America and India. In 1758, the Scottish general, John Forbes, captured Fort Duquesne and naturally renamed it Fort Pitt. But he was a Scotsman from the Edinburgh area and he named the settlement about it *Pittsburgh*, using the Edinburgh suffix, though in this case it is pronounced "berg" and not "bur-oh."

Portugal

When the peninsula south of the Pyrenees was first explored by Greek colonists, they came across a river which they called the Iberus. That name has changed, with the centuries, to *Ebro River*. From the river, the region and then the entire peninsula received the name *Iberia*.

To the Romans, however, the peninsula was "Hispania," probably from the native name "Hispa," of uncertain meaning. With the centuries, the initial *H* dropped off so that to the inhabitants of most of the peninsula, the land is "España." We drop the *E* also and call it *Spain*.

In 711, the peninsula was invaded by the Moslems. The northernmost portions rallied against the conquerors and, through centuries of battle, slowly drove the Moslems southward. In the process a number of kingdoms were set up and by the fifteenth century all but one had united to form modern Spain. The remaining nation, still independent, makes up 15 per cent of the peninsula and is located along the western seacoast.

It had its beginnings in a region north of a river that ran through a province which in Roman times was called Cale. The town at the mouth of the river, serving as the port for the district, was therefore called Portus Cale by the Romans. Its name in modern times is *Porto* or *Oporto*. In the Middle Ages, however, the city was still known by its full name and this was eventually applied to the nation that had formed about it which became known, in slightly twisted form, as *Portugal*.

The region in pre-Roman times had been inhabited by a Celtic tribe called Lusitanians and for that reason, Portugal is sometimes called, poetically at least, *Lusitania*. A Lusitanian city, "Olisipo," was supposed, according to legend, to have been founded by Ulysses with the original name of "Ulyssippo." More likely, it is from a Phoenician word meaning "fortress." In modern times, the initial *O* dropped off and the city became "Lisboa" and is the capital of Portugal. In English, the city is known as *Lisbon*.

Provence

THE GREEKS had difficulty in settling west of Italy since Phoenicians and Carthaginians were powerful in those waters. One successful Greek colony in that area, on what is now the Mediterranean coast of France, was nevertheless founded. However, it must have been on the site of a prior Phoenician town, for its name was "Massalia," a Phoenician word for "settlement." To the Romans it became "Massilia" and to the French, in later days, it became *Marseille* (mahr-say'). In English, a final *s* is added and there is a tendency to pronounce it "mahr-saylz'."

In the second century B.C., Rome, which had defeated Carthage, was supreme in the western Mediterranean, and Massalia called upon it for help against the surrounding Celts. In 124 B.C. Rome answered the call and defeated the Celts. Rome then set up a special territory including the Greek city and sent out an administrator whose duty it was to govern under Roman law.

The word for such a duty in Latin was "provincia" and that was eventually applied to the territory that was being governed. Although, in the end, the Romans ruled over many provinces, the one that included Massalia, as the nearest and oldest, was always *the* province. It is still called that today, for the region of France including Marseille is still spoken of as *Provence* (pro-vahns').

During the early Middle Ages, Provence and the rest of southern France was far in advance of northern and central France in many ways. More of the old Roman influence and tradition survived. A special Provençal language and literature flourished until the thirteenth century when a northern invasion crushed it. A typical difference in language was that the southerners said "oc" for "yes" while northerners said "oil," a word which later became "oui." The southerners were therefore said to speak the "langue d'oc" ("the language of 'oc' "). The region of southern France west of Provence is still spoken of as *Languedoc* (lang-dok').

Prussia

IN MEDIEVAL times, the south shore of the Baltic Sea was occupied by a tribe called the Borussi who were more or less under the domination of the Poles to the south of them. The Borussi were heathens and, in 1226, the Poles invited a German, heathen-fighting organization, called the "Teutonic Knights," from "Teutones" (probably meaning "people"), the name of an ancient Germanic group, to take over the fight against the tribe.

The Teutonic Knights were glad to oblige and, having conquered the Borussi, they naturally remained in the area and became a far worse problem to the Poles than the heathen had ever been. The dominions of the Teutonic Knights became known as *Prussia* ("Preussen" in German), a distortion of Borussi.

In theory, the Teutonic Knights held the area as vassals of the Pope, but at various times Poland established power over the region. In 1466, Poland had the strength to retake the western portion altogether, which became known as *West Prussia*, leaving the Teutonic Knights only *East Prussia*.

In 1525, the head of the Teutonic Knights was Albrecht of Brandenburg (see BRANDENBURG). This was the time of the Protestant Reformation and Albrecht had become a Protestant. He no longer considered that Prussia belonged to the Pope, so he annexed his portion to his own dominions, though between the two still lay Polish West Prussia.

In 1701, the ruler of Brandenburg, Frederick III, decided he wanted to have the title of king. Brandenburg was part of the Holy Roman Empire and so Frederick was subject to the Emperor and could not be king. However, his East Prussian province was outside the Empire, so he assumed the title of Frederick I, King "in Prussia." *Prussia*, instead of *Brandenburg*, came to be the name applied to the whole realm of the descendants of Frederick even when this realm came to include almost all of northern Germany. Prussia merged into Germany in 1870 and, though Germany still exists, the original Prussia is no longer German. After World War II, the northernmost portion became part of the Soviet Union, the rest, Polish.

Queensland

ALTHOUGH specific kings and queens are honored plentifully on the map, it is usually through use of their reigning names. It is not usually considered sufficient to name a place simply after "the king" or "the queen." In this respect, the British were an exception, particularly during the reign of Queen Victoria, who ruled the British Empire for sixty-four years during the height of its power. Most Britons must have grown to feel that "The Queen" could only mean one thing.

Thus, in 1859, when the northeastern portion of Australia was organized into a separate state, there was a desire to name it in Victoria's honor. The southeasternmost region of Australia had already been named *Victoria*, but even then, at the beginning of the great reign, it was felt quite sufficient to name the new state *Queensland*.

To be sure, not all people felt about the British monarch as the British themselves did. For instance, in 1849, Queen Victoria visited Ireland for the first time and disembarked at a southern port named *Cobh* (pronounced "cove" and referring to the harbor, perhaps). With great ceremony, the name of the place was changed to *Queenstown* and the name was kept for over seventy years. However, when Ireland achieved dominion status and self-government in 1922, their respect for the memory of the British queen proved nonexistent. They went back to *Cobh* at once.

Similarly, there are a number of places named *Kingston* in the English-speaking world. The largest in the United States is Kingston, New York, which was a Dutch settlement till 1667. When the English took over, they deliberately named it Kingston in order to add insult to injury, since Holland was a republic at the time. The same feeling led to the naming of Kingston, Ontario, which was founded in 1783 by Tories fleeing the new republic of the United States. The largest Kingston, however, is the capital of Jamaica in the West Indies, founded in 1692 and therefore honoring William III.

Reunion Island

GEOGRAPHIC place names sometimes change more than once to match political changes. An amusing example is that of an island east of Madagascar that was first discovered by the Portuguese in 1513. It remained uninhabited and unclaimed until 1649, when the French colonizer, Étienne de Flacourt arrived from Madagascar, claimed the island for France, and named it *Bourbon Island* after the French kings then ruling, who were of the House of Bourbon.

However, in 1793, the Bourbon king, Louis XVI, was beheaded by French revolutionaries and the name of the island was changed to *Reunion Island*, indicating the reunion of government and people under a republic. But, then, when Napoleon Bonaparte became Emperor in 1804, it naturally became *Bonaparte Island*, and when Napoleon was overthrown in 1815 and the Bourbons, in the person of Louis XVIII, returned, it was Bourbon Island again.

In 1830, the Bourbons were out again in favor of the related house of Orléans, which was, in turn, overthrown in 1848. The island then became Reunion Island again, and although the Bonapartes returned and again departed there were no more changes.

In the Soviet Union, something of the same sort has taken place now and then. There is the case, for instance, of a fortress city founded in the Ukraine in 1754 and named *Elisavetgrad* (ee-liz'uh-vet-grad) after the reigning Czarina, Elizabeth.

After the Revolution in 1917, it seemed improper to have a city named after a czarina so it was renamed *Zinovievsk* (zi-nuv'yevsk) after one of the early revolutionary leaders, Grigori Evseevich Zinoviev. However, Zinoviev in later years was accused of having helped engineer the assassination of another official, Sergei Mironovich Kirov, in 1934, and was executed for this in 1936. As added disgrace, his name was removed from the city, which, in 1935, was renamed a second time and became *Kirovograd* (ki-ro'vo-grad) in honor of the assassinated official.

185

Rhode Island

TWELVE ISLANDS in the southeastern Aegean Sea, called the *Dodecanese Islands*, from the Greek word for "twelve," remained Turkish through the nineteenth century, when other Aegean islands had been ceded to Greece. After a war with Italy in 1911, defeated Turkey ceded the islands to the victors. Italy appropriated *Rhodes*, a larger Turkish island, in 1912, plus another much smaller island in 1920. Although the "twelve islands" thus became fourteen in number, they retained their name. After World War II, defeated Italy ceded them to Greece.

The island of Rhodes, according to legend, received its name because the population worshiped the sun-god and therefore honored the rose ("rhodos" in Greek), which they considered his particular flower.

This had a later consequence in the New World. Although the colony of Massachusetts had been settled by people searching for religious freedom, they wanted it only for themselves. Those who disagreed with them were driven out. One of these was Roger Williams, an idealist who believed in true freedom for all religious views. In 1636, he founded a settlement south of Massachusetts which he named *Providence*, so certain was he that all would be well.

Other nonconformists also settled in the area, some on an island off the coast named Aquidneck, an Indian name. In 1644, the name of that island was changed to *Rhode Island* because (some people think) an early explorer, the Italian Giovanni de Verrazano, had described it a century earlier as about the size of Rhodes. When the different sets of nonconformists finally joined forces it was under a combination of both names: *Rhode Island and Providence Plantations*. That is still the official name so that the longest name belongs to the smallest state. It is universally called simply Rhode Island, however, even though most of it is on the mainland.

It was one of the thirteen original states but was the last to ratify the Constitution and, even then, only under the threat of being treated as a foreign nation with tariff walls choking its trade.

Rhodesia

CECIL JOHN RHODES was a kind of British Theodore Roosevelt. Plagued by bad health, he lived an outdoor life, and devoted himself to a variety of tasks in business, politics, and exploration with almost superhuman energy.

In 1870, while a boy in his teens, he traveled to Cape Colony in South Africa for his health. There, he developed the grandiose notion of a railroad running the full length of Africa from north to south ("Cape-to-Cairo") and having it through British territory all the way.

At the time, British territory was far from forming a connected link, and Rhodes got to work to rectify that situation. In 1885, he engineered the British annexation of *Bechuanaland* (bech-oo-ah'nuh-land), north of Great Britain's South African dominions. This name is from that of a local native tribe called the Batswana, of which "Bechuana" is a distorted version.

Then, in 1889, Rhodes negotiated treaties with native rulers for territory north of Bechuanaland and the British started a northerly penetration into territory which, in honor of Rhodes, was named *Rhodesia*. Rhodes's next step was to help stir up the Boer War in order that Great Britain might take over the independent Boer Republics that lay between South Africa and Bechuanaland. However, he died, just before that war was over, at the age of forty-nine. After World War I, Great Britain finally could say that it controlled a connected strip of territory the length of Africa, but no railroad was built.

At first Rhodesia was administered as two territories, *Northern Rhodesia* and *Southern Rhodesia*. In 1953, however, the two were joined and to it was added the small territory of *Nyasaland*, east of northern Rhodesia. The whole is the *Federation of Rhodesia and Nyasaland*. "Nyasa" is a corruption of the Bantu word "nyanza," meaning "lake," and *Lake Nyasa* (nee-as'uh), from which Nyasaland gets its name, thus means "Lake lake" really.

Richmond

IN YORKSHIRE, in northern England, a castle was built by the Norman invaders on a high cliff, probably as a defense against the Scots to the north. The town that grew about it was named *Richmond* (originally "Richemont" in Norman French, or "rich mountain," perhaps only as a kind of good-luck name). The keeper of the castle had a considerable responsibility in the defense of northern England and the title "Earl of Richmond" was an important one. Henry Tudor was Earl of Richmond in 1485, when he defeated Richard III and became king of England as Henry VII.

In 1498, a town on the Thames about nine miles west of London burned down and Henry VII had it restored. In his own honor, he changed its name to *Richmond*. This second Richmond had been famous earlier as a favorite residence of royalty and it continued to be so, giving the name a very fashionable sound.

For this reason there are a number of Richmonds across the width of the United States. On the east coast, there is the Borough of Richmond, now part of Greater New York (see MANHATTAN), and on the west coast, there is a Richmond that is a suburb of San Francisco.

The most important Richmond, however, is one on the James River in Virginia, founded in 1737 by William Byrd and named for Richmond on the Thames. *Richmond* is now the capital of Virginia and was once capital of the Confederate States of America.

Byrd had a similarly royal fancy for another town he planned twenty miles south of Richmond. There was a trading station there founded by a Peter Jones and called, very plainly, Peter's Point. Byrd changed the name to *Petersburg*. This means "Peter's town" and does not seem much of a change except that it seems likely Byrd was influenced by the fact that thirty years earlier a new royal city had been founded in Russia by Peter the Great and that, too, had the name Petersburg (with a "Saint" before it, which Byrd, a Protestant, couldn't use).

Rio de Janeiro

On New Year's Day of 1502, the Portuguese navigator André Gonçalves, making his way down the coast of Brazil, entered a bay on the southeast coast which he mistook for a river. In view of the time of the year, he called it Rio de Janeiro, meaning "January River."

The area was first settled by French Huguenots (fleeing religious persecution) in the 1550's. In 1567, however, the Portuguese drove them out. This was on January 20, the feast day of St. Sebastian, so the Portuguese named their own settlement São Sebastiao do Rio de Janeiro. On the maps, however, it appears simply as *Rio de Janeiro* and in common speech it is often called simply *Rio*.

Rio is now the largest city in Brazil and from 1763 was the capital. Second in size is a city 300 miles west and slightly inland, founded by Jesuits in 1554 and also given a saint's name, *São Paulo* (sown-pow'loo) which, in English, is "St. Paul."

In 1822, Brazil declared itself independent of Portugal under Pedro, son of the Portuguese monarch. For sixty-seven years, it was the *Brazilian Empire*. In 1889, however, the second emperor, Pedro II, was deposed and Brazil became a republic.

The republic consists of a number of divisions with considerable powers of self-government (like the states in our own country) and, as a matter of fact, the official name of the land is "Estados Unidos do Brasil" or *The United States of Brazil*.

Through all this, Rio remained as capital. However, after World War II, Brazilian leaders began to plan a completely modern city to be hacked out of the wilderness. They chose a spot some 600 miles northwest of Rio and, in 1956, began construction. By 1960, it was sufficiently completed to be made the new capital. Its name is, in Portuguese, "Brasilia," and in English, *Brazilia*. From this position, as base, the Brazilians hope to speed up the development of their so far largely untapped interior.

Romania

FOR MANY centuries, the Danube River was the northern boundary of the Roman Empire in the east. Barbarians from the north, whom the Romans called Dacii, raided the Empire beginning about A.D. 85. The Roman emperor Trajan invaded their land, *Dacia*, in 101 and made it a Roman province. It represented the last new conquest of the Romans.

As barbarian pressures rose through the third century, the Roman colonists were gradually withdrawn back across the Danube and Dacia was abandoned. However, Roman culture and the Latin language remained in the area and were never entirely forgotten.

About 1300, a group of people called the Vlachs moved into the area. Their racial background is uncertain, but they also called themselves Armani or Romeni and apparently thought of themselves as descendants of the Roman settlers. Their language is related to Latin, moreover.

They founded the principality of *Walachia* (wah-lay'kee-uh), a name derived from the word "Vlach," on the Danube. North of it was Moldavia, a name of obscure origin. The two together were in later years lumped as the *Danubian principalities*.

They came under Turkish control by 1600, but as a result of nineteenth-century wars between Russia and Turkey, they finally gained their independence in 1861 and united to form a kingdom which, because of their insistence upon descent from Romans and their use of a Latin-descended language, they called *Romania* (often spelled *Rumania* or *Roumania* in the West). There are some Romanians in the extreme southwest of the Soviet Union, where the *Moldavian Soviet Socialist Republic* has been organized in consequence.

Another memory of Rome lies in the name *Rumelia*, which was given by the Turks to their European possessions. For a while, between 1878 and 1885, a district south of the Danube was given semi-independence under the name of *Eastern Rumelia*. In 1885, however, it was annexed to Bulgaria.

Rome

PROBABLY THE most influential city in the history of the world was *Rome*. The ancient Romans derived the name from Romulus, the legendary founder of the cities, but there are suggestions it comes from an ancient Italian word for the river on which Rome stands or from an old tribal name.

The plain on which Rome is located was called *Latium* (lay'-shee-um). Roman legend derives this from an early king by the name of Latinus, but there is speculation that it comes from a word meaning "wide" because it was a wide plain for that narrow and hilly land. In any case, the name of the Roman language, Latin, comes from the name and the modern Italian province containing Rome is *Lazio* (lah'tsyo).

Rome remained a rather insignificant city-state until about 350 B.C., but then it began a long career of conquest that brought it the control of the entire Mediterranean world. The name came to be applied not to the city alone but to all the vast territory it controlled. It was the *Roman Republic* until Augustus became the first emperor, in 27 B.C., and the *Roman Empire* thereafter.

As Roman society decayed and its problems grew more complex, it became very difficult for any one emperor to hold his vast lands together. The emperor Diocletian, in 286, therefore divided the Empire in two, himself ruling the eastern part (which was the richer) and a colleague the western part. In this way the *Western Roman Empire* and the *Eastern Roman Empire* arose. Sometimes (since Europeans recognized only one empire during ancient and medieval times) they were referred to simply as the *Western Empire* and the *Eastern Empire*.

The Western Empire came to an end in 476, when the last Roman emperor in the west, Romulus Augustulus, was dethroned and a Germanic leader, Odoacer, ruled in Italy. The Eastern Empire maintained an unbroken line of rule for another thousand years, until 1453, calling itself the Roman Empire to the very end.

Russia

IN THE ninth century, tribes of Swedes crossed the Baltic Sea and invaded the vast lands of eastern Europe. One of the tribes was called Rus, and although it was absorbed by the native population before long, it gave its name to the entire region, which became known as *Russia*.

In the thirteenth century, Russia suffered the far more serious invasion of the Mongols from Central Asia. The eastern portions of Russia remained under Mongol domination, while the western portion came under Polish rule and the southern portion was gradually taken over by Turkey.

In the center of Russia is a river called Moskva, a name of obscure origin, except that it contains part of the Russian word for "water." On it grew up the town of Moskva, which in English is *Moscow*, as the capital of *Muscovy*. In 1480, the rulers of Muscovy finally shook off the Mongol yoke and slowly regained control of the western and southern portions of the land (to say nothing of lunging eastward across the frozen plains of northern Asia all the way to the Pacific and into North America). By 1800 all of Russia was united once more.

However, cultural differences remained. The eastern portion, with its Mongol heritage, is the largest of the three and is *Great Russia*. The southern portion, with its Turkish background, is *Little Russia*. It is also called the *Ukraine*, a word meaning "frontier" since for several centuries it was the Russian frontier, and *Ruthenia*, from an old Latin term for the Russian tribes of the region.

The western portion, once under Polish influence, is *White Russia*, so called because the national costume is rather heavy on white material. A closer version to the native name, sometimes used in English, is *Byelorussia*, the word "byel" meaning "white" in Russian.

Even the autocratic czars recognized that Russia was not quite all one piece when they spoke of themselves as czars "of all the Russias."

Sacramento

Two RIVERS approach each other in central California, one from the north and one from the south. They veer west and enter the San Francisco Bay. They received names in the old Spanish days, the river coming from the south being the *San Joaquin River* (san-wo-keen'), named for the father of the Virgin Mary, and that from the north being the *Sacramento River*, this being named for the Holy Sacrament; that is, the Mass.

In 1839, while California was still Mexican, a German-born immigrant, John Augustus Sutter, established a domain on the Sacramento River. In 1848, just as California became American after Mexico's defeat in war, gold was discovered on his land and a mad horde of prospectors moved in. A town was laid out and it became *Sacramento*. In 1854 it was made the state capital.

But not all of California's towns and rivers bear Spanish names. The gold rush resulted in the establishment of towns that were named in English. For instance, the town of *Stockton*, established on the San Joaquin River, was named for Robert Field Stockton, an American naval officer who had gained fame in the conquest of California from Mexico.

A very undramatic case is that of another town that was founded in 1852 by a man called Horace W. Carpentier, who bought land across the bay from San Francisco in order to establish a ferry service. Groves of oak trees grew in the area and Carpentier called the town he laid out *Oakland* in the best suburban tradition. It is now the third largest city in California.

Just to the north of Oakland is *Berkeley*, founded the year after Oakland and named in far more literary fashion. One of the founders, Frederick Billings, had just been reading a book by the Irish philosopher George Berkeley, and in a fit of admiration suggested the city be named in his honor, which it was. The honor grew greater when a chemical element discovered in a university in that city was named "berkelium."

Saint Lawrence River

ON AUGUST 10, 1534, the French explorer Jacques Cartier arrived at a large ocean inlet to the west of Newfoundland. Since it was the day dedicated to St. Lawrence, he named the inlet *Gulf of Saint Lawrence*. Apparently, he then tried to find out from the local Indians their name for the territory in which he found himself, and through some misunderstanding they must have thought he was asking what certain structures were. They gave him their word for "huts," which was something like "canada." Consequently, Cartier named the river flowing into the Gulf of St. Lawrence the "Canada River." In later times, however, it came to be called the *Saint Lawrence River*, while *Canada* was applied to the land it watered and, eventually, to the entire upper third of the North American continent (minus Alaska).

Nearly a century later, in 1608, another French explorer, Samuel de Champlain, founded a settlement on the St. Lawrence River and named it *Quebec*, possibly from an Indian word meaning "contraction" because the river narrows at its site. He also discovered the lake south of the St. Lawrence River, which now forms part of the boundary between New York and Vermont and is, therefore, called *Lake Champlain*.

In 1642, the French administrator Paul de Maisonneuve founded another city, about 150 miles upriver from Quebec. He called it Ville Marie ("Mary-town") but the name was changed to *Montreal* ("royal mountain"). That was originally the name of the dominating hill of the area, named in loyal monarchist fashion. When the English took over in 1763, the hill became *Mount Royal*, but the city kept its French name.

Great Britain, once it was in control, divided Canada into two provinces. The region including Quebec and Montreal, along the lower reaches of the St. Lawrence River, was called *Lower Canada;* the part about the upper reaches and the Great Lakes, *Upper Canada*. When Canada became a dominion, Lower Canada became the *Province of Quebec*.

San Francisco

CALIFORNIA, having been under the domination of Spanish-speaking people for the first three centuries of its existence, is covered with Spanish names. Many of them are the names of saints and therefore include "San" or "Santa" as part of the name. Examples, along the southern coast, are *Santa Barbara, Santa Monica, Santa Maria,* and *San José,* which in English would be "St. Barbara," "St. Monica," "St. Mary," and "St. Joseph."

Farthest south of all is *San Diego,* named in 1602 for a Spanish friar who had been canonized fifty years before and on whose day those naming the town had first entered the harbor.

The most famous example is farther north, however. The mid-California coast was just about as far from civilization in the sixteenth century as any place on the earth. A number of people landed there or passed there but did not stay. (There are even legends that Chinese navigators reached it in the fifth century, though this is doubtful, to say the least.)

In 1542, a Portuguese explorer, Juan Rodrigues Cabrillo, reached the area, noted that the ocean inlet would make a fine harbor, and called the area La Bahia de los Pinos ("The Bay of Pines").

Nearly forty years later, in 1579, the English navigator, Francis Drake passed by during his circumnavigation of the world. He named the area New Albion. *Albion,* you see, is a poetic name for England. It comes from the Latin word "albus" meaning "white" (see ALBANIA) and may have reference to the well-known white cliffs of Dover. Another theory is that it is in reference to the white metal, tin, for which England was famous in ancient times.

Finally, in 1595, a Spanish explorer, Sebastian Rodrigues Cermeño, passed that way en route from the Philippines. A Franciscan friar on board named the area La Bahia de San Francisco ("The Bay of St. Francis") and the inlet is still called *San Francisco Bay.* The great city settled on its shores in 1776 was named *San Francisco* in consequence.

195

San Salvador

IT WAS a common habit among the Spanish to give names inspired by religion to the new lands they discovered, and they set the precedent at the very beginning.

When Columbus sighted land on October 12, 1492, he named it *San Salvador,* which, translated, means "Holy Savior." The native name, Columbus reported, was "Guanahani." San Salvador turned out to be one island of a large group beginning near Florida and running southeast parallel to the coast of Cuba. They are now known as the *Bahama Islands* through a distortion of the native name.

Although the Spaniards had been the first to land in the Bahamas, they made no attempt to settle there and, in 1627, the English took over. The name *San Salvador* dropped out of use and, astonishingly enough, its identity was forgotten. Nobody is quite certain exactly what piece of land was first sighted by Columbus.

However, if the Bahamas lost its "Holy Savior," the Spaniards took care to see that due honor was observed elsewhere. In 1524, the Spanish soldier Pedro de Alvarado, exploring Central America (and bringing the Indian tribes under the subjection of Spain), found a city on the Pacific coast which he named San Salvador. That city still exists. In fact, when general independence was won by the Spanish American areas in the 1820's, the area about San Salvador became a separate nation, the smallest in Central America, and took the name *El Salvador* (which, in English, means "The Savior").

The Portuguese were not behind the Spaniards in naming their portions of the western hemisphere. In 1549, Tomé de Souza, first governor of Brazil, founded a city which he called *São Salvador,* which is the Portuguese version of San Salvador and, despite the spelling, is pronounced much the same. It is now the fourth largest city in Brazil, has dropped the *São* prefix and is known simply as *Salvador.* An alternate name, used in earlier days, was *Bahia* (buh-ee′uh), which means "Bay."

Santa Fe

IN THE sixteenth century, Spaniards already well entrenched in Mexico sent explorers northward in search of a "New Mexico" as rich in gold as the old one had been. In 1541, for instance, a Spanish explorer, Francisco Vásquez de Coronado, went slogging over what is now the southwestern United States in a vain search for gold. However, when Mexico gained her independence she retained the "New Mexico" in the north until 1848, when she went to war with the United States and lost.

The name remained, however, and a section of the American Southwest entered the Union in 1912 as the 47th state, with the name of *New Mexico*. The capital of the state is the oldest state capital in the United States, having been founded by Spaniards in 1609 with the resounding name "La Villa Real de la Santa Fe de San Francisco," meaning "the royal city of the holy faith of St. Francis." Only part of it was kept and the city is today *Santa Fe* (san-tuh-fay').

The city of *Albuquerque* (al'buh-ker'kee), which is fifty-five miles west of Santa Fe and is the largest city in the state, is a puzzler at first glance. There was a Portuguese soldier, Affonso de Albuquerque, who in the early sixteenth century virtually founded the Portuguese Empire singlehanded. But why should Spaniards founding a city in 1706 name it for a Portuguese soldier? The answer is they did not. They named it in honor of the viceroy of the Spanish colonies in North America who was, at the time, the Duke of Alburquerque (Alburquerque being a province in southwestern Spain). The first *r* somehow dropped out, creating the confusion.

The town of *Los Alamos*, which has become famous since World War II as the site of nuclear experiments, has a name that has the quiet pastoral meaning of "poplar trees." And, in that connection, the *Alamo*, the fort made famous by its to-the-death defense during the war for Texan independence, was a mission building named for the poplar grove near which it had been built.

197

Santiago

CITIES NAMED after saints are usually named straightforwardly enough in two words, Saint something (or Sainte, Santa, San, São, depending on the language). For instance, *Saint Paul*, the capital of Minnesota, is clearly named for the Apostle Paul. The name was suggested by a Catholic priest in 1841, after the name of the chapel he had built in the town. Accepting the suggestion was a good idea, too, for the town had previously been called Pig's Eye.

Again, *Saint Joseph*, Missouri, was founded in 1826 by an American of French ancestry, Joseph Robidoux, who named the town after his patron saint (and consequently after himself).

Sometimes, however, a foreign name will collapse a saint-name into a single word which, to English and American ears, obscures the origin.

For instance, the Apostle James, brother of John, is considered the patron saint of Spain because, according to legend, he went to Spain to bring Christianity and was there martyred. However, the Spanish version of "James" is "Iago." (And why not? They have as much right to "Iago" as we have to "James," considering that the Hebrew name of the apostle and of all others named James in the New Testament, was "Jacob.")

For that reason, "Saint James" in Spanish would be "San Iago" except that Spanish custom runs the words together to form "Santiago." There are a whole series of towns named Santiago in the Spanish-speaking world. The original one, in northwestern Spain, is *Santiago de Compostela* (san-tee-ay′go-dee-kom-po-stay′lah). Beneath its cathedral, the bones of St. James are supposed to be buried.

There are larger Santiagos in the western hemisphere. There is, for instance, *Santiago de los Cabelleros* (day-los-kah-vah-yay′ros) in the northern Dominican Republic, and a still larger one, *Santiago de Cuba*, in southeastern Cuba. The largest of all is *Santiago de Chile*, which is the capital of Chile and the fourth largest city in South America.

Saragossa

Two of the most famous men in Roman history were Gaius Julius Caesar and his nephew Gaius Octavius Caesar. The first brought peace to the Roman Republic after half a century of on-and-off civil wars. After he was assassinated in 44 B.C., so that the wars began again, the second seized control, established the Roman Empire, became the first emperor, and ushered in two centuries of peace. As emperor, he called himself Augustus.

So revered was the memory of these two men that, ever since, the names of Caesar and the adjective "august" have been applied to rulers. Naturally, a number of Roman cities were named (or renamed) in honor of these two men, especially Augustus, but in almost every case the names changed with the centuries so that one could barely see, if at all, the men they were intended to honor.

A city in the Spanish peninsula, to use an example, was renamed Caesaraugusta by the Romans. The first and last syllables were lost, however. The modern Spanish name for the city is "Zaragoza" and we call it *Saragossa* (sar-uh-gos′uh).

Another city, farther to the southwest, was founded by Augustus in 23 B.C. and named Augusta Emerita ("Augustus, the retired soldier," to indicate that peace had come and would remain). However, the first word was dropped and the city is now *Merida* (may′ree-dah).

The chief towns of a number of Celtic tribes received the "Augusta" prefix. Thus, there was "Augusta Suessiones," "Augusta Trevirorum," and "Augusta Taurinorum." In each case the "Augusta" was dropped. The modern names are *Soissons* (swah-son′) in northern France, *Trier* (treer) in Western Germany, and *Torino* (taw-ree′no) in northwestern Italy. The French version of the second is *Trèves*, which, with the English pronunciation of "trevz," is more often used by us, while Torino is more frequently called *Turin*. Augustus's luck wasn't all bad, though. "Augusta Praetoria" became *Aosta* (ah-os′tah) in northwestern Italy and "Augusta Vindelicorum," *Augsburg* in southwestern Germany.

Saudi Arabia

Soon AFTER the great days of its conquering armies, the Arabian peninsula fell back into the backwoods of history, while conquered countries like Persia and Egypt took over the leadership of the Moslem world. This is not surprising since much of Arabia is a barren desert.

The southeastern section, particularly, is called, in Arabic, Al-Rah al-Khali ("the empty quarter") while in English it is the *Great Sandy Desert*. The northern part of the peninsula, also dry, is sometimes referred to as *Arabia Deserta*, while a strip to the southwest, where the climate is wet enough for agriculture, is *Arabia Felix* ("happy Arabia").

The Arabs themselves refer to the interior as "Najd" or, in English, *Nejd* (nejd), meaning "plateau," because that is what it is. A mountain range along the western shore is called al-Hi-jaz, which becomes *Hejaz* (heh-jaz') in English, and means "barrier." This gives its name to the coastal region itself.

In the eighteenth century, a new kingdom arose in Nejd under the energetic house of Saud. In 1906, Abdul-Aziz ibn-Saud became king. After World War I, the Hejaz was declared independent under Husein ibn-Ali. However, ibn-Saud attacked in 1924 and by 1926 had conquered Hejaz and made himself king of both nations.

At first the combined domain was called *Nejd and Hejaz*, but ibn-Saud had also taken over *Asir* (a-seer'), meaning "inaccessible." This lay south of Hejaz and since ibn-Saud now controlled most of Arabia he gave his kingdom an inclusive name, calling it *Saudi Arabia* (sah-oo'dee), honoring his family at the same time.

Great Britain still controls the southern and southeastern coast of Arabia, and there is one other independent nation on the peninsula. The independent nation is *Yemen*, the present name of the old Arabia Felix. Its name means "right hand" and this may signify the fact that from Africa, as one faces Mecca, Yemen is on the right hand; that is, to the south.

200

Savannah

GRASSLANDS, free of trees, have names that appear on the map in a variety of languages. The old English word "field" is incorporated in the names of many towns. There are a dozen towns named Springfield, for instance. The largest is *Springfield*, Massachusetts. Although Springfield, Illinois, is smaller, it is the capital of its state. Then there are half a dozen towns named *Greenfield* (again the one in Massachusetts is largest), and so on.

The French word is "prairie," which comes from the Latin "pratum," meaning "field." The French reached the Midwest before the English and Americans did and the flat, treeless plains that fill the center of North America have received that name. We speak of the *Prairie States* to signify the Midwest sometimes, while the *Prairie Provinces* are Manitoba, Saskatchewan, and Alberta, which lie between the Rocky Mountains and the Great Lakes.

The Spanish word for a treeless plain is "sabana," which has entered the English language as "savannah." It is particularly used along the coastal regions of the southeastern United States where early Spanish influence was strong. In fact, when James Oglethorpe founded a settlement on the shores of his new colony of Georgia in 1733, he named it *Savannah* from the appearance of the surrounding countryside.

Another Spanish word for it is "pampas" and this is used in Argentina especially, where one speaks of the "pampas" as we speak of the "prairies." There is a town in northern Texas called *Pampa* for the same reason that Savannah received its name.

In South Africa, such an area is called "veldt" just as in Australia it is called "the bush."

In southern Russia, it is called *steppe*, a Russian word meaning "wasteland." The region east of the Caspian Sea, which is arid and semidesert, is sometimes referred to as *the Steppes*. Because the Kirghiz tribe roams those regions, it is sometimes called the *Kirghiz Steppe*.

Savoy

THE HOUSE of Savoy began as lords of a district southwest of Switzerland called *Savoy* from an old word meaning "fir-tree," in which the country abounded. Amadeus III became a count in 1111 and his descendant, Amadeus VIII, was made a duke in 1416.

The Dukes of Savoy expanded their power southward into northwestern Italy. This new territory was *Piedmont*, meaning, in French, "at the foot of the mountains," since it lay just south of the Alps, and the Duke took the title of "Prince of Piedmont."

Piedmont sided with the Austrians in the War of the Spanish Succession (1701–1715) and, as a reward, ended with the island of Sardinia to the south. (Greek legend has it that the island was first settled by Carthaginians under the leadership of a man named Sardo, whence the modern name.) Consequently, in 1720, Victor Amadeus II called himself King of Sardinia.

After Napoleon's downfall (Savoy was on the right side again) Sardinia gained the coastal city of Genoa (see MONACO).

In 1859, with the help of Napoleon III of France, King Victor Emmanuel I of Sardinia began a war with Austria that ended in the union of the whole Italian peninsula, so that he became King of *Italy*. According to one theory, the word "Italy" comes from an old Latin word for "calf" because Italy was rich in cattle in pre-Roman times.

For his help in uniting Italy, Napoleon III had a price and that price included Savoy, which became part of France and is still French. So, in gaining Italy, the House of Savoy lost Savoy itself.

The price may have seemed small, and Italy continued to choose the right side and gain territory. Finally in 1935–36, Italy, under Benito Mussolini, conquered Ethiopia (see ETHIOPIA) and King Victor Emmanuel III became "Emperor of Ethiopia." And that was the final height, for Italy chose the wrong side in World War II, and in 1946, the House of Savoy ceased its rule altogether and Italy became a republic.

Saxony

AMONG THE most important of the German tribes remaining in Germany after the barbarian movements that followed the breakup of the Roman Empire were the Saxons. They are supposed to take their name from their favorite war-weapon, the "seax," a short, thrusting sword. Charlemagne conquered *Saxony*, the region of central Germany in which they lived, only with great trouble and after many wars.

During the middle Ages, Saxony broke up in a very complicated fashion. In central Germany, a region maintained itself intact as Saxony ("Sachsen" in German) and remained an independent nation until 1870, when it was absorbed into the German Empire. It now forms the southeasternmost province of East Germany. The section near the North Sea became *Lower Saxony* ("Nedersachsen" in German) and a province of that name still makes up most of the northern portion of West Germany.

Between the two Saxonies were a number of smaller pieces named for the towns they contained, such as *Saxe-Coburg, Saxe-Weimar, Saxe-Altenburg* and so on. After World War I, most of these were included in the province of *Thuringia* ("Thüringen" in German), named for a tribe living in the region in ancient times. Thuringia is now the southwesternmost province of East Germany, while north of it is "Sachsen-Anhalt" (*Saxe-Anhalt*).

In the fifth century, Germanic tribes invaded the island of Britain (see ENGLAND) and among these were Saxons. Three of the seven kingdoms set up by the invaders were founded by the Saxons. The region north of modern London was *Essex* ("east Saxon"). South of that was *Sussex* ("south Saxon") and to the west of both was *Wessex* ("west Saxon"). After Danish invasions in the ninth century had wiped out the kingdoms to the north, Wessex, under Alfred the Great, took over the leadership and eventually united England.

Essex and Sussex still form counties (shires) of England, but there is no Wessex. Instead, there is *Middlesex*, which lies between Essex and Sussex (though it borders only on the former).

Seattle

THE CHIEF cities of Washington State take their names from Indian words. The largest is *Seattle*, named for a friendly Indian chief ("Seathl") of the area. About fifteen miles to the south is *Tacoma*, which derives its name from the native name of the mountain, meaning "big snow," about forty miles southeast of the city. That mountain is the highest point in the state.

A controversy surrounds the mountain. It was first sighted by the English navigator George Vancouver, in 1793, and he named it after Admiral John Sprat Rainier of the British Navy. Most people, including those of Seattle, call it *Mount Rainier* ("ruh-neer'" or "ray'-nyer") but the citizens of Tacoma call it *Mount Tacoma*. (One of Vancouver's officers, Peter Puget, explored the ocean inlet in which Seattle and Tacoma both stand, and it is named *Puget Sound* in his honor.)

In the western part of the state is the city of *Spokane* (spo-kan'). Its name comes from an Indian tribe of approximately that name and means "children of the sun." Now it so happens that the coast of Washington, where Seattle and Tacoma are located, is about the rainiest part of the North American continent. Spokane has only one third as much rainfall and the Indians there, thinking of the coast, must really have thought of themselves as "children of the sun."

On the other hand, "walla" is the local Indian word for "water." "Much water" would naturally be "walla walla" and *Walla Walla* is the name of a city in southwestern Washington.

In northwestern Washington is a mountain only half the size of Mount Rainier (Tacoma). The English navigator John Meares, who discovered it in 1788, fancied he saw a resemblance to the famous Greek mount of the gods and named it *Mount Olympus*. As a result the peninsula to the west of Puget Sound is the *Olympic Peninsula*, and the small town at the southern end of Puget Sound, founded in 1851, is named *Olympia*. It is now the capital of the state. (The Greek *Mount Olympus* bears a name with a meaning that is lost in antiquity.)

Siberia

AFTER RUSSIA's long subjection to Mongol domination from the thirteenth to fifteenth centuries, the tide slowly began to turn. Under Ivan IV (commonly called "The Terrible") the last remnants of Mongol land were captured in 1552. The Mongols (also called Tatars, a word that means "archer" in their language, for the bow was their chief weapon) did not, however, perish but maintained their culture and their Moslem religion. In 1920, after the Russian Revolution, the region was organized as the *Tatar Autonomous Soviet Socialist Republic*.

The big attraction of the almost empty stretches at the *Ural Mountains* (a Russian name of unknown origin) and beyond was the fur trade. A Russian family called Stroganov were the tycoons in this respect. They hired Cossacks to explore eastward. A Cossack named Yermak led a band across the Urals in 1582 and began by overcoming a small Tatar khanate just across the mountains. The khan's residence was in a place the Tatars called Sibir and that (in English, *Siberia*) became the name of the entire northern stretch of Asia. The name even passed to far-distant islands off Asia's north coast which were discovered in 1773 and named the *New Siberian Islands*. The largest islands of the group are the *Lyakhov Islands*, after the discoverer.

By 1700, Russian dominions had reached across six thousand miles of Asia to the Pacific and toward the end of his reign, Peter the Great employed a Danish navigator, Vitus Bering, to explore eastern Siberian waters to see if Siberia were connected to North America. Bering conducted explorations over a period of fifteen years and found that the answer was no. Between the two continents was fifty-six miles of water that is now called *Bering Strait*. The stretch of water south of the strait is the *Bering Sea*.

In 1741, Bering died on an island off the Siberian coast which is now called *Bering Island*. Together with other islands in the vicinity they make up the *Komandorski Islands* ("Commander Islands"), also named in his honor.

Sicily

AT THE very toe of the Italian boot is an island that seems like a triangular football ready to be kicked. The triangular shape is so remarkable that an old, rather poetic name for the island is "Trinacria," which, in Latin, means "three-cornered." However, that is not its name on the map, however descriptive it might be.

When Greek colonists began to arrive at the island about 750 B.C., they found tribes of natives who called themselves Sicels. The Greeks therefore called the island Sikelia, which the Romans made into "Sicilia" and we into *Sicily*.

The chief city of Sicily, founded in 734 B.C., according to Greek tradition, was named *Syracuse*, a name of obscure origin. It became the largest and richest city in Greece when it was at its height, and at times controlled almost the whole island. Toward the end of the third century B.C., however, it was absorbed into expanding Rome.

The name traveled across the ocean, for, in 1825, a town in New York was settled which had as its first postmaster John Wilkinson. He was a romantic soul who read about the Sicilian Syracuse and liked the ring of the name. The New York town became *Syracuse*, too, therefore, and it is now the fourth largest city in the state.

Sicily remained Greek in character till 827 when the Moslems conquered it. About 1050, Norman adventurers from France took it from the Moslems and by that time its Greekness was gone. In 110, the Normans invaded southern Italy, extending their power to the city of Naples and beyond. Southern Italy seemed so like Sicily in character that they called their realm the *Kingdom of the Two Sicilies*, though it is more commonly known as the *Kingdom of Naples*.

Southern Italy and Sicily continued on through history, sometimes united and sometimes under separate rule. Through the early nineteenth century it was combined as the Kingdom of Naples, but in 1860, all of it was absorbed into the united kingdom of Italy.

Singapore

SOUTHEASTERN Asia extends southward in a long neck of land nearly to the equator. The native inhabitants call themselves "melayu" and from this comes the name of *Malay Peninsula* for the stretch of land. The southernmost part consisted in the nineteenth century of a group of small units which had formed the center of a strong empire about 1400. The capital of this empire had been the city of *Malacca*, a name also derived from that of the people.

In 1511, the Portuguese soldier and explorer Affonso de Albuquerque captured Malacca, and Portuguese influence was dominant for a while. By 1786, however, when Great Britain had established control over India, it was the British who were in charge. In 1819, the Englishman Thomas Stamford Raffles purchased an island off the southern tip of the peninsula from the local sultan. There had once been a native town there by the name of "Singhapura," which, in Sanskrit, meant "lion city." It was refounded now as *Singapore*.

In the late nineteenth century, British influence spread over all the small *Malay States*. Some were united under direct British rule as the *Federated Malay States*, the rest making up the *Unfederated Malay States*, and the whole being referred to as *British Malaya*.

Singapore, some islands across the narrow *Singapore Strait*, and sections of the adjacent mainland were lumped together as *Straits Settlements*.

The Japanese conquered the whole peninsula in 1942 and though after the war control was restored to Great Britain, matters were no longer the same. In 1946, the Straits Settlements were broken up. The mainland portions were joined with the Federated and Unfederated Malay States to form the *Malayan Union*, which, in 1948, became the *Federation of Malaya*. In 1957, the area achieved complete independence as *Malaya*.

In 1963 Malaya joined Singapore and most of the British possessions in nearby Borneo to form a new independent nation, *Malaysia*.

Solomon Islands

DURING World War II, a number of Pacific Islands that had been thought of vaguely by the American public as dreamy Utopian sort of places became painfully and unpleasantly real. It was in this area, in January 1942, that American forces mounted their first counterattack against the conquering Japanese.

These first attacks were aimed at the *Gilbert Islands* and *Marshall Islands*. These were first visited by an English navigator named John Byron in 1765, but they received their names from later visitors, two sea captains, Gilbert and Marshall, who visited the islands in 1788. Later in the war, marines fought bitter battles on the islands of both groups.

However, fighting was most long-drawn-out and dramatic in the *Solomon Islands*, consisting of a pair of rows of islands running parallel to the New Guinea coast. They were first discovered by a Spanish navigator, Alvaro de Mendaña de Neyra, who felt that they would be loaded with wealth of all sorts (unknown lands are always expected to be wonderful) and named them after King Solomon, who, according to legend, owned fabulous gold mines somewhere. Unfortunately, they turned out to be like all other Pacific islands, rich only in what people can make out of them.

Both French and British were involved in later individual islands of the group. The largest and most northwesterly of the islands is Bougainville Island (see OCEANIA). Another island, midway along the western chain, was discovered by the Englishman John Shortland, in 1788. He named it *New Georgia*, after the reigning British king, George III.

Later still, there was fighting in the *Bonin Islands*, just south of Japan. This name is a corruption of the Japanese "Munin To," meaning "empty of men," because when the Japanese first reached it, the islands were uninhabited. The word "jima" or "shima" is Japanese for "island," so *Iwo Jima*, in this group, means "Iwo Island."

Somalia

THE EASTERNMOST projection of Africa, southeast of Ethiopia, was invaded in the early fifteenth century by a group of people related to the Ethiopians, but with some Negro admixture. They called themselves the Somalis. In the early nineteenth century, the region they inhabited therefore came to be called Somaliland (so-mah′lee-land).

In 1885, at the height of the European penetration of Africa, Italy began to occupy the Somali coast and finally, over succeeding decades, managed to bring under control the entire coast east of Ethiopia. This became *Italian Somaliland*. West of that, a section of coast came under the control of Great Britain and still farther west a small section became French. These were *British Somaliland* and *French Somaliland*. The southeastern portion of Ethiopia, lying between British Somaliland and Italian Somaliland, is also inhabited by Somalis.

The Italians also penetrated the coast to the west of French Somaliland and, by 1890, had organized a colony north of Ethiopia, which came to be called *Eritrea* (e-ri-tree′uh). This name arose from the fact that it bordered on the Red Sea, which had been "Erythraean Sea" (from the Greek "erythros," meaning "red") to the ancients.

After the conquest of Ethiopia in 1936, Italy combined Eritrea and Italian Somaliland with Ethiopia as *Italian East Africa*. In the very early days of World War II, Great Britain was forced to evacuate British Somaliland, while the French remained helpless after the defeat and occupation of France by Germany. For the winter of 1940–41, Italy was supreme in the region. Then, in the spring of 1941, the British returned and quickly defeated the Italians, sweeping East Africa clean.

After World War II, Eritrea was ceded to Ethiopia, while Italian Somaliland was held in trust under the United Nations. In 1960, Italian Somaliland was united with British Somaliland and the two became the independent nation of *Somalia*. Only French Somaliland remains of prewar European holdings.

Soviet Union

Russia remained under an autocratic form of government long after western Europe had gained democracy to varying extents. In 1905, however, after Russian defeats in a war with Japan due to the corruption and inefficiency of the government, the Russians revolted. Councils of workers and revolutionaries formed in the large cities. These were called "soviets," a Russian word meaning "councils."

The 1905 Revolution was put down, but in 1917, after even worse Russian defeats in World War I, there was a new Revolution and this time the Czar was overthrown and, eventually, the various soviets took charge. The new government lacked a monarch, it established a socialist economy, and it was run by the soviets. It was therefore a "soviet socialist republic."

In 1918, the new Russia was forced to sign a peace treaty with victorious Germany by which Russia lost Byelorussia and the Ukraine (see Russia). However, when Germany was itself defeated by the western Allies later in the year, Russia regained most of the lost sections. In order to content those sections and non-Russian peoples in the south and east, Russia established a number of different republics, in each of which the local language and customs were encouraged. Thus there was founded the *Ukrainian Soviet Socialist Republic*, the *Byelorussian Soviet Socialist Republic*, and so on. All were gathered together under a central government which was the *Union of Soviet Socialist Republics*.

This long name is often cut simply to *Soviet Union*, or abbreviated as *U.S.S.R.* Great Russia, itself (see Russia), which dominates the Union, consists of portions which possess some self-rule so that it has a federal structure and is called the *Russian Soviet Federated Socialist Republic*. This is usually abbreviated as *R.S.F.S.R.* The term *Soviet Russia* can be used for this part of the country but it is incorrect to use it for the entire Soviet Union. It is certainly incorrect to use the old name "Russia" for the nation in its present form.

Spitsbergen

THE EASTERN hemisphere is not as rich in Arctic islands as is the western hemisphere.

Nevertheless, islands do exist north of Europe and Siberia. Thus, the Dutch navigator Willem Barents, in 1596, spied a group of islands 360 miles north of Norway. Because of the mountain peaks he first made out, he called it *Spitsbergen,* meaning "mountain peaks." Ownership of Spitsbergen was disputed by Norway, Sweden, and Russia for many years, but by the 1920's it was decided that they were to be Norwegian. It so happens that the Vikings, during their voyages in the Middle Ages, reported the existence of northern islands in 1194. These may have been the Spitsbergen group. Norway assumes it was and has given the old Viking name of those islands to the ones which Barents discovered. For that reason, the Spitsbergen group is known officially as *Svalbard* (svahl'bahr). However, one of the smaller islands of the group is *Barents Island.*

In his voyages, Barents also discovered two long islands north of the Siberian coast about 600 miles east of Spitsbergen. These are now called *Novaya Zemlya* (no'vah-yah-zem'lyah), which is Russian for "new land." The portion of the Arctic Ocean lying north of Europe between Spitsbergen and Novaya Zemlya is called *Barents Sea.*

A group of islands off the northernmost portions of the Siberian coast were not discovered until 1913. They were named *Nicholas II Land,* after the reigning Russian Czar. However, within four years, Nicholas II was overthrown and executed and in a spirit of revolutionary fervor, the new government renamed the group *Severnaya Zemlya* (seh'ver-nuh-yah), meaning "northern land," while individual islands became *Bolshevik Island, October Revolution Island,* and *Komsomoletz Island* (kom'so-mo'lets). A "komsomol" is a Communist Youth Organization and, as a matter of fact, a sizable city in the Soviet Far East, first laid out in 1932 by young volunteers of such organizations, is called *Komsomolsk* (kom-so-molsk').

Sudan

THE ARABS as well as the Europeans (see NIGERIA) were impressed with the dark skins of the inhabitants of Africa below the Sahara. They applied the name "Bilad-es-Sudan" ("land of the blacks") to the entire stretch south of the Sahara, from the Atlantic to the Indian oceans.

During the partition of Africa among the European nations after 1870, France obtained most of this region. That section of French-owned territory south of Algeria was known specifically as *French Sudan* ("Soudan" in the French spelling).

In 1960, the French Sudan, together with *Senegal* (sen'e-gawl'), the coastal territory to the west, named for the Senegal River that forms its northern boundary, gained independence as the *Soudanese Republic*. Within two months, however, the confederation split up. Senegal became independent in its own right. What had formerly been the French Sudan then took the name of *Mali*. This comes from a native word for "hippopotamus" and signifies strength and power.

The easternmost portion of the Sudan, along the banks of the upper Nile south of Egypt, was conquered by Egypt in 1822 and remained under the domination of that country for sixty years. In 1883, there was a Sudanese revolt against the Egyptians, and when the British tried to restore order, one of their armies, under General Charles George Gordon, was destroyed after a dramatic siege in *Khartoum* (kahr-toom'). That name comes from the local word for "elephant's trunk," because of the shape of the riverbank at that point.

Ten years later, another British army defeated the Sudanese and re-established control. Egypt and Great Britain theoretically shared sovereignty over the upper Nile in a "condominium" ("mastery together," in Latin). Great Britain was, of course, in actual control, but the territory was known as the *Anglo-Egyptian Sudan* until 1956. In that year it became an independent nation under the name of *Sudan*. It is the largest, in area, of the new African nations.

Switzerland

In ROMAN times, the area just north of Italy was inhabited by a Celtic tribe known as the Helvetii and the area is still sometimes referred to, poetically, as *Helvetia*. After the fall of the Roman Empire, Teutonic tribesmen moved in. As early as 972, a particular village was referred to as "Suittes," a name of unknown origin. This became *Schwyz* (shveets) and was applied to the region about the city as well.

The small states in the area joined with Schwyz in 1291 in a league to combat Austrian attempts to dominate the territory. They were successful, and still more neighboring regions joined. Speaking three different languages, they were united only in their desire for self-rule. In all three languages, the name of the federation was taken from *Schwyz*. In German, it became "Schweiz," in French, "Suisse," and in Italian, "Svizzera." In English, it is *Switzerland*, or, sometimes, the *Swiss Confederation*.

Only once in its history was Switzerland occupied by a foreign power and that was during Napoleon's time, when, for a while, the ancient name was restored (in accordance with Napoleon's classical fantasies) as the *Helvetic Republic*.

The largest city of Switzerland is *Zürich* (Zoo'rik), which derives its name from the Roman town of Turicum that existed there.

Another more complicated borrowing is that of *Bern*, which, since 1848, has been the capital. The city was founded by Berchtold of Zähringen in 1191. Berchtold was, apparently, descended from a family that had lived in Verona, in northern Italy. The German name for Verona is "Bern" and this German form, Berchtold took over for his new town.

The town of *Basel* (bah'zel) in northern Switzerland marks the site of a royal castle built by the Roman emperor Valentinian I, in 374. Since the Greek word for "king" is "basileus," a residence of the king can be called a Basilea and from this to *Basel* is but a step. The French form is "Bâle."

213

Sydney

OF ALL the distant lands colonized by the British, the lands "down under" — Australia and New Zealand — have remained most British. Canada has a strong French minority, South Africa a Dutch majority, and the United States is a melting pot. The very names on the Australian and New Zealand map testify to Englishness, however.

Australia's largest city, Sydney, was founded in 1788 (as a penal colony to begin with) and was named for Thomas Townshend, Lord Sydney, who was then the British home secretary. The next largest is *Melbourne*, founded in 1842, and named for William Lamb, Viscount Melbourne, who was the British Prime Minister at the time. *Brisbane* was founded in 1824 (another penal colony) and was named for the Scottish general Thomas Makdougall Brisbane, who was governor of that section of Australia at the time. *Adelaide* had a more exalted origin than any of these, for, when founded in 1836, it was named for Queen Adelaide, wife of Great Britain's then-reigning king, William IV.

The largest city in the island of Tasmania, off Australia's southeast coast, is *Hobart*. It was founded in 1804 and named for Robert Hobart, who was then secretary of state for the colonies.

To break this parade of names in honor of British notables, however, comes the capital of Australia, which was established in its modern form in the 1920's and was named *Canberra*, a native word for the region.

As for New Zealand, its largest city is *Auckland*. That was founded in 1840 and named for George Eden, Earl of Auckland, then governor-general of India. Auckland was capital of New Zealand till 1865. Then the capital was shifted to the more centrally placed *Wellington*, also founded in 1840, and named for Arthur Wellesley, Duke of Wellington, who had been the final conqueror of Napoleon in 1815 and who had served as British Prime Minister from 1828 to 1830. *Christchurch* was named for the Oxford school of Christ Church, which had graduates among the original settlers (the old school tie!).

Syria

IT SOMETIMES happens that the name of a small tribe is spread out, unfairly, over a large group, simply because the small tribe was first met with by those who did the naming.

Thus, a group of people speaking a Semitic language spread out over the area north of the Arabian desert about 1500 B.C. The land was called *Aram* and the people Arameans. According to the Bible, this was after an ancestor called Aram, but it is likely that it comes from a Semitic word meaning "highlands," signifying the mountainous regions north of the Euphrates from which they may have first come.

A small district in the north had the name "Suri" and apparently Greek travelers met the Arameans first in that area. They called them Syrians, therefore, and then applied the name to the whole area occupied by the people. *Syria* is the word used in most cases, even in the Bible (as translated), and Aram has disappeared from the map.

Syria became part of the Persian Empire, then of the Seleucid Empire, then of the Roman Empire, then of the Arab dominions, and then of Turkey. After World War I, it became a French possession. In 1946, it became independent but in 1958, it voluntarily abandoned that independence to join with Egypt to form the *United Arab Republic*, more commonly known in abbreviated form as *U.A.R.* Yemen (see SAUDI ARABIA) joined in a far looser manner and the U.A.R. plus Yemen may be referred to as the *United Arab States*. In 1961, however, Syria broke away and was independent again.

On the Syrian coast, Seleucus I, who succeeded Alexander the Great in the control of the area, built a city which he named for his mother, Laodice. (He was obviously a devoted family man, for he named another city for his son; see ANTIOCH.) This mother-named city was *Laodicea* (lay-od'i-see'uh) and it gave its name to the whole Syrian coast. The name persists today as *Latakia* (lat-uh-kee'uh) or, in Arabic, "El Ladhiqiya," and is famous chiefly for its tobacco.

Tangier

MANY NORTH African cities which once shared fully in Western culture under the Roman Empire, fell to the Moslem conquerors and were lost to the Western world until modern times. The city of *Tangier* (tan-jeer′), sometimes called and pronounced "Tangiers," is an example. Although farther west than London and Paris, its very name brings up romantic notions of the "mysterious East." The name, however, is a corruption of the Roman "Tingis," which is derived from the original native name (of obscure origin), "Tingi." In Roman times, it was the capital of western Mauretania and that section was called *Mauretania Tingitana* in consequence.

Portugal took Tangier from the Moslems in 1471 and Spain seized control in 1580. After World War I, however, Tangier and some of the immediately surrounding territory was internationalized as *Tangier Zone*. The section of coast outside that zone remained under the control of Spain as *Spanish Morocco*. In 1956, when Morocco gained its independence the Tangier Zone was ceded to it.

The town of *Constantine* in eastern Algeria is another reminder of Roman times and a pretty direct one, too. Its original name was "Cirta," but it was rebuilt by Constantine the Great in 313 and bears his name.

Some North African towns bear names that testify to European origins after the Moslem incursion. For instance, on the Morocco coast about 200 miles southwest of Tangier, the Portuguese, in 1468, built a town they called Casabranca ("white house"). It was abandoned but, in 1770, the Moroccans built a town on the site, which they called Dar-el-Beida (Arabic for "white house"). Now it is known as *Casablanca* (Spanish for "white house"). During World War II, when President Roosevelt was meeting with Prime Minister Churchill at Casablanca, reports that he was at the White House, intended to mislead the Germans, were actually not fake reports at all — if the phrase was read in Spanish instead of in English.

Tennessee

AMERICA HAS honored only one of its great men (George Washington) with the name of a state. Another, however, missed this honor only narrowly. At the time the United States became independent, the coastal states laid claim to vast tracts of land all the way west to the Mississippi. Fortunately for future harmony, the western tracts were ceded to the nation as a whole and ultimately formed separate states.

When North Carolina ceded its western claims to the United States in 1784, settlers in those regions at once formed a state which they called *Franklin*, after Benjamin Franklin, the great American scientist and statesman. This state existed for four years but it wasn't recognized by the other states and came to an end in 1788. Finally, in 1796, the region entered the Union as the 16th state but was called *Tennessee*, which was the name of the largest Indian settlement in the area, and of which the Indians themselves did not know the meaning.

However, America's great men are copiously honored at stages below the state level. Twenty-five states have counties named Franklin and there are a number of small towns by that name. Thirty-one states have counties named *Washington*. Twenty-six states have counties named *Jefferson* (after Thomas Jefferson) while *Jefferson City* is the capital of the state of Missouri.

Twenty states have counties named *Madison* (after James Madison). The town of *Madison* is the capital of the state of Wisconsin. Twenty-four states have counties named *Lincoln* (after Abraham Lincoln) and that is also the name of the capital city of Nebraska. Seventeen states have counties named *Monroe* (after James Monroe) and twenty-four states have counties named *Jackson* (after Andrew Jackson). The town of *Jackson* is also the capital of Mississippi.

For that matter, two southern states have counties named *Jeff Davis* and one has a county named *Jefferson Davis* after the man who was the only president of the Confederate States of America.

217

Texas

Not all Indians spent their time in nothing but scalping settlers. We have evidence for that in the name of the state which for a century was the largest in the Union.

Spanish settlers from Mexico moved north of the *Rio Grande* (Spanish for "Great River" — and there are half a dozen or so other Rio Grandes in Latin America) into what is now the territory of the state as early as 1689. This was partly because the explorations of La Salle (see Louisiana) seemed to them to be bringing the French too far south. In this northern trek the Spanish pioneers came across Indians who greeted them with the cry of "Techas," meaning "friends," thus announcing their peaceful intentions. The Spaniards named the new province Tejas, and to Americans this became *Texas*. (Another theory, however, is that the word means "allies" and that it originally applied to a confederation of Indian tribes in the area.)

Texas remained quite thinly populated until after 1800 when Americans began to flood in. In 1821, Mexico gained its independence from Spain, and Texas became a Mexican state. In 1835, the American settlers in Texas rebelled against Mexican control. They were led by such men as Stephen Fuller Austin, who was one of those who supervised and encouraged American colonization of Texas. The Mexican president, Antonio Lopez de Santa Anna, reacted by destroying a small group of Texans holding out in the Alamo. Shortly after that, however, a Texan army under Samuel Houston defeated and captured Santa Anna, and Texas gained its independence. Houston was the first and only president of independent Texas and Austin was the secretary of state. In 1845, Texas was admitted as the 28th state of the Union.

The result is that the largest city in Texas, founded in 1836, is *Houston* (hyoos-tun). The capital city, founded in 1838, and 150 miles west of Houston is *Austin*. Oddly enough, there is a town 150 miles northwest of Austin which is named *Santa Anna* (though after St. Anne, rather than after the enemy).

Thailand

IN THE centuries before Christ, what is now southern China was inhabited by a non-Chinese people who called themselves Thai, from a word meaning "free." As the Chinese expanded southward, the Thai were shoved into southeastern Asia. The coming of the Mongols accelerated that movement. By 1300, they had established a kingdom in the new region which they called Maung Thai ("land of the Free") and which, in English, becomes *Thailand* (tie'land).

The English in India made slow movements eastward during the nineteenth century, fighting three wars in *Burma* (a native name of obscure origin). After the first two, the British controlled the coastal areas, *Lower Burma* (along the lower courses of the river), and by 1886, they controlled *Upper Burma* as well and were on the boundaries of Thailand. By that time the French were to the east of Thailand in French Indochina (see INDOCHINA) and neither nation was willing to see the other take Thailand, so Thailand remained free. (The French often referred to Burma as *British Indochina*.)

The Burmese referred to the tribes on their eastern boundaries as "Shan." In 1948, Burma became independent as the *Union of Burma* and its eastern region is the *Federated Shan States*. The Shan are related to the Thais, and the British twisted the first word and applied it to the Thai nation, calling the latter *Siam*.

Siam has always remained the more popular name for the country in the western world, but in 1939, with the Japanese in control, and western ideas unpopular (and dangerous), the nation insisted on the official designation of *Thailand*. After the defeat of Japan, Thailand went back, discreetly, to Siam. However, by 1949, it felt sufficient confidence in the friendliness of the world to feel that the real name of the country would not be resented and it is Thailand once more. The inlet of the Pacific Ocean on its southern shore is called the *Gulf of Siam* and, sometimes, the *Gulf of Thailand*.

219

Tibet

THE GREATEST mountain range in the world curves in a huge arc between India and China. It is called the *Himalaya* (him'uh-lay'uh or hi-mah'luh-yuh), from Sanskrit words meaning "home of snow." North of the Himalaya is a high plateau, averaging three miles above sea level, and called Bod by the natives. Because of its great height it is often called To-bod ("High Bod") and this was twisted by the European explorers, who first reached the land about 1600, into *Tibet*.

Tibet first came under Chinese control in 1720. The control remained rather loose and through the nineteenth century, the British maintained a sphere of influence over the area. In 1959, the new rulers of the People's Republic of China suppressed a Tibetan revolt and brought it under tight Chinese control for the first time.

The highest mountains in the world are to be found in the Himalaya, most of them having native names. The highest of all, however, does not. That is *Mount Everest*, with its peak 29,002 feet above sea level. It was named for an English military engineer, George Everest, who, in 1841, headed the survey that fixed the position and height of the mountain.

Eighty miles to the east is *Kanchenjunga* (kun'chen-jung'guh), with the highest of its five peaks reaching 28,146 feet above sea level. The name of this third highest mountain comes from native words meaning "five treasure houses of the great snows."

The *Karakorum Range* derives its name from Mongol words meaning "black camp." (*Karakorum* was also the name of the Mongol capital in the days of Genghis Khan and his sons, because of the black tents in which the Mongol leaders dwelt.) The range, on the northwestern edge of the Himalaya contains the second highest mountain (28,250 feet high). Its European discoverer, Thomas George Montgomery, named it K^2 in 1856 and it has no other official name. However, it is sometimes called *Mount Godwin-Austin*, after the English explorer Henry Haversham Godwin-Austin, who surveyed the region in 1861.

Tokyo

In the days since World War II, the great western cities of London and New York have had to yield pride of place in population to an Oriental city, one that is the capital of Japan. Its population declined during the war but has zoomed since and by 1960 was at the nine million mark.

The city is relatively young, having been founded in 1456 under the name of "Yeddo." It was the residence of the Shogun, who was nominally merely an official of the emperor, but actually the absolute ruler. The figurehead emperor held his lonely powerless state in an inland town west of Yeddo.

In 1853, the American naval officer Matthew Calbraith Perry sailed into the city's harbor and Japan (hitherto closed to foreigners) was opened to commerce with the outside world by force. (To Americans, looking back at this in the early 1940's, this did not seem such a shrewd move after all.)

To meet the sudden change, Japan decided to Westernize. There was an uprising under the leadership of the emperor and the Shogunate was overthrown. The emperor moved into Yeddo which became the official capital. Its name was changed to *Tokyo*, meaning "eastern capital" and the ocean inlet that was its harbor became *Tokyo Bay*.

Nor is Tokyo the only giant city of the Orient. China's largest city is *Shanghai*. Its exact population is not known but it must be approaching that of New York in size. Its name is from Chinese words meaning "at the sea."

The largest city of southern China bears the most un-Chinese name of *Canton*. Actually it is in the province of "Kwangtung" and "Canton" is only the English twisting of that Chinese word. The China trade of the early American merchants led to several Cantons in the United States. The largest is *Canton*, Ohio. It is thought that a Canton in Illinois was so named because the founder was convinced that its site was directly opposite Canton, China, on the globe. (He was wrong.)

Transcaucasia

THE EXPANDING Russian Empire continued expanding while Europe was occupied with Napoleon. For a whole century, beginning in 1774, Russian armies worked their way through Caucasia (see KHERSON) and across the mountain ranges there until, by 1878, they had reached to almost the southern shore of the *Caspian Sea.* This sea, the greatest inland body of water in the world, has a name (of obscure origin) that goes back to the Greek "Kaspia."

After the Russian Revolution, the Russian hold weakened and for a while, with the help of the Turks, it seemed as though the area might break away. However, by 1921, the new Soviet government had gained control. In 1923, the area south of the Caucasus Mountains was organized as the *Transcaucasian Federation,* or simply *Transcaucasia* (meaning "across the Caucasus," which, from the standpoint of the rest of the Soviet Union, it was).

In 1936, however, the Transcaucasian Federation was broken up into three soviet socialist republics. The westernmost is the *Georgian S.S.R.* The similarity of its name to that of the American state is caused by the fact that, in Greek, "georgos" means "farmer." A stretch of good farming land might receive the name "Georgia" as the Caucasian territory did. Or the proper name "George" (meaning "farmer," of course) might arise and then a territory might be named after such a George, as the American state was (see MARYLAND). The Russian name for the Caucasian Georgia is "Gruziya" while the Georgians call their land Sakartvelo.

The capital of Georgia is *Tiflis.* This was originally founded by the Persians in 379 as a stronghold against the Georgians, who were themselves expanding southward at the time. The original Persian name was "Tphilis" and the official Georgian name for the city is now "Tbilisi." In all its forms, however, the name means "hot springs" because such springs occur in the vicinity.

Transvaal

ALTHOUGH THE Portuguese had discovered the southern tip of Africa, they did not colonize it. The first to do so were the Dutch, in 1652, who needed it as a way station for ocean trips to the East Indies. They founded the city of "Kaapstad," which, in English, is *Capetown*. (It was, after all, located at the Cape of Good Hope.)

During the Napoleonic Wars, the Netherlands was occupied by Napoleon, and Great Britain played it safe by occupying Dutch overseas territory. By 1814, Great Britain took over South Africa officially and Capetown became the capital of *Cape Colony*.

English settlers flooded into the colony and the older Dutch settlers (or "Boers," this being a Dutch word for "farmers") resented them. They withdrew to Natal (see NATAL) in the northeast.

Under the active leadership of the governor, Benjamin D'Urban, the British followed. *Port Natal*, the chief city of Natal, was taken and renamed *Durban* in 1835. The Boers then took the drastic step of moving north far beyond the borders of Cape Colony to set up their own independent republic. They crossed the *Vaal River*, so called from a Dutch word meaning "colored" because the river was yellowish with sediment. The new republic was therefore called *Transvaal* ("across the Vaal").

In 1854, Boer settlers south of the Vaal, but north of the *Orange River*, organized a second independent Boer state, which they called the *Orange Free State*. It might seem that the Orange River, too, was named for its color, but it wasn't. It was named in 1777 by a Dutch officer, R. J. Gordon (he was of Scotch extraction), who named it for the Dutch ruling house, the House of Orange.

In 1902, after a bitter war and narrow victory, the British annexed the two *Boer Republics*. In 1908, however, all four provinces were given dominion status as the *Union of South Africa*. Since then, Boer influence has gradually outweighed the British, and in 1961, the Union withdrew from the Commonwealth of Nations altogether.

Transylvania

ROMANIA WAS formed in 1861 by the union of Moldavia and Walachia (see ROMANIA) but there were other territories that remained in dispute with neighboring, and larger, powers. To the east of Moldavia is a strip of land called *Bessarabia*. This name is derived from the family name ("Basarab") of the Romanian princes that ruled it in earlier days.

Russia has taken it and been forced to give it up a number of times. Since World War II, however, it has been firmly in the grip of the Soviet Union.

To the west of Moldavia is a beautifully forested region inhabited mainly by Romanian-speaking people. To the Hungarians, who were still farther west, this section was the land "across the woods" and by the twelfth century the Latin version of this phrase, *Transylvania*, became the name of the region. The Hungarians conquered it about 1000, and the Turks took it over in 1540, along with most of Hungary. The Austrians in 1699 defeated Turkey and took over both Hungary and Transylvania.

After World War I, Transylvania became part of Romania for the first time and has remained so ever since, except for a period in the early 1940's when Hitler gave half of Transylvania to Hungary. This was an attempt to make both nations contented allies but, actually, as anyone might have predicted, both sides felt cheated.

Transylvania is separated from Moldavia by the *Carpathian Mountains* and from Walachia by the *South Carpathian Mountains* (a name stemming from the Latin "Carpates," applied to the ranges in ancient times). The South Carpathians are sometimes called the *Transylvanian Alps*. Just north of Transylvania and south of the Carpathians is a territory in which Ukrainian is spoken. This is the *Carpatho-Ukraine* (or *Carpatho-Ruthenia*, an old Latinized name for Russia). It was part of Czechoslovakia between the World Wars, but in 1945 was ceded to the Soviet Union.

Tripoli

BEGINNING IN 632, Arab tribes erupted from their large peninsula of Arabia and conquered vast territories to the north, east, and west. *Arabia* is a word of uncertain origin, but may come from a Semitic word meaning "noble men." As usual, people think well of themselves.

As conquest continued, the vanquished peoples were converted and became Moslems. They joined the victorious armies and by the time the Moslems invaded Spain in 711, the army consisted of North Africans chiefly.

These North Africans were called Berbers, a name dating back to ancient times and which is derived from "barbarian." The ancient Greeks called anyone who didn't speak Greek a barbarian and it did not imply, in those days, that a non-Greek was uncivilized. He just didn't speak Greek. The ancient Romans applied the name to anyone who didn't speak Greek or Latin. In Roman times, the North Africans learned to speak Latin, but after the Arabic conquest, Arabic became their language and they were "barbarian" again.

The Moslem north coast of Africa from Egypt westward was called *Barbary* by the Europeans of the Middle Ages and early modern times. The Moslem states that were established there were called the *Barbary States*.

One of these, however, retained a Greek name. A group of three cities had been founded by the Phoenicians on the African coast due south of Sicily. The name "Tripolis" came to be applied to them, the word meaning "three cities" in Greek. It is still called *Tripoli* today. It was one of the Barbary states in the early nineteenth century, but came under the control of Turkey in 1835. After the Italo-Turkish war of 1911, it was ceded to Italy. Though it formed part of the colony (now nation) of Libya, the area just about the city is *Tripolitania*.

There was another "Tripolis" on the Lebanese coast. Both it and the North African Tripoli are known as *Tarabulus* (tah-rah′boo-loos) to the Moslems.

Troy

IT WOULD seem inevitable that among the thousands of towns and cities founded in the United States, some would be established by people who wanted to impart a learned flavor to the new place by giving it a classical name. For instance, a city founded in 1789 on the east bank of the Hudson River just north of Albany, was named *Troy*, after the famous ancient city in Asia Minor which had been besieged for ten years by the Greeks. The Greeks had derived the name from a mythical founder of the city named Tros.

(There is a city in France named *Troyes* — pronounced "trwah" — which was the site of famous fairs in the Middle Ages, and from which the Troy system of weights is supposed to be derived. It has nothing to do with ancient Troy, however. In Gallic times, it was the principal settlement of a Celtic tribe called the Trecassi by the Romans, and *Troyes* is an example of the usual incredible twisting the French gave to Latin names.)

Central New York State has other classical reminders. There are a *Rome* and an *Athens* (and there is one of each in Georgia as well). There is also a Syracuse (see SICILY). At the southern tip of *Lake Cayuga* (named for an Indian tribe of the region and one of a group called the *Finger Lakes* because of their long, slender shapes), is the town of *Ithaca*. This was settled in 1788 and named for the island home of Odysseus, the hero of Homer's *Odyssey*.

Halfway between Syracuse and Albany is *Utica*, which is another classical echo. It was founded in 1797, and was named after the town of that name which had once existed near Carthage (see NAPLES). *Utica* is supposed to have been selected as the name by a blindfold drawing from a hat.

There is also a *Corinth* in New York, named for the famous ancient Greek city, and another in Mississippi which was made famous through being the site of a Civil War battle. There are several towns named *Sparta*, another famous Greek city, the largest being in Wisconsin. On the other hand, there are Indian names, too. The city of *Schenectady* in east-central New York is from Indian words meaning "end of the trail."

226

Tunis

NEAR THE great and flourishing ancient city of Carthage was another Phoenician settlement named Tunes, a disregarded village. For nearly 1500 years, all through the Roman epoch, Carthage was the great city of the region.

But the wheel of fortune turns. In 698, the conquering Arabs swept over the region and, for some reason, they preferred Tunes. Carthage declined and vanished and Tunes, or as it is now called, *Tunis*, became a great city, and lent its name to the surrounding area, which is called *Tunisia*, or, in French "Tunisie." In 1882, it came under French domination but, in 1956, it gained its independence.

The chief port of Tunisia is *Bizerte* ("bee-zurt'" or "bi-zurt'ee"). Its name is a corruption of the Roman name "Hippo Zarytus."

About 500 miles west of Tunis is a city built on the site of an old Roman town named Icosium. The Arabs built the new city in the tenth century and called it Al-jezair, meaning "the islands" from the islands located off-shore. This has come down to us as "Alger" in French and *Algiers* in English. The whole region between Morocco and Tunisia is known as "Algérie" to the French and *Algeria* to us.

The French took over Algeria in 1830 and that was the first building block of what was to be eventually a vast African empire. The immediate seacoast is *Northern Algeria* and is considered an integral part of France by everyone, apparently, but the natives. To the south are the *Southern Territories* ("Territories du Sud") which comprises a large section of the *Sahara Desert*. "Sahara" is from the Arabic word "sahra," meaning "desert," so that "Sahara Desert" is "desert desert," which is a good description after all.

Algeria remained part of France's African empire when virtually all else was freed. It was the first and almost the last. After being in revolt since the early 1950's, it, too, gained its independence at last in 1962.

Turkistan

CENTRAL ASIA has been a breeding ground for hardy horsemen who have on occasion ridden out of their homeland to plunder and raid the settled cities on all sides. Thus, Europe felt the force of the Huns in the fifth century and of the Mongols in the thirteenth century. Nor was Asia exempt. The Huns invaded China, for instance, as early as 200 B.C., and the Mongols conquered China as well as Russia.

Through the Middle Ages, Central Asia served as a reservoir for a group of people who called themselves by a name which, in English, is expressed as "Turks." This may come from a native word meaning "strong."

The original home of the Turks is referred to as *Turkistan* or *Turkestan* ("land of the Turks"). It is a large, ill-defined stretch of territory lying east of the Caspian Sea and north of Iran and Afghanistan. The ancient Persians called the area *Turan*, from the same native word from which we derive "Turk," and the old name is preserved since Turkish is listed as a "Turanian language."

Turkistan is chiefly divided between the two large nations on whose borders it lies. The eastern half, *East Turkistan*, came under vague Chinese control about 1600, and in 1870, the control became sufficiently tight to warrant the region being termed *Chinese Turkistan*. The Chinese themselves call it *Sinkiang* ("new territory") and that has replaced the former name even in the West.

The western half, *West Turkistan*, was invaded from the north in the 1860's by the ever-expanding realm of the czars, and became *Russian Turkistan*. After the Russian Revolution, it was divided into four soviet socialist republics named for the chief tribes. One of them, the *Turkmen Soviet Socialist Republic*, sometimes called *Turkmenistan*, retains the word "Turk" in the name. The whole area is sometimes lumped together, self-explanatorily, as *Soviet Central Asia*.

A small section of northern Afghanistan is sometimes called *Afghan Turkistan*.

Tuscany

IN ITALY, in the days before Rome grew powerful, there was a strange civilization to the north, and a people called by the Romans "Etruscans." The origin of the name is unknown and so is almost everything else about them. Their language has not been deciphered and they were so completely absorbed by the Romans later on that very little is left for modern archaeologists to work with. About all that can be said is that they arrived from somewhere in Asia Minor about 800 B.C. and were at the height of their power in 500 B.C., at which time they even controlled Rome, which was only a small town then. By 300 B.C., Rome had grown strong enough to be nibbling away at *Etruria*, as they called the district, and by the beginning of the Christian era, the Etruscan culture was about gone.

In their heyday, they shared control of the western half of the Mediterranean Sea with the Carthaginians, and the Greeks could make little headway against them. The Greeks called the Etruscans "Tyrrhenians," which is rather closer to what the Etruscans called themselves than "Etruscan" is. In consequence, the section of the sea southwest of Italy dominated by Etruscan ships was, and still is, called the *Tyrrhenian Sea*.

Although Etruria disappeared, it left a trace on the map, for in its place appeared the Italian district of *Tuscany* ("Toscana" in Italian), which resembles "Etruscan" closely enough.

In the days when Napoleon was reorganizing Italy and amusing himself by reviving ancient names, he reshaped Tuscany and some surrounding areas into a new *Kingdom of Etruria* in 1801. It didn't last long (none of Napoleon's artificial creations ever did) and, in 1807, he incorporated it into the *French Empire*. After Napoleon's downfall, it became *Tuscany* again. Napoleon had a good chance to witness that, for, in his first exile, he was sent to the small island of *Elba* (a distortion of the Roman name "Ilva") just off the Tuscan coast.

United States of America

THE WORD "state" can be used for any territory which is governed by rulers considered by the population to be akin to themselves. It comes from a Latin word meaning "to stand." A state stands by itself.

A "colony" on the other hand, comes from the Latin word for "farmer," because the Romans sent out groups of farmers ("coloni") to cultivate distant areas and governed them from Rome. A colony came to mean any territory under the control of a distant state.

Before the American Revolution, the eastern coast of North America was covered by thirteen separate colonies which were, to a large extent, ruled by England. During the Revolutionary crisis, however, the subject of independence came to the fore and finally, on June 7, 1776, the Virginian, Richard Henry Lee, rose in the Continental Congress and made the motion that "these united Colonies are, and of right ought to be, free and independent States."

The colonies declared and won their independence and the states joined in a "federal union." The word "federal" comes from a Latin word meaning "league." The nation therefore became the *United States of America* or, as commonly abbreviated, the *U.S.A.*

It is a rather all-embracing term. Actually, there are four other nations in the Americas that consider themselves to be leagues of self-governing states. These are the *United States of Mexico*, the *United States of Brazil*, the *United States of Colombia* and, at one time, the *United States of Venezuela*. Each of these, however, is known commonly by the last part of the name. Only the United States of America is commonly known by the first part as, simply, the *United States*.

The people of the United States call themselves Americans. The people of Latin America naturally feel we have no right to monopolize the term, since they are Americans, too. They refer to us as "North Americans."

Utah

In 1824, a twenty-year-old American explorer, James Bridger, trekking through the West, came upon a large lake, saltier by far than the ocean. The name it deserved was obvious. It was named the *Great Salt Lake*.

The area was first settled by a group of men and women following a new version of the Christian religion. They were "Mormons" or members of the "Church of Jesus Christ of Latter-Day Saints." In 1830, a man named Joseph Smith claimed he had discovered golden plates covered with an unknown language which had been miraculously translated for him and this proved to be the basis for a new sect. The followers of Joseph Smith believed in a few practices that were frowned on by most men — such as marrying more than one wife. The Mormons were driven from one place to another. Finally Joseph Smith was killed by a lynch mob and a group of Mormons under a new leader, Brigham Young, traveled far westward.

They arrived in the area of the Great Salt Lake in 1847, and there they founded a city which was naturally called *Great Salt Lake City*. In later years, this was shortened to *Salt Lake City*.

In 1849, the Mormons organized themselves as a state, to which they gave the name *Deseret*, claiming this to mean "honeybee" in the language of the golden plates. The honeybee, of course, implies the state to be a land flowing with honey, and that was what the careful Mormons, as industrious as any honeybees, made of it.

However, their custom of plural marriages made them unpopular with non-Mormons, and the government of the United States kept up a running struggle with them. The Mormon state was not recognized. After Brigham Young's death, most of the Mormons finally gave in and abandoned polygamy. In 1896, the state, properly purified, entered the Union as the 45th state.

Even then, it did not enter as "Deseret" but as *Utah*, named for the Utes, a tribe of Indians of the region. However, one of the state's nicknames is still "Honeybee State."

231

Uzbekistan

ONE OF the line of rulers that descended from Genghis Khan, the dreaded Mongol conqueror, was Uzbeg Khan, who died in 1340. A tribe of Mongol-Turkish people living in Central Asia called themselves Uzbegs after him, and the area in which they dwelt was called *Uzbekistan* (ooz'bek-i-stan'), meaning "land of the Uzbegs." The area was conquered by Russia in the 1860's and, after the Russian Revolution, was reorganized as the *Uzbek Soviet Socialist Republic.* (It is part of Soviet Central Asia — see TURKISTAN.)

On the northern borders of Uzbekistan is a shallow lake, dotted with islands, which bears the name *Lake Aral,* from the native term "Aral Denghiz," meaning "sea of islands." Into it flow two rivers, the "Amu-darya" and "Syr-daria," which, in ancient times, were known as the Oxus River and the Jaxartes River. The region which is now Uzbekistan was, to the Greeks and Romans, the region across the Oxus, and in Latin that is *Transoxiana.*

The ancient Persian name for the area was "Sughuda" and this the Greeks called *Sogdiana.* Whatever the name of the area, the capital city was "Maracanda." This city was captured and destroyed by Alexander the Great in 329 B.C. It recovered only after centuries and when it did, the name had become twisted to *Samarkand.* In 1370, Samarkand became world-famous as the capital of the last of the great Mongol conquerors, Tamerlane, but it sank again to obscurity after his death.

Southeast of the Uzbek S.S.R. is a smaller area inhabited by a tribe called the Tajiks. Their land is *Tajikistan* (tah-jik'i-stan'), often spelled *Tadzhikistan.* This, too, was reorganized after the Russian Revolution as the *Tajik Soviet Socialist Republic.*

The capital of the Uzbek S.S.R. is *Tashkent,* a name of obscure native origin. The capital of the Tajik S.S.R., which used to be "Dyshambe," was, after the Revolution, changed to *Stalinabad,* in honor of Joseph Stalin. Stalin lost favor after his death, and the name was changed back in 1961.

Vatican City

THE LATIN word "vatis" means a "soothsayer." At temples to Apollo, in particular, soothsayers would chant their prophecies ("vaticinate") so that a hill in Rome, on which the temple to Apollo stood, was called the Vatican Hill. St. Peter was supposed to have been martyred there and, in the time of Constantine the Great, the Roman bishop (that is, the Pope) was given a castle upon that same hill. This seemed appropriate since the Pope considered himself the successor of St. Peter.

After the Roman Empire fell, the Pope gradually emerged as the strongest native ruler of the Italian peninsula. In A.D. 755, the Frankish king, Pepin, donated tracts in central Italy to the Pope and this served as the nucleus of the *States of the Church* ("Lo Stato della Chiesa" in Italian), which, however, are far more commonly known as the *Papal States*. These expanded with the centuries and, at one time, covered the entire mid-section of the peninsula.

During the 1860's, when the small states of the peninsula were being united into the Kingdom of Italy, most of the Papal States were incorporated, too, over the protests of Pius IX, who was then Pope. The city of Rome and the region about it were kept under Papal jurisdiction through the agency of French troops sent out by Napoleon III. In 1870, however, the French were defeated by Prussia, and Italy took over what was left of the Papal States. Pius IX and the popes after him stubbornly refused to leave their palaces, considering themselves "prisoners of the Vatican."

In 1929, however, Pope Pius XI reached an agreement with Benito Mussolini, who was then the Italian leader. The Pope was once more to be the head of an independent state, consisting of a hundred acres about the Papal palace. This state, *Vatican City* ("Citta del Vaticano" in Italian), is the smallest in the world, only one eighth the size of Central Park. Its name recalls at the same time the present power of the Roman Catholic Church and the long-dead soothsayers of Apollo.

Venezuela

In the fifth century, times were bad for Italy. The Roman Empire in the west was falling apart and the barbarians were on the march. The Huns particularly were sacking in the north and working their way down toward Rome. Some of the inhabitants of northeastern Italy fled before them and made their way into the marshy lagoons on the coast, waiting for the Huns to pass on.

They built a town there, while waiting, which came to be known as *Venice* ("Venezia" in Italian), being named after the "Veneti," a pre-Roman tribe that lived in the region.

Venice became a powerful city, with time. Her ships dominated the Mediterranean and could fight on equal terms against the Turks. There were periods when she owned Crete and Cyprus, and in 1204, Crusaders under her leadership even sacked the city of Constantinople.

However, what always caught people's fancy about the town, even down to this day, is that, being built on lagoons, its streets are waterways, with gondoliers taking the place of coachmen or taxicab drivers.

This association of Venice and waterways carried over into the western hemisphere. In 1499, Amerigo Vespucci skirted the northern coast of South America and came across native villages built in the shallow water on wooden piles. To Vespucci, this was reminiscent of Venice (and Vespucci was Italian, remember), so he named the new area "little Venice" or *Venezuela*. That is now the name of the most northerly nation in South America, and the ocean inlet on the westernmost portion of its shore is the *Gulf of Venezuela*.

Until recently, Venezuela had a federal organization and called itself the *United States of Venezuela*. Since 1953, however, it has been simply the *Republic of Venezuela*.

Its capital was founded in 1567 as "Santiago de León de Caracas," but only the last word, *Caracas* (kuh-rak′us), is now used.

Veracruz

At the time of the coming of the Europeans, the nearest approach to a civilization in North America was that of an Indian tribe known as the Aztecs. About 1300, they had migrated to a plateau they had named, in their language, "place of Mexitli," Mexitli being one of their war gods. The region is now known as *Mexico*. The capital city, which was "Tenochtitlan" to the natives, is *Mexico City*, and the large body of water that bathes the eastern shore of the region is the *Gulf of Mexico*.

Mexico was conquered between 1519 and 1521 by a small band of Spaniards, under the leadership of Hernando Cortes, thanks to their guns and horses, and to the disunity and superstitions of the natives. The Spaniards had two motives for their conquest: gold and religion. In Mexico there was the opportunity for both. The Aztecs had accumulated plenty of gold and, being heathen, they were excellent targets for conversion. Cortes himself showed the double motive plainly in the port city he founded in 1519. He called it La Villa Rica de la Vera Cruz ("The Rich City of the True Cross"). Nowadays it is known simply as *Veracruz* (ver-uh-krooz').

In other cases in Latin America, it was the gold motif, rather than the religion motif, that shone through in the final names. The island to the west of the Dominican Republic was named, in 1519, *Puerto Rico* ("rich port"). The name had been spread out over the island from a city which was eventually renamed *San Juan* ("St. John") and which is now the capital of Puerto Rico. (The island is sometimes called Porto Rico but this, though easier for English-speaking people to pronounce, is incorrect.)

Another example is the Central American nation north of Panama, which has a name that was given it by Columbus himself, in 1502, when he skirted the coast on his fourth voyage. He saw natives with gold earrings on the shore and named the land *Costa Rica* ("rich coast").

235

Victoria Nyanza

THE NINETEENTH-CENTURY growth of the British Empire gave Britons an excellent chance to spread the name of their queen all over the map (see QUEENSLAND).

For instance, in 1858, the British explorer John Hanning Speke discovered a large lake in east-central Africa that proved, indeed, to be the third largest inland body of water in the world. He named it after Queen Victoria and so it is *Lake Victoria*. It is sometimes called, more exotically, *Victoria Nyanza*, "nyanza" being the Bantu word for "lake." Going on the basis of information gained by Speke, another explorer, Samuel Baker, found, in 1864, a second and smaller lake 200 miles northwest of Victoria. He named it *Lake Albert*, or *Albert Nyanza*, after Prince Albert, Queen Victoria's husband, who had died three years before.

Queen Victoria appears elsewhere, too. The third largest of the frozen islands north of Canada is *Victoria Island*. The southeastern tip of Australia was constituted as the *State of Victoria* in 1851. The city of *Victoria*, on Vancouver Island in Canada's extreme southwest, had its beginnings in 1843. (*Vancouver Island* and the city of *Vancouver* on the mainland near by are named for the English navigator George Vancouver, who first explored the territory in 1792.)

Then, too, a great cataract, larger than Niagara, was discovered along the Zambesi River in southeastern Africa by the Scottish explorer David Livingstone, in 1855. (This is the man who, lost in the jungle in 1871, was found by the explorer Henry Stanley and greeted with the now famous expression, "Dr. Livingstone, I presume.") Livingstone named the cataract *Victoria Falls*.

The Canadian province of *Alberta* was not named after the Prince Consort directly, but received its name in 1882 in honor of the wife of the governor-general of Canada, the Princess Louise Caroline Alberta, who happened to be one of the daughters of Victoria and Albert.

Vienna

No RIVER passes through so many cities of renown as does the Danube. It rises in Bavaria and passes into Austria where it flows through the Austrian capital, a city which was known to the Romans as "Vindobona." The Austrians keep merely the first syllable of that old name and call it Wien (veen). To us, it becomes *Vienna*.

This is a source of confusion, because the Romans had a "Vienna" of their own that was an entirely different city, one in Gaul, on the Rhone River. It is now called *Vienne*.

The name "Vindobona" is of Celtic origin and may mean the "white city" (always a flattering name, implying, as it does, cleanliness and purity). If that is doubtful, there is no doubt in the case of another city 300 miles downstream. This is *Belgrade*, the capital of Yugoslavia ("Beograd" to the Yugoslavs themselves), which definitely means "white city." (There is also a *Belgorod* in the Ukrainian S.S.R., which means the same.)

Between Vienna and Belgrade are *Bratislava* and *Budapest*. The former is the chief city of Slovakia and is probably named after some leader named Bratislav, a favorite name for the early kings of Bohemia and Poland (who took turns dominating the region).

Budapest was originally two cities: *Buda* on the west bank and *Pest* on the east bank of the Danube. "Pest" means "oven" though why that should be the name of the city is uncertain. "Buda" is of obscure origin but has no connection with "Buddha" at any rate. In 1872, the two were combined under one city government and became Budapest.

About forty miles north of the lower Danube is the Romanian capital, *Bucharest*. There is a tradition that it was founded by a shepherd named Bucur (the Romanian version of the city's name is "Bucuresti") and another tradition derives it from the Romanian word for "pleasure." Both traditions are doubtful. Near the Danube mouth is the port of *Constanta*, another city (see CONSTANTINOPLE and TANGIER) named for Constantine the Great.

Vietnam

AFTER World War II, when the French were forced out of Indochina, the territory was divided once again into the three states which France had originally taken over in the 1880's.

In the southeast was *Cambodia,* a name derived from the legendary ancestor "Kambu," from whom the natives, who call themselves Khmers, trace their descent.

North of Cambodia is *Laos* (louse), named for the tribe inhabiting it.

Running down the coast to the east of Laos and Cambodia is the the dumbbell-shaped *Vietnam,* thick in north and south, but thin (only thirty miles across in spots) in the middle. The name means "far south" in Chinese, and to the Chinese, of course, the land is far south indeed. To the West, however, it is only recently that that name has become familiar. It has been preceded by several others.

Back in the third century a Chinese general conducted a victorious campaign in southeastern Asia and he was given the title of "Annam," meaning "Pacified South." This title was transferred to the land he pacified. Thereafter *Annam* was the preferred Chinese name for the Indochinese coast and Westerners picked it up when they first grew acquainted with the region.

The southernmost portion of Vietnam was known to the Japanese by a name that sounded like "Cochin" to European traders. To avoid confusion with a province called Cochin in India, they called southern Vietnam *Cochin-China.* Northern Vietnam was called *Tonkin* or *Tonking,* from the Chinese name, "Dong Kinh," for the capital city.

In the early 1950's, Vietnam was racked by civil war and, in a compromise peace in 1954, the country was divided into two regions. The southern half, which is pro-Western, is the *Republic of Vietnam,* usually called *South Vietnam.* The northern half, which is pro-Chinese, is the *Democratic Republic of Vietnam,* usually called *North Vietnam.*

238

Virginia

THE FIRST British attempts to colonize the coast of what is now the United States were made in the 1580's under the patronage of the English courtier Sir Walter Raleigh. Landings were made at a place now called *Roanoke Island* (from an Indian word meaning, perhaps, "place of white shells").

The settlers wished to name the land in honor of the English monarch who, at the time, was Elizabeth I, the unmarried "virgin Queen." It seemed suitable, therefore, to name the coast *Virginia*.

Unfortunately, the colonies at Roanoke didn't survive but were destroyed by the Indians. It wasn't until 1607 that a successful colony was established in Virginia and by that time, Elizabeth was no longer alive. Her successor, James I, was on the throne. The new colonists established *Jamestown* on the banks of the *James River*, both named in his honor.

Virginia had only vague boundaries at first but, by 1700, had narrowed down to about the boundaries possessed by the modern state. Roanoke Island was not included but now belongs to North Carolina, Virginia's southern neighbor. The capital of North Carolina is Raleigh, in honor of the patron of that ill-fated venture.

At the start of the Civil War, when Virginia seceded from the Union (it was one of the thirteen original states, of course, and the tenth to ratify the Constitution), fifty-five of its western counties, firmly against secession, voted to remain in the Union. On June 20, 1863, just before the Battle of Gettysburg, they were admitted to the Union as *West Virginia*, the 35th state.

A city at the northern tip of West Virginia bears what seems the eminently English name of *Wheeling*. This is an illusion. The name is actually of Indian origin, coming from "wil-ing," meaning "place of the head," presumably because an execution had taken place there involving a decapitation.

Virgin Islands

EAST OF Puerto Rico, there is a chain of small islands that curves down to the South American continent. The most northerly of the group were discovered by Columbus in 1493, during his second voyage, and were named by him in honor of Saint Ursula and her companions, who were supposed to have died about 450, defending themselves against the Huns. They were all virgins and the islands are therefore the *Virgin Islands*.

The Virgin Islands have had an unusually mixed history as far as European colonization is concerned. The Dutch, British, Spanish, and French have all, at one time or another, established themselves there. The largest island, a little south of the rest of the group, bears the name of *St. Croix* (sant-kroy) or *Santa Cruz* (san'tuh-krooz), both (the former French, the latter Spanish) meaning "Holy Cross."

In 1753, Denmark purchased St. Croix from the French and also occupied two islands to the north, which bear the names of *St. Thomas* and *St. John*, after two of the apostles. This was one of Denmark's very rare excursions into colonization outside the Arctic. These three islands were lumped under the name of *Danish West Indies*.

In 1917, the United States was worried lest Germany might win World War I, then raging, and force weak Denmark to cede the islands, thus gaining a foothold in the western hemisphere. Playing it safe, the United States bought the islands from Denmark. The official title is now the *Virgin Islands of the United States*. (They are usually called simply Virgin Islands, but this is inaccurate because a couple of dozen small islands to their east are also part of the group, but belong to England. Those are called the *British Virgin Islands*.)

Marks of a century and a half of Danish ownership remain on the map of the islands, however. Since the fifteenth century, Denmark has been ruled by kings that have alternately borne the names of Frederik and Christian. Well, the two chief towns on St. Croix are *Frederiksted* and *Christiansted*, meaning "Frederik's town" and "Christian's town" respectively.

Washington

IN 1805, the American explorers Meriwether Lewis and William Clark reached the Pacific Coast, after having been sent out by President Jefferson to explore America's new acquisition of Louisiana. This, together with even earlier explorations, formed the basis for an American claim to that section of the coast. This region was called *Oregon*, a name that arose through misspellings of words of Indian origin on old, poorly engraved maps. Oregon was also claimed by the British and for a while it looked as though war might result.

In 1845, however, the dispute was settled peacefully, with the United States obtaining the southern portion. The region north of the Columbia River (see DISTRICT OF COLUMBIA) was called the Territory of Columbia, but Congress disapproved because of possible confusion with the District of Columbia. It therefore became the territory of Washington, after George Washington, of course. For some reason, Congress didn't worry about the confusion between this and *Washington*, the city that fills the District of Columbia and is the capital of the nation. The city is almost invariably called *Washington, D.C.*, to prevent confusion, while the territory, which entered the Union in 1889 as the 42nd state, is usually called *Washington State*, for clarity's sake.

The area south of Washington forms the state of Oregon, while the remainder of the American portion of the region wrested from Great Britain is the state of *Idaho*, from Indian words meaning "gem of the mountains" (it is thought). Oregon entered the Union in 1859 as the 33rd state; Idaho in 1890 as the 43rd.

Nearly half of the American states have names that are derived from Indian words, but one state honors the original Americans in English. That, of course, is the state of *Indiana*, which entered the Union in 1816 as the 19th state. By a very crooked route, the Sanskrit word for "river" (see INDIA) thus ends up in the heart of the American Middle West.

241

Wilkes-Barre

THE industrialization of the United States was made easier by the fact that it possessed rich coal fields and large deposits of iron ore. The coal was used to power factories by steam engine and also to smelt iron ore. The earliest coal fields in America center about Pennsylvania.

In the 1840's, George Whitfield Scranton, an American manufacturer, first smelted iron ore with a special hard grade of coal ("anthracite coal") available in certain eastern Pennsylvania regions and made millions out of it. In 1840, he and his brother bought a section of the anthracite coal country and founded a town they called Scrantonia. By 1851, that had been simplified to *Scranton*.

About twenty miles southwest of Scranton is another city of the coal area that was named not after one, but after two men. The city was founded in 1769 at a time when the question of the rights of the American colonies to be free of taxes not imposed by themselves was much in the air. There were many stout champions of American rights in the British Parliament and two of them were John Wilkes, an ardent foe of George III, and Isaac Barré, an English soldier of French parentage, who had nevertheless fought against the French in the French and Indian War. The Pennsylvanian city was named *Wilkes-Barre* (wilks'bar-ee) in their honor. (In 1788, a town was founded in Vermont which was named *Barre* [bar'ee] after the second man alone.)

The capital of Pennsylvania, like Scranton, was named for its founder but only after a struggle. In 1785, the owner of the land in that region, John Harris, was commissioned to lay out a town, and was directed to name it Louisburg after Louis XVI, who had helped the colonies win independence. Harris did this, but in 1791, he refused to sell the town additional land unless the name were changed to *Harrisburg*. The town gave in, but the county in which it is located is still called *Dauphin*, in honor of Louis XVI's oldest son (who never reigned, thanks to the French Revolution, but who is sometimes called Louis XVII).

Wilmington

THE EASTERNMOST projections of the Carolina coast are subject to stormy weather and to the lashings of occasional hurricanes. The South Carolina coast has a graphically named *Cape Fear* as a result, a name given it in 1585 by a colonizing ship that feared shipwreck there. The North Carolina coast is marked by *Cape Hatteras*, which comes from an Indian word, "Hatrask." Just south of Cape Hatteras is *Raleigh Bay,* named for Sir Walter Raleigh, who sponsored the unsuccessful early colonizations of the area (see VIRGINIA).

On the North Carolina shore, well south of Raleigh's colonies, is a city named for another British courtier and politician. The city was founded in 1734, and, at the time, the Lord Privy Seal (who was a powerful friend of the governor of North Carolina) was Spencer Compton, Earl of Wilmington. The town was therefore named *Wilmington.*

There is another and larger *Wilmington* in northern Delaware, famous as the site of the DuPont industries. This was originally named in far more plebeian fashion. In 1731, a Thomas Willing laid out the town and named it Willington after himself. But with the Earl of Wilmington so prominent in the government, the attraction was overwhelming. It, too, became Wilmington.

By the time that North Carolina's western neighbor, Tennessee (see TENNESSEE), was experiencing the founding of cities, the United States was independent and there were American Cabinet members to honor. There was no longer any need to look overseas. In 1791, a town in Tennessee was founded and named for Henry Knox, Secretary of War in Washington's Cabinet. It was the period of French popularity (see LOUISVILLE) and the town was named *Knoxville,* using the French "ville," as a result.

A city in southwestern Tennessee is *Chattanooga,* which is neither American nor British, but Indian. It means "rock rising to a point" and refers to *Lookout Mountain* (a self-explanatory name), which is in the vicinity.

Wisconsin

MANY OF the place names in America are originally Indian words that were spelled out as well as possible by the first explorers, who were often not English, and then misspelled or mispronounced by the English-speaking settlers when they arrived.

For instance, the Midwest was first explored by the Frenchmen Marquette and Joliet (see ILLINOIS). They worked their way into Lake Michigan, in early 1673, and then into a narrow bay angling off westward from that lake. By the time they reached the end of the bay it was spring and the trees were green, so they called it Baie Verte, which later settlers translated into the English equivalent, *Green Bay*. So far, so good.

Striking into the interior along rivers, they came to one which the natives called something like "Mesconsing," which may have meant "meeting of the waters" because the area is riddled with small lakes. The French spelled this "Ouisconsing" and the Americans made that *Wisconsin*. The area was admitted to the Union in 1848 as the 30th state.

The *Wisconsin River* flows into the Mississippi and on the other side, Marquette and Joliet found an Indian tribe that were called the Ayuhwa, which perhaps means "sleepy ones." (It isn't usual for people to call themselves uncomplimentary names, but perhaps the name was used for these Indians by neighboring tribes. Neighbors will call you anything.) The region finally became American and entered the Union in 1846, as the 29th state, under the name of *Iowa*.

In 1679, the French explorer La Salle passed down Lake Michigan and found an Indian village with a name which members of his party spelled "Melleoki," meaning, perhaps, "good land." There were various other spellings recorded by later explorers. When an American town was established on the spot in 1810, it adopted a variant of these spellings and became *Milwaukee*.

244

Wyoming

In a number of cases, place names of the eastern part of the United States were passed on westward as new territories opened up.

Thus, in eastern Pennsylvania there is a region called *Wyoming Valley*, from an Indian word, "mecheweami-ing," meaning "at the big plains." At this location, the State of Pennsylvania also possesses a county named Wyoming, while a town of Wyoming is in an adjacent county.

In 1778, during the Revolutionary war, British and Indians attacked the Wyoming Valley, killing and torturing in an atrocious way. The young nation was shocked and the name *Wyoming* gained a new kind of fame.

In 1868, a portion of the northern Rocky Mountain area was being organized as a territory and the suggestion was adopted that it be named *Wyoming* after the eastern valley, associated as it was with the Indian menace. (It was the time of the Indian Wars which had to be fought before the West could be opened to settlement.) The area entered the Union in 1890 as the 44th state. The state capital, located in the southwest corner of the state, is *Cheyenne*, named for a tribe of Indians who lived in that area.

A name might move westward on a tide of patriotism. Thus, in 1775, a group of settlers in the wilderness west of Virginia, in what is now Kentucky, received the news that the Revolutionary war had begun with a battle at Lexington, in Massachusetts. At once they named their own settlement *Lexington*. The new Lexington ended up much larger than the old one.

Or the reason might be personal vanity. In 1845, Asa L. Lovejoy of Boston, Massachusetts, and Francis W. Pettygrove of Portland, Maine, were laying out a town site on the Pacific coast. Each wanted to name the new settlement for his home town. Rather than coming to blows, they decided to toss a coin. Pettygrove won and we now have a *Portland*, Oregon, and again the new town is larger than the old.

Xeres

THE LATIN word for a flat field is "campus" (used today for the carefully tended grounds about a college) and so the flat fields about Naples were called *Campania*, both by the ancient Romans and modern Italians. The chief city of the area in ancient times was *Capua*, another form of the word, one in which the *m* has dropped out.

Campania is not as flat as all that actually, but a section of France east of Paris is quite flat and it took the same name, spelled in French fashion as *Champagne* (pronounced "sham-pane'" in English). Champagne is most familiar to us because its vineyards are the source of a famous sparkling wine called by the name of the province.

Other provinces of France have an association with alcoholic drinks. For instance, there was a Gaulish god named Borvon, who was considered to rule over hot springs, which were always considered important by the ancients (see AACHEN). A district in Gaul was named for him which, in later France, became *Bourbonnais* (boor-buh-nay'). The lords of the district formed the "House of Bourbon," which gave France its most famous kings, including Louis XIV, Louis XV, and Louis XVI. It also lends its name to a kind of whisky from a Kentucky county named *Bourbon* (in honor of Louis XVI) at the time of the Revolutionary war.

An unusual example is the case of a city in southern Spain, founded by the Romans and named Ceret, perhaps from an earlier Celtic name. In 1264, it was retaken from the Moslems by Spanish forces and by that time it had the name *Xeres*. Because for two more centuries it lay on the boundary of the last Moslem possessions in Spain, it was called *Xeres de la Frontera* ("Xeres of the Frontier") to distinguish it from another Xeres farther north. The pronunciation of "Xeres" was "sher'ris" and the wine produced in the area, highly popular in England, was named "sherry."

Eventually, the Spaniards took to pronouncing the town's name "hay'res" and spelled it Spanish-fashion to suit that pronunciation, so that it is now *Jerez de la Frontera*.

246

Yenisei

IN SOUTH-CENTRAL Siberia, exploring Russian fur traders came across a large lake in 1643, which turned out to be the deepest in the world. It was the only body of water outside the ocean, where deep-sea fish existed. The Mongol tribes of the vicinity called it Dalai-nor, meaning "holy sea," but Turkish tribes called it Bai-kul and it is the latter name that stuck, for it is *Lake Baikal* (bie-kal') on the maps, while a range called the *Baikal Mountains* lines its west shore.

From the mountains arises a great river that flows north into the Arctic Ocean. It is the *Yenisei* (yen-i-say'), from a native word meaning "great river." In its middle course there is a town named *Yeniseisk*. A second river almost as large flows to the east, also toward the Arctic, passing through frigid lands inhabited by Mongol tribes who call themselves Yakuts. On that river is the town of *Yakutsk*.

Still farther east, Russian traders came across another tribe, the Kamchadales. From them arose the rather twisted name *Kamchatka*, applied to the long peninsula stretching southward from the eastern end of Siberia. One of the cities on its east coast is *Kamchatsk*.

Not all east Siberian names are native, however. The Russian czars were properly honored, too. There is a *Nikolaevsk* (ni-koh-lah'-yevsk) on the east Siberian shore, named for Nicholas I, who ruled from 1825 to 1855. On an island south of Kamchatka is the town of *Aleksandrovsk*, named for Nicholas's son, Alexander II, who ruled from 1855 to 1881.

The easternmost section of Siberia, just across the strait from Alaska is called *Cape Dezhnev*, after Simon Dezhnev, a Cossack explorer who traveled along its coast in 1648, and who actually passed through the Bering Strait before Bering did. The cape is sometimes known, in English, as *East Cape*, which is descriptive, to be sure, but far less mouth-filling.

Yugoslavia

THE EASTERN half of Europe is occupied by the "Slavs." There are two theories as to the origin of the word. One is that the Germans, expanding eastward during the Middle Ages, found the Slavs gentle, unwarlike people who were easily enslaved. By this theory, "Slav" is merely a form of "slave."

However, it may be that "Slav" comes from the Slavic word "slovo," meaning "word." The Slavs might call themselves that because they felt that they spoke words whereas other groups of people spoke only incomprehensible gibberish. Then, too, early Slavic monarchs used names containing the Suffix "-slav." Examples are Yaroslav, Sviatoslav, and Bratislav. This is from "slava" meaning "glory" and that offers a third possibility for the origin of "slav."

In any case, since those early days, the Slavs have spread east to the Pacific and south to the Mediterranean and form a numerous and powerful group. The Germans found Slavs to be no longer gentle and unwarlike when they advanced eastward in 1941.

One of the Slavic nations in the south, before World War I, was *Serbia*. Again this may be derived from the Greek "serbos," meaning "slave," from which we get our own words "serf" and "servant." In 1918, Serbia was united with Montenegro (see ALBANIA) and with Slavic-speaking remnants of the disintegrated Austria-Hungary to form an enlarged nation named *Yugoslavia*. Since "yug" is a Slavic word for "south," the name means the "land of the Southern Slavs." (The name can be written *Jugoslavia*, but the pronunciation remains "Y.") Neither Germany during World War II nor the Soviet Union afterward found the land particularly serf-like.

The northernmost region of Yugoslavia, bordering on Austria, is *Slovenia*. This means "land of the Slavs." So does *Slovakia*, which is a stretch of territory north of Hungary and which now forms part of the nation of Czechoslovakia.

Yukon

THE HIGHEST peaks of the Rocky Mountains are in the far north. There is one mountain in south-central Alaska, for instance, which the Russians, during their domination of the area, called Bolshaya ("large"). It was indeed large but exactly how high its peak was remained unknown till 1896, when an American explorer, W. A. Dickey, surveyed it and found it stood 20,300 feet above sea level. That made it the highest known mountain in North America and none higher has been found since. Dickey named it after William McKinley, who had just been elected President of the United States, so that it is now *Mount McKinley*.

North America's second highest mountain is *Mount Logan*, in Canada, just off the Alaskan boundary. It was named for a Canadian geologist, William Edmond Logan.

The northwestern portion of the American continent is large in other respects, too. The fifth largest river on the continent runs across the upper edge of Canada and through Alaska. In 1846, a Canadian explorer, John Bell, reached it and was told by the Indians that it was "yukon-na" ("a big river"). It has been the *Yukon River* ever since. The northwesternmost corner of Canada, north of British Columbia, is *Yukon Territory*.

First commissioner of the territory was George M. Dawson, in whose honor the city of *Dawson*, on the upper reaches of the Yukon, was named. In 1896, gold was discovered along the Yukon and Dawson's population rose to a frenzied 20,000. It has since shrunk to less than a thousand.

On a tributary of the Yukon, in central Alaska, is the city of *Fairbanks*, now as large as Dawson at its best. It was founded in 1902 by gold-miners and named, for some reason, after a senator from the state of Indiana, Charles Warren Fairbanks. (Fairbanks went on to greater glories, for in 1905, he became Vice-President of the United States under William Howard Taft.)

Zanzibar

AFTER THE death of Mohammed, the victorious Arab armies carried Arab influence across the breadth of northern Africa and deep into the Sahara. But Arabia is just across a narrow sea from East Africa, and Arab influence was felt there too.

A number of states under Mohammedan leadership grew up on Africa's east coast, and these were collectively called Zenj or Zenj-bar, meaning "coast of the Negroes" in Persian. The latter term was corrupted gradually to "Zanquebar," then "Zanguebar," and finally *Zanzibar*.

When the Portuguese appeared along Africa's eastern coast, the Sultan of Zanzibar held sway over a large section of the coast in a loose way. In the nineteenth century, the European nations took over. In the 1880's both Germany and Great Britain snatched at unoccupied areas (unoccupied by Europeans, that is). The northern portion, just south of Ethiopia, became British and was called *British East Africa*. South of that was *German East Africa*.

After World War I, defeated Germany was forced to cede its share of East Africa to Great Britain. Great Britain's enlarged area was now given native names. What had formerly been German East Africa became *Tanganyika* (tan'gan-yee'kuh), after the native name for the great lake that formed much of its western boundary and that had been discovered in 1858 by the English explorers Richard Burton and John Speke. In 1961, Tanganyika received its independence.

The coastal section of what had formerly been British East Africa was renamed *Kenya* (ken'yuh) after *Mount Kenya*, Africa's second highest mountain, with a name derived from a native word meaning "gray mountain" or "spotted mountain." West of Kenya is *Uganda*, which receives its name from the native tribe "Buganda," which, in the nineteenth century, had established a strong control over the area. In 1962 Uganda received its independence.

The dominions of the Sultan of Zanzibar have been reduced to a few small islands off the Tanganyika coast. In 1963 both Kenya and Zanzibar gained their independence, and in 1964, Zanzibar and Tanganyika joined to form a single nation.

Index of Names

Carteret, George, 149, 155
Carteret, Philip, 151
Cartier, Jacques, 194
Catherine I, 166
Catherine II, 55, 166
Cermeño, Sebastian Rodrigues, 195
Champlain, Samuel de, 150, 194
Chancellor, Richard, 144
Charlemagne, 11, 22, 25, 45, 77, 89, 93, 119, 160, 172, 180, 203
Charles I (England), 45, 89, 125, 130, 155
Charles II (England), 45, 149, 155, 157, 175
Charles II (Spain), 129
Charles III (France), 160
Charles Martel, 45
Charles the Bald, 119
Charles the Bold, 37
Charlotte of Mecklenburg, 134, 150
Charnock, Job, 41
Chiang Kai-shek, 174
Chouteau, Pierre, 61
Christian IV, 54
Christian IX, 168
Churchill, John, 49
Churchill, Winston, 49, 216
Cincinnatus, Lucius Quinctius, 50
Clark, George Rogers, 122
Clark, William, 241
Claudius, 51
Clay, Henry, 8, 89
Cleaveland, Moses, 164
Coen, Jan Pieterszoon, 92
Columbus, Christopher, 10, 13, 33, 42, 44, 63, 64, 68, 86, 94, 102, 120, 196, 235, 240
Compton, Spencer, 243
Conant, Roger, 105
Constantine the Great, 16, 53, 216, 233
Cook, Captain James, 21, 67, 90, 151, 163
Cornwallis, Charles, 27
Coronado, Francisco Vásquez, 197
Cortereal, Gaspar, 153
Cortes, Hernando, 94, 235

Crespit, Juan, 148
Cunha, Tristan da, 16

D

Dallas, George Mifflin, 57
Dardanus, 3
Darwin, Charles Robert, 58
David, 100, 105
Davis, Jacob, 143
Davis, Jefferson, 217
Dawson, George M., 249
Dayton, Jonathan, 58
Dearborn, Henry, 20, 96
Defoe, Daniel, 47
De Long, George Washington, 123
Denver, James William, 60
Dezhnev, Simon, 247
Dias, Bartolomeu, 41
Dias, Dinis, 23
Dickey, W. A., 249
Diocletian, 191
Dodge, Henry, 76
Dorus, 84
Drake, Francis, 195
Dreyfus, Alfred, 87
Dubuque, Julien, 106
Dunk, George Montague, 161
D'Urban, Benjamin, 223

E

Eden, George, 214
Edward I, 83
Edward, Prince, 150
Edwin, 180
Eisenhower, Dwight David, 49
Elizabeth I (England), 83, 239
Elizabeth (Russia), 185
Eric the Red, 85
Evans, R. M., 58
Everest, George, 220

F

Fages, Pedro, 148
Fairbanks, Charles Warren, 249

Odysseus, 226
Oglethorpe, James, 20, 130, 201
Ojeda, Alonso de, 86
Omri, 80
Orellana, Francisco de, 9
Othman, 169

P

Pauw, Michael, 127
Peary, Robert Edwin, 95
Pedro I, 189
Pedro II, 189
Penn, Richard, 175
Penn, Thomas, 175
Penn, William, 65, 175, 177
Penn, William (Senior), 102
Pepin, 233
Perry, Matthew Calbraith, 221
Peter the Great, 12, 71, 115, 166, 188, 205
Pettygrove, Francis W., 245
Philip (Burgundy), 37
Philip II (Macedon), 70
Philip II (Spain), 147, 178
Philippe (Orleans), 156
Picault, Lazare, 133
Pike, Zebulon Montgomery, 8
Pitt, William, 180
Pius IX, 233
Pius XI, 233
Pizarro, Francisco, 117
Plato, 13
Plautius, Aulus, 118
Pliny, 40, 71
Polk, James Knox, 57
Polo, Marco, 48, 103, 104, 112, 124, 126
Ponce de León, Juan, 74
Poo, Fernando, 39, 41
Portola, Gaspar de, 120
Pratt, Charles, 149
Pribylov, Gerasim, 5
Prony, Jacques, 124
Ptolemy, Claudius, 4
Ptolemy Philadelphus, 2, 177
Puget, Peter, 204

Pu-Yi, Henry, 126
Pyrene, 29
Pyrrhus, 70
Pytheas, 85

R

Raffles, Thomas Stamford, 207
Rainier, John Sprat, 204
Raleigh, Walter, 239, 243
Rehoboam, 100
Reno, Jesse Lee, 60
Retez, Ynigo Ortiz, 88
Rhodes, Cecil John, 187
Richard I (the Lion Hearted), 2
Richard III, 188
Robidoux, Joseph, 198
Rochester, Nathaniel, 46
Roggeveen, Jakob, 67
Romulus, 191
Romulus Augustulus, 191
Roosevelt, Franklin Delano, 49, 216
Ross, John, 144
Rostislav, 111

S

St. Botolph, 31
St. Clair, Arthur, 50
St. Francis, 120
St. James, 198
St. Marinus, 73
St. Paul, 198
St. Peter, 233
St. Ursula, 240
Saljuq, 169
Santa Anna, Antonio Lopez de, 218
Schouten, Willem Cornelis, 47
Scranton, George Whitfield, 242
Seleucus I, 14, 24, 215
Selkirk, Alexander, 47
Septimius Severus, 53
Seville, Diogo de, 23
Seward, William Henry, 5
Seychelles, Morau de, 133
Shortland, John, 208
Siggurdson, Harold, 54
Smith, John, 31, 152
Smith, Joseph, 231

Smith, Thomas A., 76
Smith, William, 12
Solis, Juan Diaz de, 15
Soto, Hernando de, 38, 139
Souza, Tomé de, 196
Speke, John Hanning, 236, 259
Stalin, Joseph, 49, 115, 232
Stanley, Henry Morton, 52, 236
Stockton, Robert Field, 193
Stuyvesant, Peter, 86
Sutter, John Augustus, 193
Suvorov, Alexander Vasilievich, 55

T

Taft, William Howard, 249
Tamerlane, 232
Tariq ibn-Zayid, 81
Tasman, Abel Janszoon, 21
Theseus, 3
Torres, Luis Vaez, 21
Townshend, Thomas, 214
Trajan, 190
Treat, Robert, 149
Trent, William, 149
Tros, 226
Trujillo, Rafael Leonidas, 64

U

Ulysses, 181
Uzbeg Khan, 232

V

Valentinian I, 213
Van Amstel, Giesebrech, 92
Vancouver, George, 204, 236
Van Diemen, Anton, 21
Varthema, Ludovico di, 104
Velasquez, Diego, 102
Verrazano, Giovanni, de, 186
Vespucius, Americus (Vespucci, Amerigo), 10, 63, 234

Victor Amadeus II, 202
Victor Emmanuel I, 202
Victor Emmanuel III, 202
Victoria, 35, 63, 89, 128, 150, 184, 236
Vladimir, 111

W

Waldseemüller, Martin, 10
Wallis, Samuel, 163
Washington, George, 8, 27, 50, 180, 217, 241
Wayne, Anthony, 76
Wellesley, Arthur, 214
Wentworth, Benning, 143
West, Thomas, 175
Wilhelmina, 131
Wilkes, John, 242
Wilkinson, John, 206
William I (England), 155
William I (Germany), 93, 131
William II (Netherlands), 86
William III (England), 184
William III (Netherlands), 131
William IV (England), 214
Williams, Roger, 186
Willing, Thomas, 243
Winston, Joseph, 105
Worth, William Jenkins, 76
Wrangel, Ferdinand Petrovich von, 123

Y

Yaroslav the Wise, 111
Yermak, 205
Young, Brigham, 231
Young, John, 58
Yussuf ibn-Tashfin, 132

Z

Zarco, João Gonçalves, 40
Zinoviev, Grigori Evseevich, 185

Index of Places

Sardinia, 202
Saskatchewan, 128
Saskatoon, 128
Sassanid Empire, 24
Saudi Arabia, 200
Sault Sainte Marie, 62
Savannah, 201
Savoy, 202
Saxe-Altenburg, 203
Saxe-Anhalt, 203
Saxe-Coburg, 203
Saxe-Weimar, 203
Saxony, 203
Scandinavia, 160
Scania, 160
Schleswig, 69
Schwaben, 119
Schweiz, 213
Schwyz, 213
Scotia Sea, 12
Scotland, 83
Scranton, 242
Sea of Galilee, 80
Seattle, 204
Seine River, 173
Seleucia, 14, 24
Seleucid Empire, 24
Senegal, 212
Serbia, 248
Serendib, 44
Sevastopol, 55
Severnaya Zemlya, 211
Seychelles Islands, 134
Shanghai, 221
Shetland Islands, 168
Siam, 219
Siberia, 205
Sibir, 205
Sicily, 206
Sierra Nevada, 148
Sindh, 171
Singapore, 207
Sinkiang, 228
Skane, 160
Slave Coast, 23
Slesvig, 69
Slovakia, 248

Slovenia, 248
Snow Mountains, 131
Society Islands, 163
Sofia, 36
Sogdiana, 232
Soissons, 199
Solomon Islands, 208
Somalia, 209
Somaliland, 209
Soudanese Republic, 212
South America, 63
South Andaman, 27
South Carolina, 45
South Carpathian Mountains, 224
South Dakota, 61
Southeast Asia, 98
Southern Kingdom, 100
Southern Rhodesia, 187
Southern Territories, 227
South Georgia, 90
South Korea, 112
South Orkney Islands, 12
South Platte River, 146
South Sandwich Islands, 90
South Sea, 170
South Sea Islands, 170
South Shetland Islands, 12
South Vietnam, 238
Soviet Central Asia, 142, 228
Soviet Russia, 210
Soviet Union, 210
Spain, 181
Spanish Guinea, 88
Spanish Morocco, 132, 216
Spanish Netherlands, 147
Spanish Sahara, 23
Sparta, 226
Spice Islands, 140
Spitsbergen, 211
Spokane, 204
Springfield, 201
Stalinabad, 49, 232
Stalingrad, 49, 115
Stalinir, 49
Stalino, 49
Stalinogorsk, 49
Stalinsk, 49

Isaac Asimov

Isaac Asimov was born in the USSR in 1920 but was brought up in Brooklyn, New York and has been an American citizen since 1928. He attended Columbia University, from which he received his B.S. in 1939, his M.A. in 1941, and his Ph.D. in 1948. He has been a chemist with the Naval Air Experiment Station in Philadelphia and since 1949 a member of the faculty of the Boston University School of Medicine.

Prof. Asimov began writing in 1938. "I had been reading science fiction since 1929 and I gradually developed the desire to write my own. So I did."

Since that time his science-fiction short stories and novels have made him one of the country's most famous names in the field. But he is also the author of many very successful factual books on scientific subjects for readers of all ages.

His earlier book *Words of Science* led him into a wide-ranging study of the derivations of words that has taken him to the Greek myths, the Bible, and now to the whole world itself.